The Occult I Ching

.

"In an extraordinary piece of esoteric scholarship, Maja D'Aoust has crafted one of the most intriguing investigations of the I Ching you are ever likely to read. Like many such examinations, *The Occult I Ching* contains a complete presentation of the oracle itself, but it is in her exploration of I Ching history that D'Aoust shines brightest. Her presentation of evidence for a connection between the I Ching and DNA is worth the cover price on its own. Highly recommended."

J. H. BRENNAN, AUTHOR OF *THE MAGICAL I CHING* AND *OCCULT TIBET*

"Maja D'Aoust's diamond mind has created another gem. *The Occult I Ching* is an illuminating brew of divinatory mythos, elegant wisdom, fascinating theory, and practical advice. This witch-kissed twist on a legendary tool has already proven its gold for me in lightning-bolt synchronicities from the moment I began using it."

LIBERTY LARSEN, MAGICIAN AND MUSICIAN

The Occult I Ching

The Secret Language of Serpents

Maja D'Aoust

Destiny Books
Rochester, Vermont

Destiny Books
One Park Street
Rochester, Vermont 05767
www.DestinyBooks.com

Text stock is SFI certified

Destiny Books is a division of Inner Traditions International

Cataloging-in-Publication Data for this title is available from the Library of Congress

ISBN 978-1-62055-904-8 (print)
ISBN 978-1-62055-905-5 (ebook)

Printed and bound in the United States by Lake Book Manufacturing, Inc.
The text stock is SFI certified. The Sustainable Forestry Initiative® program
promotes sustainable forest management.

10 9 8 7 6 5 4 3 2 1

Text design by Priscilla H. Baker and layout by Virginia Scott Bowman
This book was typeset in Garamond Premier Pro with Civane and Futura used as
    display typefaces
Artwork by Maja D'Aoust unless otherwise indicated

To send correspondence to the author of this book, mail a first-class letter to the
author c/o Inner Traditions • Bear & Company, One Park Street, Rochester, VT
05767, and we will forward the communication, or contact the author directly at
www.witchofthedawn.com.

◘

This book is dedicated to my I Ching teacher, Dr. Stephen Karcher, whose genius work with the I Ching changed my life. I am grateful for his sharing spirit, whose insights transformed my view of reality. I also gained many revelations through Dr. Kelvin DeWolfe in our discussions of Chinese philosophy and consciousness. I am grateful for Brooke Schooles and her assistance putting the work together and for Baza Novic's support through the pitfalls. I am also grateful for the wise editors Jamaica Burns Griffin and Kate Mueller who lifted up the quality of this work through their keen perceptions; thank you.

Contents

PART 3

The Future of Ancient Technology

◨

The Daimonic
Path to Inner Knowing

We live in a world of nature. We bear witness to so many wonders, forms, animals, and plants around us. We try to count and catalogue them all. We number the stars and name them. We look at all the myriad shapes that matter takes, all the stages it goes through, and the ways in which it behaves. We study Earth and the universe.

Some who have grown wise in their studies of the world around us, the wise ones, need not extend their scope as far as the stars. Some wise ones have been able to see the truth of the entire universe in the shape of a single turtle shell laid before their feet at a riverbank. There, in the lowly, unassuming mud, they saw and knew all of Nature, her truth and what she is. Wise ones see that there is a pattern in nature, and that pattern is reflected in all the forms. The Taoist masters who created the I Ching were able to see such patterns reflected in the inner and outer worlds, and they recorded their wisdom.

In the occult traditions, most divination systems are referred to as mirrors of reality. From the ancient ways of scrying, where one gazed into a reflection in the water, to modern computer apps, every divination system acts as a mirror to reflect situations and the contents of our outer and inner lives to us.

We often experience outer reflections of ourselves if we are not self-reflective. We see ourselves in the way others treat us, look to others for definitions of our identity, and find comfort in teaming up with affiliations and ideologies that help us define ourselves. We look to the outer world to provide reflections of our inner selves and try to find what we are in the things we look upon.

A divination system offers a mirror for our inner selves rather than one that reveals our face. Our internal selves can often be blocked from our view because of our need to engage in survival behaviors and to constantly direct our attention outward. The Janus face of our subconscious on the back of our heads is always out of reach of our forward-facing vision. To see who we truly are as a whole, instead of the egoic reflection that is thrown back at us during our everyday lives, we can only reflect within.

When our inner reflections reach a point of clarity, like a still pool of water, we can calm our minds in peace by coming into knowing who we are. When we know who we are, we are able to know a great many things, including the answers to questions we may have.

> *Without opening your door,*
> *you can open your heart to the world.*
> *Without looking out your window,*
> *you can see the essence of the Tao.*
>
> LAO-TZU, TAO TE CHING

One of the ways we can connect to ourselves is through divination systems. This is the daimonic path to inner knowing. When we shift to our internal existence, we know exactly who we are, and so fewer doubts arise, which allows us to gain a profound confidence. We *feel* things and *know* them. This is gnosis. We see what is inside us and act from within rather than from an external viewpoint. In an early Greek myth of Hermes he walks along a beach and thinks to himself, "I wish I could play some music." At that very same moment, a turtle shell appears out of nowhere, washed up on the shore by the waves. When he sees it, Hermes exclaims, "Symbol!"—for what he wished for inside was reflected on the outside. He turns the shell into a lyre, the first musical instrument, and plays a song. Living life from the inside out affords a shift in perspective. The ability to come into gnosis through self-reflection is related best in the myth of Medusa. In the myth, Perseus kills Medusa by decapitating her, with the help of Athena's polished shield to reflect her face, which enables him to avoid her baleful gaze that turns men to stone. When Medusa is made to gaze upon her own ego (her facade), she sees her darkness, which she had previously projected, like arrows, toward her perceived enemies. When her inside self meets her outside self through reflection, she literally loses her head, decapitated by the sword of truth, wielded by Perseus, and her ego is separated, revealing her true form. The truth of the soul of Medusa emerges as Pegasus, who springs up from her blood and takes flight, representing the liberated mind freed through self-reflection.

The Reflection

Those things you hide from your own eyes,
safe from the firelight called "realize,"
they carve themselves upon the mask that is your face,
each evening when the light goes down in bows of grace.
The dark emerges, hungry in all directions,
seeking that which has not reached perfection.
With morning light comes but the chance
to face the mask again, again repeat the dance.
Prying eyes must upon themselves use force,
remembering their ancient source.
The ones who have nothing from this place to fear
have shed all snakes, and through the venom freedom
     made clear.
The destination can be found on any ground from womb
     to tomb.
It drips within our hearts in phoenix tears of honeycomb.

MAJA D'AOUST

The mirrors of divination can be used in many ways. There are those who ask the oracles questions regarding their everyday lives. Concerns surrounding money, relationships, and health make up the bulk of divination requests. This is to be expected, for what else do we deal with in our lives? Divination systems can also be used as a guru, which can guide the user through his or her spiritual path and give advice as a conscience. All daimonic activity was used this way in ancient times. One might say there is no substitute for our own conscience, so why engage a divination system? The purpose of divination systems is to amplify the voice of our daimon, who is our guide throughout our life. Engaging with a divination system is one way to gain access through dialogue with your own daimon located deep within your inner heart.

The I Ching contains a mirror world made up of possible scenarios that can evolve through time. All things in nature contain one repeated pattern—the golden rectangle of phi—which means that we find ourselves in a limited number of experiences as we travel through life. Although the environment may grow and evolve and we may invent new things, the basic archetypal scenarios remain. For this reason, the I Ching remains a viable oracle, and its hypothetical scenarios are still applicable today.

I have drawn from many mythologies and histories in this book. All the Western myths you read here have their Chinese counterparts, as the archetypes are the same no matter where on Earth you find yourself. The symbols of the archetypes exist in a universal location, within us and outside us simultaneously. They are perennial and eternal, independent of location and era. These stories of the hexagrams and their archetypes form the esoteric mystery school traditions. In this magical I Ching, it is my wish to display the hexagrams as mystery keys and components of the teachings of the initiate as he or she goes through the unfolding path of gnosis. Discovering Sophia—the Greek concept and goddess of wisdom—within occurs in the same fashion for all, no matter what language we speak. The archetypes are the unifying factor that extend beyond language and exist in symbolic form to be enjoyed by all of humanity.

> *The beginning of the sustenance of life*
> *Is all in yin and yang.*
> *The limitless can open up*
> *The light of the great limit.*
> *Diligently polished, the mirror of mind*
> *Is bright as the moon;*
> *The universe in a grain*
> *May rise, or it may hide.*
>
> SUN BU'ER

PART 1

Secrets of
the Ancient Serpents

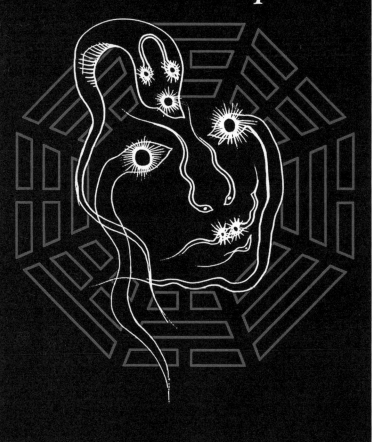

Origins of the I Ching and Serpent Divination

The I Ching as a divination system works through producing changes and evolutions within the individual, using stories and symbologies. As Stephen Karcher observes in his book *Total I Ching: Myths for Change,* "change is articulated through words. These words keyed a stream of memories in the old diviners, setting off a chain of interconnecting associations. They carry the myths and act as centers for their ongoing development."[1] The I Ching is, then, essentially a sacred language that allows for an intercourse between the diviner and the spirits.

The tradition of the divination system known as the I Ching goes back long into antiquity. It has been used in China for thousands of years to open a dialogue with divinity and pull aside the curtain of reality revealing the light of the heavens. Touted as one of the oldest books in the world, the I Ching began as a divinatory language made up of symbols used on turtle shells and oracle bones, dating from about 6500 BCE,[2] first codified formally in the Zhou dynasty circa 1500 BCE. The first translation of the I Ching into English was only in the 1950s, about the same time DNA was discovered by Watson and Crick.

The earliest diviners to use the I Ching were the shamans of China. Chinese shamans are known by many names but are generally referred to as *wu* or *wu-his,* a Chinese word commonly translated as "witches."[3] The wu were in charge as intermediaries between the spirit world and the human world and developed systems involving divination techniques, such as the I Ching. Divination was always consulted on matters of great import, and for the wu it acted as their guidance system. The wu were consulted for best war strategies and agricultural

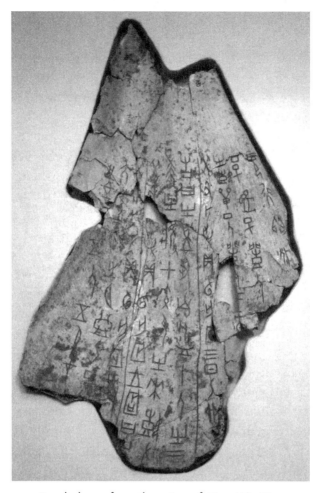

Oracle bone from the reign of King Wu Ding
(late Shang dynasty), circa 1200 BCE
Collection of National Museum of China. Photo by BabelStone, CC BY-SA 3.0.

practices. They were also versed in medicine and complex herbal remedies, performed birth and death rituals, and engaged in ecstatic states. From them the earliest Taoist philosophies were developed, and from that grew the alchemical studies in Asia. The driving force behind their practices always remained the I Ching and its basic principles of cosmology. It was the wu who brought us the I Ching, and its origins are buried deeply in their history of nature worship.

According to Chinese mythology, the discovery of the I Ching predates the wu shamans. Fu Xi or Fu Hsi, the mythical first emperor of China, who reigned from 2852 to 2737 BCE, is credited with discovering the I Ching. A mysterious half-man, half-serpent entity, Fu Xi is credited with, among other things, the invention of hunting, fishing, and cooking. The contributions of Fu Xi are recorded in the Baihu Tongyi, compiled by the Chinese historian Ban Gu.

> In the beginning there was as yet no moral or social order. Men knew their mothers only, not their fathers. When hungry, they searched for food; when satisfied they threw away the remnants. They devoured their food hide and hair, drank the blood, and clad themselves in skins and rushes. Then came Fu Xi and looked upward and contemplated the images in the heavens, and looked downward and contemplated the occurrences on the earth. He united man and wife, regulated the five stages of change, and laid down the laws of humanity. He devised the eight trigrams in order to gain mastery over the world.[4]

Fu Xi, according to tradition, discovered the I Ching on the back of a turtle shell while he was standing in the Yellow River receiving direct ecstatic communication from a higher consciousness. Fu Xi saw eight original trigrams, called the *bagua,* on the tortoise shell. These trigrams, which make up the body of the I Ching, are the basis of nearly all Taoist philosophy of nature, medicine, martial arts, mathematics, and alchemical knowledge.

Fu Xi was so struck by what he had received that he knew he had to write it down immediately so that he could share it with others, but this was before written language, so he did not know what to do and sat down thinking. According to the stories, a giant serpentine dragon appeared in that moment and granted him the oracle scripts of the I Ching, which Chinese language is now based upon, and Fu Xi was able to complete his task. Some scholars say that this dragon was the daimon of Fu Xi.

The Worldwide Wisdom of Serpents

The name Fu Xi in Chinese (伏羲) means "the great bright one." This meaning is derived from a special Taoist secret about light. There were immortal entities referred to as "the august ones," and they were said to shine with light as brightly as the sun. Fu Xi was one of these entities, and so he was said to shine with light. Some interpret this to mean someone who has become enlightened or a spiritual master. References to these entities can be found all through modern qigong practices, which focus on generating a sunlike state of light within the body. They were referred to as the august ones because of their supposed relationship to the light of the rising sun, or the dawn. The august mystery is tied to the origins behind the words *augury* and *auspicious* and the chemical symbol for gold, which is Au, from *aureate,* whose root, *aus-,* means "to shine." There are some variations in Chinese mythology regarding who is considered an august one. Sometimes Fu Xi is included in the five emperors in addition to being an august one. The five emperors were considered the founders of China and its people; they brought the knowledge of civilization to humanity, which was trapped in the dark times of the cave man. Fu Xi had a female counterpart and consort who was named Nü Wa, with similar magical powers and achievements in terms of ushering in civilization.

The two were depicted as an intertwined pair whose lower serpent bodies formed an interspiraling shape, much like DNA (see illustration on the next page). These two were considered the original parents of humans, much like Adam and Eve in the Judeo-Christian mythology, who also had a serpent affiliated with them, usually called Satan or Lucifer. Fu Xi and Nü Wa hold in their hands the iconic symbols of the compass and the ruler, now recognized in Freemasonry buildings across the globe.

The emblem of Freemasonry is none other than these two objects, which Fu Xi and Nü Wa hold in their hands, formed together over the letter *G,* as was pointed out to me by my qigong teacher Dr. Kelvin DeWolfe. It is hard not to recognize the obvious similarity of the objects, which Freemasonary may have appropriated from the Chinese. In the practice of feng shui, also developed by the wu shamans based on the teachings of the serpent couple, these instruments were used to obtain information from the stars in heaven as well as to build and develop architecture and agriculture. The Miao people of Southern China claim to be descendants of this famous serpentine couple, Fu Xi and Nü Wa. The Miao believe Fu Xi to be their ancestor.

Fu Xi and Nü Wa. Hanging scroll. Color on silk.
Located at the Xinjiang Uighur Autonomous Region Museum.
Nü Wa is on the left; Fu Xi is on the right.

Tales of serpentine or eellike human hybrids bringing civilization to cultures extend around the globe. They can be found in hermetic literature and in the myths of Africa, Mesopotamia, and India, so as odd as a story of a serpent being coming up with a divination system might be, it is hard to ignore its prevalence. In India, the most famous snake hybrid entities that performed this function were known as the *nagas,* who influenced the majority of religions in Asia, including the current religion of Tibet.

The teachings of the nagas are still followed by the current Dalai Lama. The famous Buddhist leader known as Nagarjuna received his teachings from the nagas, which is where the *Naga* in his named is derived. Tibetan Buddhists have different sects, or lineages, which they show by the colors of their hats. There are red hats, yellow hats, black hats, white hats, and some other variations. The yellow hat sect was founded by Tsongkhapa, who includes much of Nagarjuna's teachings in his lineage. The yellow hat that the Dalai Lama wears indicates that he subscribes to this same lineage and teachings. Nagarjuna was an enlightened master who is said to have come from Kashmir, which lies between Pakistan and India. In this same region there is a race of people who refer to themselves as the nagas, and according to their history, they claim to be descended from these serpentine beings.

In the ancient Vedic texts of India, it was said that all the nagas, or serpent people, came from the *rishis,* the Vedic version of angels who came to Earth from the constellation of the Big Dipper. The rishis intermingled with the serpents of Earth and bore children. This folklore mirrors many of the fallen angel texts of the nephilim, anunnaki, and other ancient myths of some kind of entity coming to Earth to breed with animals and humans. The nagas who instructed Nagarjuna also visited Siddhartha Buddha, as symbolized in many depictions of the Buddha sitting underneath a giant cobra with many heads.

This tradition of the serpent people could be symbolic and not literal, using the snakes to simply represent wisdom conferred from a kind of guardian spirit, or daimon, and not a physical snake. The serpents in most occult teachings are angelic or demonic figures who can communicate with humans through the aetheric realm, enlightening humans through their teachings.

Divination and Serpents

The word *divination* comes from the Latin *divinare* and has two possible meanings. According to Karcher, to divine is "to discover what is hidden by supernatural or irrational means, to see things through magical insight." It also means "to make something divine, something belonging to or associated with a god."[5]

From this we may say that divination is a way of coming into contact with divinity. This is done through a form of language, although unlike most languages with which we are familiar. It is a language expressed purely through symbols. These symbols are absorbed by the diviner, and, through their presence, alter the consciousness of the diviner. It is this action, the absorbing of symbols into the consciousness, that causes the transformations. We must seek this consciousness if we are to achieve health and well-being, according to the Chinese shamans. In China, this state of awareness is called the mind of Tao.

The connection between divination and these serpent beings and the I Ching becomes infinitely more interesting when we learn about the Hebrew word *nachash*. This word is not only a reference to the serpent creature who visited Eve and tempted her in the Book of Genesis, but it is also a verb that means "to divine" or "to make a presage,"[6] which means to prophesy, exactly the function that the I Ching serves. James Strong provides the following definitions of *nachash*, also spelled *nechash*.

> **nâchash,** naw-khash; certainly, divine, enchanter, (use) enchantment, learn by experience, diligently observe; a primitive root; properly, to hiss, i.e., whisper, a (magic) spell; generally, to prognosticate— certainly, divine, enchanter, (use) enchantment, learn by experience, indeed diligently observe.[7]

Here we see a pattern forming of connections between divination, divination systems, and serpents or the serpent beings. Fu Xi the serpent being invents the divination system of the I Ching; the nachash serpent of the Hebrews is responsible for divination. In another biblical reference, the word *nechash* refers to witches, much like the Chinese shaman term *wu*, as well as sorcerers and anyone who performs divination. What follows are translations or versions of nechash from Deuteronomy 18:10.

> NAS [New American Standard]: one who practices witchcraft, or one who interprets omens, or a sorcerer

KJV [King James Version]: an observer of times, or an enchanter, or a witch[8]

The affiliation of divination with serpents is perhaps most famously known in the story of the Oracle of Delphi. The Oracle of Delphi was by far the most renowned diviner of all times, and the place in which she practiced was called the Pythia. The Pythia was so named after a giant python, or snake. The ancient Greeks believed there was a giant dragon or serpent, which they called the python, who lived at the center of Earth and emerged at the location of Delphi. Apollo bested this beast in a battle described in detail by Ovid, and its corpse remained, leaving a lingering odor that everyone smelled when entering the cave where the Oracle of Delphi dwelled. In this version of a diviner and a serpent, the oracle lives within the flesh of the snake who is defeated by the sun. The Oracle of Delphi claimed that the dragon or serpent was her familiar spirit and daimon, who conferred all her insights upon her. This story contains many similar elements to the symbolic representatives involved in the Fu Xi mythology.

The nagas and serpent beings are also featured prominently in a manuscript of divination from Mongolia, housed at the National Library of Medicine. The naga energies in this work again show an intimate connection between the serpents and systems of daimonic knowledge, even showing a half-man, half-serpent being similar to depictions of Fu Xi.

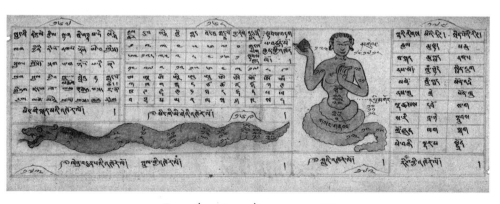

From the Mongolian manuscript
Manual of Astrology and Divination
Courtesy of the National Library of Medicine

In Egypt we see the dragon Poimandres, who is the informant of Thoth (known as Hermes to the Greeks), the one who knows. Although clouded in mystery and the subject of much controversy, Poimandres is usually depicted as a fiery serpent whom Thoth asks questions.

Hermes, while wandering in a rocky and desolate place, gave himself over to meditation and prayer. Following the secret instructions of the Temple, he gradually freed his higher consciousness from the bondage of his bodily senses; and, thus released, his divine nature revealed to him the mysteries of the transcendental spheres. He beheld a figure, terrible and awe-inspiring. It was the Great Dragon, with wings stretching across the sky and light streaming in all directions from its body. (The Mysteries taught that the Universal Life was personified as a dragon.) The Great Dragon called Hermes by name, and asked him why he thus meditated upon the World Mystery. Terrified by the spectacle, Hermes prostrated himself before the Dragon, beseeching it to reveal its identity. The great creature answered that it was Poimandres, the Mind of the Universe, the Creative Intelligence, and the Absolute Emperor of all. (Schure identifies Poimandres as the god Osiris.) Hermes then besought Poimandres to disclose the nature of the universe and the constitution of the gods. The Dragon acquiesced, bidding Trismegistus hold its image in his mind.[9]

Thoth/Hermes then in turn becomes a form of oracle to whom people pose questions in the temples. Described as many things, Poimandres was translated by some as the "mind of Re"; Greek versions interpret it as "shepherd of men," meaning a type of guide. This snake-like being is the source of knowledge that Thoth channels in his teachings to the Egyptian people. Thoth, like Fu Xi, was seen as responsible for creating language and furthering civilization. So the Egyptians too had a serpent oracle. Nowhere is this information better discussed than by Peter Kingsley in his amazing work "Poimandres: The Etymology of the Name and the Origins of the Hermetica."

After Thoth-Poimandres has introduced himself, and after the translation of his name into Greek, we have the further very simple statement: "I know what you want" (*oida ho boulei*). Once again, in terms of Egyptian theology there can be little doubt as to the identity of this god: he is Thoth, "he who knows" and, more specifically, "he who reads people's hearts" (*ip ib*). Of particular relevance to our text is a memorable passage in one of the Graeco-Egyptian magical papyri . . . "I know through and through what is in the souls of all men . . . when they put their questions to me and come into my sight, when they talk and when they are silent, so that I can tell them what has happened to them in the past, what is happening and what will happen to them in future; and I know their skills and their lifestyle and their habits and what they do . . ." Thoth's mention here of people 'putting their questions to me' (*eperotonton me*) is an obvious reference to the Egyptian practice of temple incubation, which involved the deliberate questioning of gods through the medium of visions and dreams: a practice that happens to be well attested for Thoth. But it is an equally obvious reminder of the opening to the first of the Hermetica, where Thoth-Poimandres introduces himself and immediately goes on—throughout the rest of the dialogue—to answer the questions put to him by the writer of the text. So here we come to a crucial point for our understanding of the Greek Hermetic corpus: its apparent origin in the Egyptian temple practice of consulting dream oracles.[10]

The relationship of serpents, serpent beings, and dragons with divination is extensive when one begins to examine the history of oracles and practices. The serpent beings who informed and created the I Ching in China appear to have commonalities with serpent entities in other areas who brought oracles to humans in antiquity. In his great work *Ophiolatreia; Serpent Worship,* Hargrave Jennings maps the ancient traditions of serpent worship and oracles around the globe. "The first oracle mentioned in history was dedicated to the serpent-god, who was known in Canaan by the name of OB, or AUB: hence arose the notion that the oracular response of the priestess of these serpent temples must be always preceded by a mysterious inflation, as if actuated by the internal presence of the divine."[11]

The Daimonic Power
of the Bagua

As noted earlier, the eight trigrams called the bagua formed the basis for much of Chinese knowledge and culture. The bagua was considered a mirror of the cosmos, and all knowledge and applications could be derived from it when it was understood properly. The eight gua are as follows (the first word after each trigram, for example *ken*, is the Japanese word; the second word, for example *qian*, is the Chinese pinyin transcription):

ken, qian

da, dui

ri, li

shin, zhen

son, xun

kan, kan

gon, gen

kon, kun

The word *ba* simply means "eight." But the word *gua* is completely fascinating. *Gua* means something like "oracle symbol" or "archetype," like a representative or scapegoat. It also means "to divine," "to tell fortunes," or "to read fates." In the I Ching, we form a gua by the action of making a hexagram, and this gua simply mirrors the possible reality we are currently experiencing. The gua can do this based on the theory that there are only so many possibilities to experience in reality, and chances are one of those is what we are faced with. The I Ching is made of the sixty-four permutations of the eight bagua, making the hexagrams, which constitute the various responses generated through the question process.

In some of the ancient texts, the gua were a type of dragon, supernatural spirit, or familiar who could confer special powers to humans. These gua or dragons were like guardians. If we understand the deeper meaning of the gua as being the dragons or serpents I discussed earlier, we see that the gua are daimons who constitute the divinations and are the sources of information. Perhaps Fu Xi is depicted in dragon form because he merged with his gua dragon daimon and then, in a sense, *became* the I Ching.

The gua were created by Fu Xi that day at the river. We could imagine that when we are using the I Ching we are actually connecting to the mind of Fu Xi himself through his daimon, which he left behind in the form of the gua, the pictograms or symbols that we may take into our mind and reflect upon. We could even say that the I Ching *is* Fu Xi, although I am certain less imaginative folk may take deep offense at this statement. Perhaps it is truer to say that the mind or daimon of Fu Xi accessed the I Ching, which was only really an expression of the one Tao.

Most modern interpretations of the hexagrams are based on a text called Xi-Ci-Zhuan, which explains the I Ching. Part one of the Xi-Ci-Zhuan explains how to consult the Book of Changes.

> The sage has seen the complex things in the world and imaged them in forms and symbols. Thus those forms and symbols are called images. The sage has witnessed the movements of things and observed how things meet each other. In performing a proper ritual, he can append his judgements of fortune and misfortune to lines of the *gua*. This is called judgements to the lines (yao). . . . To tell the most complex things without disliking them, to tell the most subtle movements of things without confusion. To simulate before

speaking, to reflect before acting. It is in simulation and discursive thinking that the sage can detect and make changes.[1]

Here we see that the gua can be like an image used to focus the mind upon. Much like many of the meditative techniques used in Tibetan Buddhism in which a deity is imagined so as to focus the mind upon its archetypal powers, the I Ching gua could be used in the same way to obtain their power. In some martial arts styles the animal figure is used to adapt the power of the animal shamanically. We can visualize and simulate the gua inside us, inside our heart minds, to gain through their archetypal power. This is a more esoteric usage of the gua for martial arts and combat techniques. Focusing on something for power is an ancient technique, usually referred to as idolatry, and has been used on everything from statues to mountains to archetypes to objects of affection. The I Ching provides a direct experience of a symbolic language through the energy of the archetypes or daimons: the I Ching is *experienced* not spoken. It is because of this experiential nature that the I Ching is able to circumvent the problem of translation involved in language by providing a direct experience of life energy through the hexagrams. As Karcher notes, "the oracle's signifiers are complex networks of meaning related to dream-images, which disfigure everyday language. Its truths, or unveilings, are not simple but are comprehended through a deliteralizing of language and event which moves the questioner towards mysterious depths."[2]

The energy symbols used within this oracle are known by many names: gods, archetypes, daimons, angels, djinn, spirits, and, interestingly enough, ancestors. The I Ching then can be said to be made up of daimonic ancestors. Viewed under this lens, the concept of Fu Xi and Nü Wa as the first couple and originators of the human race takes on an interesting twist. If it is ancestors and DNA we are talking to, then Fu Xi and Nü Wa become the fountainhead of our origins and live in our flesh.

The Nature of the Daimons

The exact nature of the daimons cannot easily be pinpointed. The psychologist Carl Jung described the daimons as "a psychic force, a transformational energy and source of images that cuts across boundaries."[3] For Jung, the daimon was equivalent to his idea of the archetype. The nature of the daimons can be further examined in their ability to contain forms within themselves. Psychology professor Robert Frager, in a lecture, described archetypes as "form without content . . . archetypes are basic patterns of a motif that can take many forms . . . a pattern through which energy may flow."[4]

The word *daimon* or *demon* comes to us from the Greek. According to *Plato's Symposium,* the daimon is defined as something intermediate between the human and the divine. A journey into the etymology of the word gives us two possibilities, as no one is quite sure as to its exact origin. First, it could be related to God and divinity, coming from the Proto-Indo-European root *deiwos* for God, originally an adjective meaning "celestial" or "bright, shining."[5] The daimons are gods in their own right in history and are recognized as bringing the divine into our lives.

But the etymology of the word also suggests another interpretation. The word *daimon* stems from the Greek verb *daiesthai,* meaning "to divide, distribute." M. L. von Franz also observes that "the word *daimon* comes from *daiomai,* which means 'divide,' 'distribute,' 'allot,' 'assign,'" but she also suggests that it "originally referred to a momentarily perceptible divine activity, such as a startled horse, a failure in work, illness, madness, terror in certain natural spots."[6] When we consult the I Ching, we divide yarrow sticks into lots, and so the daimon becomes our lot in life, our allotted portion. This means the daimon is a moment in time or, rather, a moment outside time, when the curtains of conditional reality are parted and we peer into divinity. Daimons are a separation of physical and divine form. They are the moment when the numinous is visible, a lifting of the veil.

Dialogues with Daimons

In the West we have few tools to access our intimate selves. What does it mean that we as a culture have lost our ability to communicate with our own souls? Why do we need an oracular tool to fish around within our murky depths? The need for a dialogue with divinity for humans is one that is timeless and sincere, but is it really necessary to commune with daimons for that to happen? In fact, it is necessary as we seem to become sick or crazy if we cease to have a dialogue with the archetypes and daimons. Karcher notes in *Total I Ching* that "dialogue with that unseen world marks the difference between serving a god or being a victim of a mania."[7]

The I Ching provides a tool to access our subconscious mind and bring it into the sphere of our awareness. From a Jungian perspective, the I Ching provides us with a tool to uncover our shadow, all the repressed parts of ourselves. The I Ching shines a light in the attic and cellar of our consciousness, uncovering all the stagnant unpleasant entities.

Part of the problem many of us have with communing with daimons is that the word *daimon,* or *demon,* has a connotation of evil. This evil association might seem odd if one was unaware of the extreme amount of labor the Christian churches have put into making sure we make this connection. In fact, there was a very systematic eradication of the archetypes/daimons by the Christian churches during the suppression of the pagan religions. Sadly enough, we as a culture have been forced into not speaking with our shadows by a religious institution. It is as if we received a lobotomy as a culture, unable to remember the language with which to contact a part of our minds. Karcher points out in his article "Re-Enchanting the Mind" that the "psychological importance cannot be overstated. The point at which the Holy Spirit demonized the pagan spirits was a decisive event for world culture. The shadow that fell on the gods, the flesh, and the cosmos fell on all races and cultures."[8]

Though not all these daimons are nasty, some of them certainly are. In the archives of the archetypes, one will find many a trickster. It seems then that contact with these daimons is not always desirable, and, if possible, a direct contact with the source of all archetypes and daimons would be the ideal. But is this even possible? Can we contact the source directly without the intermediary? Is the source different from the archetypes and daimons? We have forgotten the language of the gods, and we need interpreters. These daimons are essentially the go-betweens, translating the light of higher spirit and consciousness into something we can understand.

The truth is, the archetypes and daimons in the I Ching are in us also; we can't view them as something evil and separate from the self. Perhaps more shocking is the realization that they *are us.* They each represent an aspect of ourselves we deny. If we don't let them into our campfire circle, they will forever prank us, making us sick and feeble. We can't reach the whole of the source without taking all our undesirable bits and pieces along for the ride.

The I Ching and the Healing and Martial Arts

How exactly does talking with the spirits cure diseases and heal souls? In Chinese medicine there is a saying: *Tong zi tong bu tong zi tong,* which means "Where there is stagnation there is pain; where there is no stagnation, there is no pain." The type of change involved in the I Ching is similar in that it removes blockages, freeing stagnant energy and allowing it to flow. Things get hidden deep within our psyche and fester because we ignore them.

Just as acupuncture removes stagnations of qi and blood, allowing them to flow freely, the I Ching removes clots of stagnant daimons. The first word of I Ching is *yi,* which means "change" or "transformation." Yi can also mean mobility or fluidity, which I think corresponds beautifully to the Chinese concept behind the use of acupuncture. The change involved in the I Ching is more of a revealing, a clearing of the way to allow flow, like a constantly moving river. Once something burbles up from the unconsciousness to consciousness, we can see it for what it is and deal with it openly. You can fight much better with your eyes open than with your eyes closed.

The way both martial arts and Chinese medicine primarily follow the I Ching, in addition to theory and philosophy, is through the concept of adapting to change. In both systems, the knowledge of the I Ching assists us to adapt, much like DNA, to internal and external changes. In medicine we adapt to overcome a disease; in martial arts we adapt to overcome the opponent. The subtle use of going with the flow of change was found to bring extraordinary ability to maneuver in the worlds of medicine and physical combat. All things mirror nature, and the I Ching provides a system of understanding nature that can be applied to many situations, medicine and martial arts being among those. The effect the I Ching had upon Chinese medicine is well known and written about by many scholars throughout history, and even certain acupuncture systems are dedicated to it.

The primary text of Chinese medicine is the Yellow Emperor's work, the Huang Di Nei Jing, which is completely philosophically based on Fu Xi and the gua of the I Ching. It is to Fu Xi himself that the origin of the acupuncture needle is attributed,[1] and this is profound indeed when any question of the I Ching's influence on Chinese medicine arises. Gary Dolowich, author of *Archetypal Acupuncture,* notes how early on the I Ching influenced Chinese medicine to take a holistic approach to health.

> In the I Ching we find the seminal expression of the wisdom of ancient China, as well as a guide for inner development. By encouraging us to view the symptom as a teacher, it sets a tone that has permeated the practice of Chinese medicine throughout the ages. In fact, among the many formative teachings to be found within this classic text is perhaps the earliest statement anywhere of the wholistic approach to health. . . . Indeed, in its attitude toward healing and commitment to treat the root of the condition, the I Ching truly becomes "the soul of Chinese Medicine."[2]

The gua can be used practically in Chinese medicine in a couple of ways. You can literally ask the I Ching questions regarding treatment or diagnosis directly, which is done very often all over Asia. You may also use the gua in association with either the yin-yang theory of application (basic binary polarities) or the five-element theory of the *zhang-fu* organ system. Because all of the gua can also have correspondences with the five elements, one can make the necessary affiliations between the medicine and the yi using the elemental interpretations.

The way the I Ching is utilized in martial arts systems is also through the gua. The gua have affiliations with different body postures or poses and so are made into a system of movement in this way. If one looks deep into the roots of most martial arts systems, one will read the point at which they connect to the bagua or eight directions somehow, and it is here that the link to the I Ching can be found. The bagua influenced both internal and external forms of martial arts. Looking at different qigong systems, we can easily see the bagua penetrating the majority of the postures. Some like to debate the I Ching's relevance to martial arts, claiming that the early developers of qigong did not base it off the I Ching; however, sufficient evidence points to many qigong masters specifically deriving the postures of the physical body directly from the bagua. Though slightly controversial, the qigong concepts behind moving the body into certain postures, which formed the basis for most martial arts systems, originated with the I Ching.

Even modern martial arts systems, such as Bruce Lee's jeet kune do, are influenced by the I Ching. Lee explains this in his book *Chinese Gung Fu.*

Gung Fu is for health promotion, cultivation of mind, and self-protection. Its philosophy is based on the integral parts of the philosophies of Taoism, Ch'an (Zen), and I'Ching (Book of Changes)—the ideal of giving without adversity, to bend slightly and spring back stronger than before, and to adapt oneself harmoniously to the opponent's movements without striving or resisting. The techniques of Gung Fu emphasize not on power but in conservation of energy and moderation without going to either extreme (Yin & Yang).[3]

DNA, the I Ching, and Daimons

The first person to take public notice of the correlations between the I Ching and DNA was the molecular biologist Gunther S. Stent in 1969, sixteen years after the discovery of DNA by James Watson and Francis Crick. Stent published his findings in the book *The Coming of the Golden Age*. In this work, Stent is amazed by his own findings.

> The congruence between it [Yi Ching] and the genetic code is nothing short of amazing. For if Yang is identified with the purine bases and Yin with pyrimidine bases, so that old Yang and Yin correspond to the complementary adenine and thymine pair and new Yin and Yang to the complementary guanine and cytosine pair, each of the 64 hexagrams comes to represent one of the nucleotide triplet codons. The "natural" order of the Yi Ching can now be seen to generate an array of nucleotide triplets in which many of the generic codon relations manifest in Crick's arrangement are shown.[1]

The structure of DNA and the I Ching are nearly identical. Both DNA and the I Ching are made up of four base pairs that combine in sixty-four different combinations. In the I Ching the sixty-four combinations are the hexagrams; in DNA the sixty-four combinations are the codons. The I Ching uses combinations of whole and broken lines, much like DNA does: when DNA is replicating, or undergoing "change," the base pairs are linked or separated. Johnson Yan details the interconnections in his book *DNA and the I Ching: The Tao of Life*.

Both DNA and the I Ching are based upon a binary quaternary code that generates a system of 64 possibilities . . . both systems embody probabilistic principles . . . oracular response or amino acid. Both systems involve processes of transformation and change: in the I Ching, hexagrams change into other hexagrams through the interchange of yin and yang lines; in DNA, point mutations occur through changes in the nucleotide bases.[2]

These combinations of whole and broken lines come together through probability and coincidence to form the hexagram symbols that make up the body of the I Ching. Through a mathematical interpretation of these whole and broken lines we may derive binary number sequences. Both DNA and the I Ching can be broken down into binary number sequences formed by coincidence. German philosopher Gottfried Wilhelm Leibniz comments on the parallel nature of his own findings and the I Ching.

What is amazing in this reckoning is that this arithmetic by 0 and 1 is found to contain the mystery of the lines of an ancient King and philosopher named Fuxi, who is believed to have lived more than 4,000 years ago, and whom the Chinese regard as the founder of their empire and their sciences. . . . The Chinese lost the meaning of the *Cova* or Lineations of Fuxi, perhaps more than a thousand years ago, and they have written commentaries on the subject in which they have sought I know not what far out meanings, so that their true explanation now has to come from Europeans. Here is how: It was scarcely more than two years ago that I sent to Reverend Father Bouvet, the celebrated French Jesuit who lives in Peking, my method of counting by 0 and 1, and nothing more was required to make him recognize that this was the key to the figures of Fuxi. Writing to me on 14 November 1701, he sent me this philosophical prince's grand figure, which goes up to 64, and leaves no further room to doubt the truth of our interpretation, such that it can be said that this Father has deciphered the enigma of Fuxi, with the help of what I had communicated to him. And as these figures are perhaps the most ancient monument of science which exists in the world, this restitution of their meaning, after such a great interval of time, will seem all the more curious.[3]

This is important because binary number sequences are very good at recording information. Nearly all computers are programmed using binary numbers, and computer memory relies on this aspect of storage. DNA is very much like the stored memory (in binary form) of evolution, and the I Ching is the computer we may use to access and interpret this stored data. For example, the word-processing program Microsoft Word is essentially just a bunch of zeros and ones, but when you download it into a computer operating system, you can use it to write papers. In this way, amino acids and I Ching readings both record an instant in time and space to form something solid. They are a physical manifestation of a memory. DNA is a physical manifestation of a memory because it is a marker of an evolution or change caused by an event that really happened. As Yan notes, the I Ching is a physical manifestation of a memory because it provides access to this marker of evolution into something interpretable.

> Coincidence is not a rare event because life itself may be a coincidence. However, to search for such a coincidence in the brain library . . . a much more elaborate searching device is needed for digging out a cross reference in the stored records of memory. The I Ching may be the first example of such a device. A snapshot of the coincidence is taken in the process of divination and recorded as ritual numbers of hexagrams.[4]

Accessing the Divine through Gaps

> *The work of hunters is another thing:*
> *I have come after them and made repair*
> *Where they have left not one stone on a stone,*
> *But they would have the rabbit out of hiding,*
> *To please the yelping dogs. The gaps I mean,*
> *No one has seen them made or heard them made,*
> *But at spring mending-time we find them there.*
> ROBERT FROST, FROM "MENDING WALL"

Stephen Karcher mentions Mircea Eliade's idea that the daimon is a gap, or an interruption: "'The paradoxical point of passage from one mode of being to another' (Eliade). The daimones are gaps, holes, openings torn in the web of consciousness. This violation of the norms represents the creativity of the sacred."[5]

Calling the daimons gaps is very interesting because gaps in DNA spur it to change and evolve. When DNA gets damaged by some chaotic factor, its fabric is ripped, creating an opening. There are specific genes involved in DNA repair that then go to work reweaving the DNA, changing it to prevent the damage from happening again; this is where evolution takes place. Older genes become switched on to prevent further damage from occurring, and atavisms are accessed to evolve the organism. A 2001 scientific article explains how DNA repair can provide information about evolution.

> There is much interest in the identification and characterization of genes involved in DNA repair because of their importance in the maintenance of the genome integrity. The high level of conservation of DNA repair genes means that these genetic elements may be used in phylogenetic studies as a source of information on the genetic origin and evolution of species . . . Such alterations include DNA strand breaks and base loss.[6]

Just as DNA is prompted to fix what went wrong and fill the gap, the daimon causes the individual to reimagine the world as a result of the awareness of its presence. The daimon is meant to bring our attention to something through chaos or disease, and the gap in DNA serves the purpose of propelling us into a necessary evolution on a cellular level. Karcher goes on to describe the gap nature of the daimon: "Each daimon is the 'image of an opening.' It is an 'irruption which imposes itself from the outside' which the individual must make his own through creative re-enactment. These gaps torn in the web of conscious order represent the creativity of the sacred."[7]

The fact that it takes some kind of rift in time, a jump, a gap, or an obstacle to jolt us out of the ordinary is not a difficult concept to imagine—for how many of us voluntarily make changes unless it is an absolute necessity? Change is often chaotic and horrifying in its nature.

This concept is further detailed by a deeper meaning of the Chinese word *yi*. The very name of the oracle, the I Ching, gives us insight into its nature. The Chinese character for I Ching appears very much like replicating DNA, and the symbol that the Chinese use for yi really looks like a section of DNA undergoing "change" or transcription. As Karcher notes: "The most important word in the book is its name, Yi [I], . . . usually translated as change, or changes. Philosophically, Yi is primordial change, the mutations of transformations that initiate the process of generation and transformation in all the myriad beings, the wangwu."[8] This primordial change, which, says Karcher, "determines the generation and transformation of the myriad beings" is very much like the genetic sequences that all vertebrates share that determine whether a life-form is a man or a mouse. Change is destabilizing, chaotic. As Karcher notes: "Yi or change is usually perceived as a destabilizing change, the precursor of a paradigm shift. It is a challenge to the fixed, overdeveloped, oppressive or outmoded. It indicates sudden storms, times when the stable becomes fluid and structures fail."[9] The I Ching is a book of changes, which is exactly what DNA is too. DNA is a book of all the changes we have been through in the history of life on this planet.

Although it is nice when everything is still, calm, and peaceful, we actually need chaos for movement to occur. When there is tension and chaos it inspires friction and movement, which is the source of growth. Without chaos things can get stagnant and no change will occur. It is the chaotic that inspires action. The I Ching allows us to come into dialogue with the daimons so that we may fill the gaps created by them and evolve. We evolve through changes, transformations caused by fluid adaptation to our surroundings and chaos, expressing potentialities previously latent. Our ability to change is our main defense against death and extinction: if we can't go with the flow, we are consumed by it. Our DNA knows this and accordingly changes and transforms us subconsciously and within our bodies, operating on physical, emotional, mental, and spiritual levels.

The daimonic gaps also relate to the second word in the name of the oracle, *Ching*, which means a loom containing a warp and weft.[10] The daimons are like gaps within a loom, as Karcher explains.

Kairos represents a . . . demon of the time inscribed in each of us . . . Kairos initially described weak spots in the skeleton an arrow or spear could penetrate to reach life within. It included shifting openings in bronze plate armor which an archer aimed at, openings in battle groups through which an attack could be made, and openings in fortifications. Another root refers to the openings in the vertical web of a shuttle loom, openings which last for a limited time and through which the horizontal woof-thread must be shot.[11]

DNA too has a warp and a weft, horizontal and vertical lines that are constantly reweaving themselves through the act of replication, changing threads here and there as they go.

Here we see a good definition of DNA, a pattern through which energy (and information) may flow. DNA is a pattern of proteins (GATC in different combinations) that contains information for all the forms inside your body. In other words, contained in DNA are potential forms. If the archetype is form without content, then it is also a *potentiality* of forms, much like DNA. An archetype, like DNA, contains within it possible combinations of forms. DNA is a pattern of proteins within each cell that contains information for all the organs inside your body. One of your liver cells, for example, contains within its DNA all of the information for all the other cells in your body. Even though it contains all of this within it, it only expresses the liver cell information. I think of an archetype as a strand of DNA containing within it possible combinations of forms, expressing different ones at different times. Interestingly enough, energy also flows through DNA. DNA is very conductive because it is a liquid crystal. Archetypes or daimons have also been described in history as not only outside our bodies but also within them. We are literally made up of these archetypes and daimons, as are the hexagrams of the I Ching. In fact, the similarities between DNA and the I Ching are really rather amazing.

Poet William Butler Yeats describes the power and function of the daimon like this:

Daimon is timeless, it has present before it [a man's] past and future, or it has no present and is that past and future, and as the dramatizations recede from his waking mind and from the dreams that reproduce his waking desires they begin to express that knowledge. The daimon or timeless individuality contains archetypes of all possible existences whether of man or brute, and as it traverses its circle of allotted lives, now one, now another, prevails. We may fail to express an archetype, or alter it by reason, but all done from nature is its unfolding into time.[12]

Indeed, Jung states that the daimons have taken up residence in our bodies and our psyches and can make their presence known, when we ignore them, by causing disease.[13] According to Jung, the daimons are primarily inner, seen outwardly only as a result of our own projections of them. The shamans claim that our bodies are full of these daimons, or spirits. They inhabit every feature of our physical forms. In his book *The Cosmic Serpent,* Jeremy Narby quotes *ayahuasquero* Pablo Amaringo: "'A plant may not talk, but there is a spirit in it that is conscious, that sees everything, which is the soul of the plant, its essence, what makes it alive.' According to Amaringo these spirits are veritable beings, and humans are also filled with them: 'Even the hair, the eyes, the ears are full of beings. You see all this when ayahuasca is strong.'"[14]

Both the daimons and the gua of the I Ching are mirroring and expressing the inside of our forms. The I Ching forms a kind of hologram of our interior world that we can view with our senses, as if we were turned inside out to inspect our inner essence. The purpose of the I Ching is to open a dialogue with the daimons so that we may have an interchange. It allows us to communicate with the deepest parts of ourselves. Angus Nicholls, in his article "The Secularization of Revelation from Plato to Freud," describes this indwelling intelligence.

> *Entelechy* or *entelechia* refers to the "first actuality" of any particular organism . . . *entelechia* refers to an indwelling form or essence which determines the organism's activity and development, while at the same time containing within itself the organism's complete potential. The metaphor which perhaps best approximates the *entelechy* is the seed of a plant, which is the cause of the plant's existence, growth and characteristics, and which also holds the biological prototype or imprint of its full development. The *entelechy* is perhaps the closest thing in the Aristotelean corpus to the Platonic Daemon. In contradistinction to Plato's notion of the Daemon, the *entelechy* is immanent and substantial, rather than transcendent and insubstantial. Common to both terms, however, is an element of "fate" or "predestination." Like the Platonic Daemon, which on one level functions as the soul's "lot" in life, and which Heraclitus also specifically associates with the individual's fate or destiny, the *entelechy*

is a kind of essence which determines the future development of the organism, in what amounts to a kind of biological determinism.[15]

Why Is It Important to Access This Data and Evolve?

If, while asking ourselves what the meaning and purpose of life can be, we find that the key to accomplishing something of objective value lies in our potential for inner evolution, then we must find special methods which can teach us how to use our mind, body, and emotions to transform our inner selves.

E. J. GOLD, THE HUMAN BIOLOGICAL MACHINE AS A
TRANSFORMATIONAL APPARATUS

The word *evolution* literally means "the unfolding or unrolling of potential." The Latin root of the word is *evolutio,* which means "unfolding." Before Darwin came along, the word *evolution* was only used to describe unfolding processes, like the development of an embryo. After Darwin, people forgot its earlier meaning. Evolution is not the adding of something new but the discovery of something already contained within. For us to evolve as humans we must draw from what we already contain within ourselves. We may build ourselves by accessing our genetic tool kits, as the evo-devos would say. Evolution is a realization of our true potentiality. We will not be spurred to evolution from some outside source; it will come to us through realizing who we already are, as F. A. Popp so well expresses: "The paradigm introduced here leads to the recognition that spirit can be transformed from matter, and matter only gains in significance through the spirit. An apparently elementary, complementary truth stands behind this transformation. The genetic Yi Ching provides such a 'periodic system of the spiritual element,' and acts as a goal for human evolution."[16]

We don't know the origin of DNA. How it formed and exactly how old it is remains unknown to us even though it runs throughout our entire bodies. Crick, the codiscoverer of the form of DNA, supposes that it came to Earth from an extraterrestrial source of some kind.[17] As organisms who can't remember our individual births, much less the origin of our species, I believe we have a paramount responsibility to explore the transformational techniques of the I Ching and unlock the memory latent within our bodies to help us evolve, individuate, and manifest our deepest potentialities. To evolve our minds, bodies, and spirits through transformational psychology, we must integrate all aspects of our entire being. This integration extends to the molecular level of our bodies. It is my belief that if a person truly wishes to individuate, the integration of his or her *entire* life, right down to the moment of conception, as well integrating ancestral memories and previous lifetimes, is part of this process. Although this is a daunting prospect, to say the least, it is not impossible and has been accomplished by shamans throughout the ages. If, through transformation, we wish to individuate our souls, let us realize exactly what this entails and what is expected of us. I would like to propose a reintegration of these ancient shamanic techniques so that we may disinherit the millennia of baggage our souls have accumulated through generations of incarnations and begin anew. Karcher notes that "the creation and enshrining of an ancestor spirit is an extremely important ritual . . . [it is] one of the most important manifestations of change and its way of transformation."[18]

To rise and evolve with our ancestry, instead of having it weigh us down, is how we will grow as individuals and as a species. Frager notes, in order to individuate, we must incorporate these archetypes/daimons: "Individuation is a process of achieving wholeness and thus moving toward a greater freedom. The process includes development of a dynamic relationship between the ego, persona, shadow, anima or animus, and other archetypes."[19]

We may utilize our stored atavisms to gain more knowledge and insight into our deepest selves and get to know our DNA. Through the I Ching, we may remember what it means to be human beings. The knowledge of transformation is contained within our every cell, stored in our bodies, expressed down lineages of generations, and we must let it out.

It is the serpent who gave knowledge to Adam and Eve in the Garden of Eden and to Fu Xi and Nü Wa by the Yellow River in China. Perhaps it will be through the serpent of DNA that we may rectify this heritage and consciously inherit our ancestry. Jonathan Young notes that "Carl Jung made it his task of tasks to find the myth that was living his life. Once the general pattern of the tale becomes evident, the challenge is to participate in the rewriting of one's own story. We may not be able to create the rivers that carry us along, but we can certainly navigate the little boats of our lives."[20]

PART 2

The Serpent Oracle

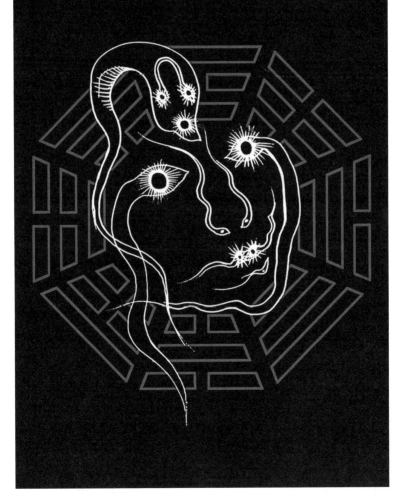

Instructions and Considerations for Using the Oracle

Several different methods have been used over the years to determine the answer to a question with the I Ching. Each one uses statistical sequences and probabilities, which could possibly influence the outcome, but that is hard to determine. A quick search on Google will yield many deeper explanations, so if you enjoy statistics and the methodologies involved, there is a plethora of information regarding those factors. However, most of the Taoist masters indicate that the outcome is generated by the spiritual sentience of the daimon, who forces your hand to do the draw at an exact moment of time, so perhaps the math is irrelevant.

Traditionally in ancient times, turtle shells were used for divination, likely because of the origin myth of the I Ching: perhaps the shamans felt it made the most sense to use these shells for divination. The shaman heated a turtle shell over a flame until it cracked and then read the resulting pattern of cracks. But this technique was harmful to the turtles, and it was also difficult to do and required a lengthy investment of time. And so, over time, other methods were developed that yielded equally accurate results. Yarrow sticks became a popular method for many years—a technique similar to the drawing of lots for fortune, which was used all over Europe.

Today, I Ching computer software programs and phone apps are common: these programs generate a response and then look up the hexagram interpretations within the I Ching. Another common, easy method is throwing coins. In my experience, the computer-generated answers are just as good, but I will briefly describe the coin technique.

For the Coin Toss

For the coin method you will need three coins. You can choose any kind of coin: pennies, quarters, farthings—they all work. Some prefer Chinese coins, and those are available for a cheap price in stores and on the web.

Some people enjoy ritualizing this method, and by all means do whatever you like. The main idea is to concentrate and focus. Setting up a ritual is a good way to focus your mind on what you are doing, which can assist with a deeper, clearer reading, especially if you have not yet established a relationship with the I Ching.

The question itself is fascinating. With my clients I often spend some time helping them to articulate the question itself. Think about the wording or phrasing of your question. A good detective can solve a case if he asks the right question. Asking the right question is a good way to get a revelatory answer. Try to be specific: think about what it is that you have been wondering about for a while and use contemplation to help you form the question. Don't forget that you can ask any question at all; it's not limited to yourself or your life. You can ask about science, the universe, spirit, daimons—whatever your mind can conceive of. You can also choose to have no focus at all and allow the daimon to deliver the message. I like to ask about "now"—and it then delivers the most pertinent thing on which I should focus.

After you have set up your space, have configured your question, and have cleared your mind sufficiently, hold the coins loosely in your hands, shake them, and then give them a throw.

You will do this six times. The hexagram will be built from the bottom up, like constructing a house. The first line will be the foundation, and the last line will be the roof.

Some people like to assign a numerical value to the head and tail sides of the coins, but I find it is easier to just read them straight as heads or tails. If you are using foreign coins that do not have discernible heads or tails, assign one side to be heads and the reverse to be tails.

The I Ching is a binary generator. There are two energies you are dealing with: yin and yang. Yin and yang are Chinese conceptions of two polarized forces. Yin is female, dark, cold, earth; and yang is male, light, hot, heaven. These are more energetic than literal. Energy manifests as two polar extremes and then a combination of the two, which forms the Tao in Chinese philosophy. If you wish to investigate this further, I recommend *A Source Book in Chinese Philosophy* by Wing-Tsit Chan. These polarized forces are also discussed at length in all the material on alchemy, so if you learn the I Ching, you will also become well versed in alchemy by default as a bonus.

Each line of your hexagram will be one of four possibilities: yin that doesn't change, yin that changes, yang that doesn't change, and yang that changes. Yin lines are written as broken, and yang lines are unbroken.

A yin line that changes will be three tails.
A yang line that changes will be three heads.
A yin line that doesn't change will be two tails and one head.
A yang line that doesn't change will be two heads and one tail.

Some people like to indicate a changing line with an X for a changing yin line or an O for a changing yang line to keep track, or you can just put a dot next to your changing lines. What follows is an example of a hexagram constructed from six tosses of the three coins.

Sixth, final toss: 3 tails (changing broken yin line, or X)   —— ——
Fifth toss: 3 heads (changing solid yang line, or O)   ————
Fourth toss: 1 tail, 2 heads (solid yang line)   ————
Third toss: 1 tail, 2 heads (solid yang line)   ————
Second toss: 2 tails, 1 head (broken yin line)   —— ——
First toss: 2 tails, 1 head (broken yin line)   —— ——

If there are no changing lines, the hexagram remains the same. Because this hexagram has changing lines, an entire second hexagram is generated. This is your relating hexagram, or what the situation is becoming or heading toward. Look up the second hexagram as well as the first, to extract the meaning of the result of your query; there will be no changing lines in the second hexagram.

In this case, you make the second hexagram by changing the sixth line into a yang line and the fifth line into a yin line, so that it looks like this:

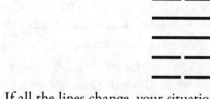

If all the lines change, your situation will undergo a lot of change; if no lines change, it will be fairly the same through time. Some people interpret the second hexagram as the future, but I would advise against such predictive divinations because they exclude growth and free will. Instead, I like to view them as potential capacities or navigational directions.

If all this is tricky for you to get the hang of, you can just do it on an app, which doesn't, in my experience, seem to change the outcome of the reading.

How to Do Your Reading Using This Book

Once you have generated a hexagram, look it up to find out which number it is, using the chart included below. Once you look it up and find out what archetype you are dealing with, turn to the page of that gua, or hexagram, in the text and read the general meaning of the hexagram and, if applicable, the specific numbered lines of the hexagram for your interpretation. While the general information for the hexagrams applies to all readings, read only the descriptions for the *changing* lines you have drawn and ignore the others. Your changing line(s) is the one that applies directly to you.

Each changing hexagram line provides a lens for interpreting your situation.

Line one, the first line you generate, which forms the base of the hexagram, is about you. If the first line is changing, this indicates something you yourself need to do.

Lower Trigram ▽ / Upper Trigram ▷	1 Heaven	2 Lake	3 Fire	4 Thunder	5 Wind	6 Water	7 Mountain	8 Earth
1 Heaven	1	43	14	34	9	5	26	11
2 Lake	10	58	38	54	61	60	41	19
3 Fire	13	49	30	55	37	63	22	36
4 Thunder	25	17	21	51	42	3	27	24
5 Wind	44	28	50	32	57	48	18	46
6 Water	6	47	64	40	59	29	4	7
7 Mountain	33	31	56	62	53	39	52	15
8 Earth	12	45	35	16	20	8	23	2

Line two is the other person or people around you and describes their situation; this line helps you navigate or understand things from their perspective.

Line three is about unification—aligning your perspective with that of the other person or people. It is also about unifying yourself with your environment or a larger issue. This line is the rectifier.

Line four is about Earth. Now we leave the smaller human perspectives and take a larger view of the situation. Four is a transpersonal line that tries to see things from a broader perspective.

Line five is about conflict. Here we have obstacles and issues that are outside us, and we need to sort them through, using some strategy or technique.

Line six is the view from above. This is the perspective of heaven, which transcends Earth and delivers the spiritual take on the situation. This line provides a bird's-eye view and helps us to transcend the issue.

For each hexagram there is an "all lines changing" section, which describes what happens when you throw a hexagram and all of the lines change, converting the hexagram into an entirely new thing. When this happens, a *lot* of change is occurring, and a different overall meaning is generated than if only one of the lines underwent a transformation. When all the lines change, the transformation will be more profound, and this section addresses that situation.

For each line in this book I also include the shadow line, or *fan yao* as it is called in Chinese. Each line has its shadow line, which transforms the line into its opposite. Look up the shadow line for each line you draw at the indicated hexgram number and line locations (44.1, for instance, indicates hexagram 44, line 1), and it will tell you what the opposite is in the situation, thus allowing you to see the issue in more totality. I have found the shadow line very helpful in my considerations and recommend looking up both the line you draw and its shadow.

The guru description for each hexagram offers a higher perspective or spiritual lesson that goes beyond the mundane or superficial interpretation. I also provide personal examples for each hexagram, generated from my years of pulling hexagrams in response to people's questions. I have noticed patterns in the answers to certain situations in which people find themselves, and I point out those patterns in this section of the text.

Hexagram Descriptions Decoded

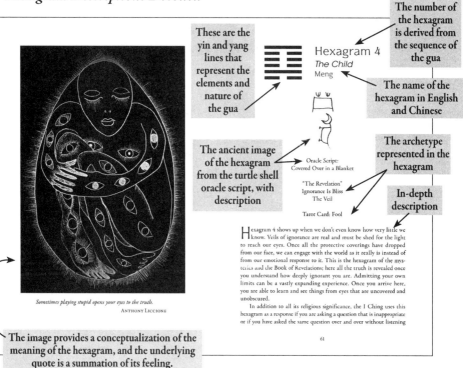

These are the yin and yang lines that represent the elements and nature of the gua

The number of the hexagram is derived from the sequence of the gua

Hexagram 4
The Child
Meng

The name of the hexagram in English and Chinese

The ancient image of the hexagram from the turtle shell oracle script, with description

The archetype represented in the hexagram

Oracle Script:
Covered Over in a Blanket

"The Revelation"
Ignorance Is Bliss
The Veil

In-depth description

Tarot Card: Fool

Hexagram 4 shows up when we don't even know how very little we know. Veils of ignorance are real and must be shed for the light to reach our eyes. Once all the protective coverings have dropped from our face, we can engage with the world as it really is instead of from our emotional response to it. This is the hexagram of the mysteries and the Book of Revelations; here all the truth is revealed once you understand how deeply ignorant you are. Admitting your own limits can be a vastly expanding experience. Once you arrive here, you are able to learn and see things from eyes that are uncovered and unobscured.

In addition to all its religious significance, the I Ching uses this hexagram as a response if you are asking a question that is inappropriate or if you have asked the same question over and over without listening

61

Sometimes playing stupid opens your eyes to the truth.
ANTHONY LICCIONE

The image provides a conceptualization of the meaning of the hexagram, and the underlying quote is a summation of its feeling.

---

to the answer it already gave you. This hexagram can be a chastising slap on the wrist.

This hexagram embodies the Book of Revelations, where symbolically the individual comes out of ignorance as the truth slowly becomes visible and the unconscious mind rises to the surface to come into gnosis. Once the covering is removed from something, the light can expose or reveal all aspects; a revelation is a disrobing, a coming out of childish foolishness into mature adulthood and wisdom. The process of the apocalypse is played out in this hexagram, which tells the story of understanding what ignorance is and how it affects humanity. This understanding begins with first recognizing what you do not know and progresses to a sympathetic awareness of the inherent state of humanity living in a world of darkness and fear.

Guru: Humility can only be arrived at by initiates if they first admit how little they could possibly know from their limited perspective. Miraculously, once you can deeply understand that you are by nature unable to be aware of all the infinite possibilities, you come into a state of joyful folly at how absurd you were to think otherwise.

Personal Example: I receive hexagram 4 consistently if I overask questions and the I Ching refuses to give me more answers. The meaning of this hexagram is also related to something not quite done developing yet, or not done cooking, like a fetus in a womb. I received it in response to someone asking if she were pregnant several times, and it turned out she indeed carried a baby in her womb. Each time a client inquires repeatedly about a subject, we invariably arrive at hexagram 4. This hexagram has also come up with clients who feel shame concerning a subject. The hexagram suggests Adam and Eve hiding in the Garden of Eden from God because they were ashamed they had disobeyed the rules. Make sure you are not hiding something from yourself because you are ashamed of it.

The Changing Lines

Line One—The Self
Your need to be protected is preventing the freedom of your own expression. The very thing that will make you feel more at ease is restricted

Advice of the hexagram from the perspective of a spiritual initiate

Experience of the hexagram from personal practice

If you had a changing line, this is the advice and meaning of the change

---

and confined due to past loss and failure. Free and liberate yourself once more and be as an innocent child.

▶ Transforms into Shadow 41.1

Line Two—The Other
Sometimes it is important to cover things over. Not everything has to be ripped apart to expose its tender underbelly. A child does not need to know the horrors of everything in order to be real. In some circumstances, it is better to keep something under wraps for the good of all. Be discreet when innocence is involved.

▶ Transforms into Shadow 23.2

Line Three—The Union
Trying to keep secrets with some people could be dangerous if their commitments to someone or something else place you in jeopardy. Some secrets are yours to keep, but others do not belong to you. When you keep your own secrets, the potential fallout is less than when you keep the secrets of others. Make sure there are no conflicts, and only keep secrets that involve your personal affairs.

▶ Transforms into Shadow 18.3

Line Four—The Earth
Accept that people will make the wrong choices; next time, present them with a better choice. Ignorance means someone didn't know any better, and we have all been there, so compassion is in order when such a situation develops. Make sure you give second chances, but don't foolishly acquiesce to constantly repeated patterns.

▶ Transforms into Shadow 64.4

Line Five—The Conflict
There is nothing like learning from your own ignorance to inspire you to teach others who are in the same boat. Once the veil is removed from your eyes, assist those around you to clear their vision as well. Someone who realizes the folly of his or her ways enough to attempt to assist others suffering the same mind-set achieves great virtue through repentance.

▶ Transforms into Shadow 59.5

The resulting line from the change; look up this hexagram and line for more meaning

The location of the line from bottom to top in the hexagram

The place where the change occurs relative to you

Some Interesting Things
about the Hexagrams

In Stephen Karcher's book *Total I Ching*, he notes that most of the hexagrams form pairs, mirroring each other in the sense that many of them when reversed form their following partner, with the exception of some of the dynamic hexagrams. For those of you interested in this amazing discovery, I highly recommend his book. Also listed in this work are ways to manipulate the hexagrams to generate the seasons, interior hexagrams, and shadow hexagrams—highly valuable tricks that can add data to your inquiry.

The hexagrams can be arranged in different ways to form sequences. Two of the most famous sequences are the Fu Xi sequence and the King Wen sequence. These are essentially ways of organizing the hexagrams that change the algorithms when you are performing the reading. Most works use the King Wen sequence, but if you want to discover more about shifting and playing with these, there is quite a bit of data available online. From the four base yin-yang combinations, outlined on page 35, you can generate a little more than ten thousand potential responses. This number is particularly intriguing in light of the old Taoist adage "Tao becomes one, one becomes two, two becomes three, three becomes the ten thousand things" (from the Tao Te Ching).

The hexagrams can also be used to generate specific dates and times and even geographical locations. Many of the folks who do feng shui use the I Ching in this fashion. There is a particularly amazing way to generate times known as the plum blossom method, which you should investigate if you seek to gain data of this sort. There is a great book by Alfred Huang on this called *The Numerology of the I Ching: A Sourcebook of Symbols, Structures, and Traditional Wisdom*.

Some Considerations

Daimonic practices have a danger of becoming compulsive. When engaging with a divination system, only you can control your impulses. Watch yourself, and do not sit there doing readings over and over. Chase down a thought, concept, or situation, but do not be excessive: take time to contemplate each answer. Avoid becoming addicted to the system as a way to make your decisions. The oracle can only give you things to consider, but you must never abandon your autonomy to anything, or you risk illness and a loss of integrity. Decide upon your own actions, and think of all oracles as advice from a friend.

You can form a relationship with a divination system that is like a dialogue. The I Ching is a sentience you can interact with. Think about it like you are talking to a person and treat it with respect and reverence. Address it as if you were soliciting advice from a friend or mentor. If you want to have a relationship with someone for a long time, how would you treat him or her? How would you share the intimacy of your innermost thoughts and fears? You do not need to change who you are with any oracle; just be honest with yourself and you will get to the truth much quicker. The I Ching provides you with the means to confront anything, and that is a gift.

Spiritual Implications for the I Ching

The I Ching is like a magic puzzle box. It is a living Lo Shu magic number square, much like the Saturn magic square magicians have used in Western occult traditions. Each line of the gua provides a key to escape the matrix cube. If we think of this puzzle like a maze or labyrinth, we can say that the I Ching provides a thread, a divine thread of the golden ratio, to navigate to the center. The maze is the human consciousness.

When you seek a solution through the I Ching, you realize that the purpose of the question you asked was to lead you to the realization that you knew the answer all along, deep within yourself. The I Ching tested you to bring your truth up against its advice: when you found a match you were delighted, and when you got a scolding you were ashamed. When you got blamed, you felt self-righteous. By paying close attention to your questions and the answers, you will become aware that you are a powerful being whose mind has no limits. You need no device such as the I Ching, for you yourself are a living oracle, living ancestor, living wisdom. Speak into your own belly when you have a question for the I Ching, and you will find that your heart whispers back the answer in its response to the feeling. You, your own inner wisdom, is responding to your feelings, not the I Ching.

What matters most when you read this book are not the words

written upon its pages. Rather, pay attention only to the feelings inside your heart. You will learn what is true not by what is written in this book but by how your heart feels. In this way, you will grow an oracle within your flesh that you can carry with you always. When you disagree with the oracle, harken to your heart: you do not need to agree with it; you only need to listen to your own response to the draw. This is called discernment. The secret of the I Ching is to pay attention to your reaction to it.

Hexagram 1
The Dragon
Qian

Oracle Script:
The Breath of Heaven

"As Above, So Below"
Creative Conception
Contact with the Muse

Tarot Card: Sun

Hexagram 1 is the mechanism of creation. Every line is yang, and it is the supreme masculine or heavenly father archetype. It is the creative force, which in the Hebrew Bible is described as the Ruach Elohim, or breath of God. The breath of God creates life through interacting with the Earth below it in a penetrating fashion. A perfect example of this concept is when the Holy Spirit breathes life into Adam, who is only a hunk of clay. It was this same breath in the form of the Holy Spirit that impregnates Mary with Jesus in the Judeo-Christian Bible. The dragon is the animating force that brings things to life, the breath that makes us live each moment and inspires us to continue with our respiration.

In the I Ching, the concept of heaven, or *qian*, is translated as dynamic tension, which can be compared to a string pulled taut, like a guitar string that, when tightened, yields a specific tone. The dragon

The Spirit of God hath made me, and the breath of the Almighty hath given me life.

JOB 33:4

is the vibrating superstring that lies at the heart of all matter, swirling and singing in the heavenly chorus. In the Chinese version, heaven is something that is stretched out or far reaching; it goes horizontally, not vertically. Hexagram 1 then is something that can stretch very far and remain tightly wound, or not lose its tension. We can think of this like the practice of martial arts or yoga: both develop flexible yet strong bodies. Something taut yet supple, strong yet flexible are the qualities of heaven and the divine masculine force.

> qian₇ "To pull / lead by a rope" (cattle) [BI, Shu], "attach" [Lü]
> ... "to lead by hand, drag along, stretch out or tighten a rope."
>
> AXEL SCHUESSLER, *ABC ETYMOLOGICAL*
> *DICTIONARY OF OLD CHINESE*

Guru: From the guru aspect of this hexagram we receive a lesson of the divine masculine and how sometimes creation requires force. Sometimes it takes a good old-fashioned knock on the noggin to get the lesson through. This is the place in our spiritual journey where we need to take direct action and learn the correct way to impose the will of heaven so that things on Earth may be accomplished. In this perfect blending of the action we take and the wish that our destiny has for us, we come into the ability to create and manifest within our lifetime. The essence of this hexagram is relating something that can exert a force upon the Earth from above.

> *Yes, Love indeed is light from heaven;*
> *A spark of that immortal fire*
> *With angels shared, by Alia given*
> *To lift from earth our low desire.*
>
> LORD BYRON, FROM "THE GIAOUR:
> A FRAGMENT OF A TURKISH TALE"

Personal Example: I received this hexagram unchanging when a client asked the oracle about her cannabis use. I thought this response was fascinating since the meaning is literally creative inspiration that enters through the breath. Some might not appreciate the depth of this response from the oracle, but one need only research the many artists, musicians, and philosophers who employ its use in their endeavors to be aware of the creative influence cannabis exerts upon the user. I also was struck by the oracle script image for qian, which looks like the chemical compound of a cannabinoid joining its receptor in the human brain. The "lock and key" biological enzymes function looks very much like the image of the dragon reaching down from heaven to join with Earth.

The Changing Lines

Line One—The Self
Keep yourself hidden. Don't act out of season, like eating flowers before they turn to fruit. Reserve your creative power. Sometimes you don't have to make a huge display. Just knowing you have it might be enough to turn the tide without action. Withholding your intention of what you know deep within and letting it grow on the inside can have more power than action.
  ▶ Transforms into Shadow 44.1

Line Two—The Other
To see a dragon is a great omen that you are on the right track. If you have a bright idea, do not fail to recognize it. Write it down; pay attention. Don't let it slip by into obscurity. Try to harness it into something for all to see. Inspiration may come to us from an outside source, but until we fashion it into something, it is just a passing fancy.
  ▶ Transforms into Shadow 13.2

Line Three—The Union
Do the work; get your hands dirty. Turning an idea into a fruit that can be eaten takes a lot of labor. Just as a seed requires care to become an apple tree, so too does your creative idea require work to manifest in the world. A baby takes a lot of time and energy to grow within a womb and must be nurtured. Do not be afraid to nurture your creations.
  ▶ Transforms into Shadow 10.3

Line Four—The Earth
Caught in the middle of making a decision is a good place to be if you are not sure which way to go. Wavering can create dynamic tension that

ensures you arrive at the correct choice. Deliberation does not have to turn into frustration if you can capture its energy. By hesitating, we are more likely to decide on an action instead of simply responding emotionally. The difference between unconscious and conscious action is that the latter is decided through deliberation.

▶ Transforms into Shadow 9.4

Line Five—The Conflict

A beautiful dragon is meant for all to see. Don't be shy or worry what others might think of you or your ideas. The most difficult demon to conquer is a lack of self-worth, which afflicts even the most noble and virtuous hearts. Realizing that you have equal worth upon Earth as other creators can make the difference between allowing yourself to express yourself and shrinking into the shadows. Be bold and fearless when showing what you are worth: you are as good as gold, after all.

▶ Transforms into Shadow 14.5

Line Six—Heaven

Sometimes heaven can be too high to reach. We must learn from Icarus that if we fly too high, before we are ready, the fall can be great indeed. No matter how great the idea is, it still does not raise you above the level of humanity. Mind your manners even in the face of your own greatness, which can be as great as a dragon but likely not greater than a dragon. Arrogance is a sure way to experience humiliation, one of Earth's greatest teachers, often experienced when doing a face plant in the dirt. Brush yourself off and get back up, but leave the chip on your shoulder in the mud.

▶ Transforms into Shadow 43.6

All Lines Changing—Hexagram 2

Only when we become a dragon can we join a flock of other dragons, equal but different, all with their own strengths and weaknesses. If we are a great and powerful dragon, we don't need to lead others but rather may find what is great and powerful within everyone. What we may, on first judgment, take to be a lesser companion could be a diamond in the rough. The great sees the great in all.

Nothing could be more irrational than the idea that something comes from nothing.

R. C. Sproul

Hexagram 2
The Mare
Kun

Oracle Script:
The Fertile Earth

"Prima Materia"
The Matrix of the Womb
Formation from Clay

Tarot Card: High Priestess

Hexagram 2 represents the divine feminine energy of holding a space for creation. This space is vacuous but at the same time filled with potentiality of all forms. It is the vessel that holds creation, much as the hermetic container that brews the seed of life. This space is a vital part of matter, although it is empty. Kun is the dark yin Earth Mother; she is the Great Goddess, sometimes called Demeter, Cybele, Hecate, and Kali. Within her caves all things are formed and all life takes its time upon her soil only to return to her embrace at the end of its journey. This hexagram is the great "womb and tomb" of all life. In Chinese this hexagram is also described as a female horse who roams Earth searching for her child, much like the myth of Demeter. The fertile mare is forever roaming, seeking to become impregnated with the creative spirit. She is Mother Mary awaiting her visit from the Holy Spirit.

The word *kun* in Chinese typically translates as earth, in a very literal fashion, meaning dirt. Some scholars have traced kun to *chthonic* and *chthon*, Greek words for "earth."[1]

The Primal Chaos

I want to speak about bodies changed into new forms. You, gods, since you are the ones who alter these, and all other things, inspire my attempt, and spin out a continuous thread of words, from the world's first origins to my own time. Before there was earth or sea or the sky that covers everything, Nature appeared the same throughout the whole world: what we call chaos: a raw confused mass, nothing but inert matter, badly combined discordant atoms of things, confused in the one place. There was no Titan yet, shining his light on the world, or waxing Phoebe renewing her white horns, or the earth hovering in surrounding air balanced by her own weight, or watery Amphitrite stretching out her arms along the vast shores of the world. Though there was land and sea and air, it was unstable land, unswimmable water, air needing light. Nothing retained its shape, one thing obstructed another, because in the one body, cold fought with heat, moist with dry, soft with hard, and weight with weightless things.

OVID, *METAMORPHOSES*, BOOK 1, 1–20

Guru: As a spiritual teaching for the individual on his or her path, hexagram 2 will appear when you must become receptive to spirit and not try to force a situation or make something happen yourself. It is about submission to a greater force and clearing a space for something to appear that is a gift from spirit. Where hexagram 1 denotes action, this hexagram is about inaction and asks you to receive from, not give to, the matter at hand. Allow spirit to come into a space you have made empty. Make your mind like a womb; empty it so that it can hold the will of spirit instead of your daily thoughts, racing to and fro.

Personal Example: I find that I consistently get this hexagram nearly every time I ask the I Ching about how I can act in a situation that does not seem to be going my way. It advises, when I most want to take control of a matter, to be receptive to some other form of action not coming from myself. When I get hexagram 2, I know I need to do some clearing, either of a space or of my thoughts, and allow something to happen that is not of my own doing. I got this hexagram when I was distraught at having no money to buy clothing for my children, and upon its advice, I decided to clear out the closet of all their old clothes and donate them to the local Goodwill. After I did this, I got several boxes of clothes from my sister that had been her daughter's: all I had to do was make room and wait.

The Changing Lines

Line One—The Self
This is the place where you can form something. Things are becoming solid: from out of the dark cave of chaos, something is starting to crystallize. Nourish it and watch it grow. If things have been ambiguous, you can now make out the shape of them. Examine them closely in this formative time; the shape something takes gets set in a mold.

▶ Transforms into Shadow 24.1

Line Two—The Other
The Garden of Eden is where everything can grow. If conditions aren't right in Eden, growth is inhibited, so keep your courtyard free from weeds. Eden is so fertile, it needs only the rain and sun to form life. Use the resources of your surroundings to help something take shape. Earth provides everything you need, even if it's not everything you want.

▶ Transforms into Shadow 7.2

Line Three—The Union
Nurture and grow things safely in a container that will give their form strength and beauty. It takes a long time to grow things; they can't be rushed. Haste makes waste, so don't force something into something you think it should be: pay close attention to what it is. Union with another can come when both parties are able to grow on their own time into what they are destined to be, even if it doesn't meet your expectations.

▶ Transforms into Shadow 15.3

Line Four—The Earth

It's all in the bag. Here the womb is full, and you can create whatever you want with it. Take time to consider beyond what you think is possible as you gratefully acknowledge that you have been given all you will need to create your deepest wish. Here we see a sack of gold to be given away in exchange for something you have always wanted.

▶ Transforms into Shadow 16.4

Line Five—The Conflict

Chaos emerges from something you thought was orderly, and you are thrown into confusion! Take a minute to consider events before you feed despair. Often trust is tested, and patience is burned to its bitter end. See what deep reserves you have contained within you before assuming you know the truth. Pursue the truth from all sides and view the situation impartially. Chaos need not destroy all the beautiful flowers you have planted in your garden.

▶ Transforms into Shadow 8.5

Line Six—Heaven

Forced up out of the earth like a volcano, you can not return to the calm and stable way things were. Change is upon you, so do not fight it; look at where the mud is flying and get out of the way. Before blood is drawn, look for peace within yourself, and don't let anyone make you blow your top.

▶ Transforms into Shadow 23.6

All Lines Changing—Hexagram 1

When the feminine force of damp earth becomes too stagnant, gas is stored beneath its surface, which can cause an eruption. The force that drives up all the darkness is so powerful it reverts back to the masculine yang energy of creative potential. Here the mother impregnates herself in a parthenogenic fashion in which the two forces are briefly in unison until the male yang has spent itself and things settle again.

Hexagram 3
The Birth
Zhun

Oracle Script:
The Power of Spring

"Birth of the New"
Bursting Forth
Manifesting Form

Tarot Card: Empress

This hexagram is the manifestation of creation in a crystallized form that is born unto the world. To me, hexagram 3 is the Christ child, born from the unification of two opposing forces. This is the result of the *hieros gamos*: something new and fresh enters into the world. In traditional texts this hexagram is represented by a fresh green shoot erupting from the earth. Every birth is unique, special, and unrepeatable, just as the dawn of each day will never be seen again. Explore each new thing as you come across it without taking it for granted, and share in its energy, which is exuberant, vital, and alive with celebration: a field of flowers shouting at the top of their lungs to greet the sun. Creation includes everything, including yourself. It is hard for new life to get off the ground, but once it picks up steam, there is no stopping its force. Establish a foundation for something that will grow well into the future.

*For the alchemist the one primarily in need of redemption is
not man, but the deity who is lost and sleeping in matter.*

CARL JUNG, *PSYCHOLOGY AND ALCHEMY*

The hexagram symbolizes the moment when the Creator formulates the golem Adam out of clay. Rabbis and alchemists attempted to be like the Creator by making things from the fertile earth by smelting metals, carving diamonds, and hewing stone. It is the chrysopoeia of the alchemists—the creation of the philosopher's stone and the completion of the Great Work.

In Chinese, the word *zhun* means "an accumulation of strength that shoots something up." It is like a sprouting plant, or an army gathering, or cells replicating to make a life-form. This hexagram embodies the idea of gathering together to grow stronger, which leads to growth, but this is hard at first until it gains enough momentum.

> *Signs are taken for wonders. "We would see a sign!"*
> *The word within a word, unable to speak a word,*
> *Swaddled with darkness. In the juvescence of the year*
> *Came Christ the tiger*
>
> *In depraved May, dogwood and chestnut, flowering judas,*
> *To be eaten, to be divided, to be drunk*
>
> T. S. ELIOT, FROM "GERONTION"

Guru: The spiritual teaching of hexagram 3 is closely related to the story of the birth of Christ. Here something new that never existed before arrives, and it is hard to accept at first because it is different. Although we all get excited upon a new arrival, it is tricky to adjust to change, so often there can be resistance to greeting the new. This story is about being able to make a new thing and release the old so that the new may grow. This is difficult at the beginning until we are able to repent. A new plant's hardest task may be the job of breaking through the soil so that it is free to grow. Similarly, if we wish to create a new thing, we must repent and change our old ways every day.

Personal Example: I received a profound realization regarding the true nature of this hexagram. It was about the power of life itself and what a certain shade of green represents—the bright and vibrant yellow-green of spring, like chartreuse, when the first green leaves emerge. The name Chloe, which is associated with Demeter, means "blooming" or "young green shoot." Synchronistically, I was shown the meaning of the name when it happened to pop up alongside "Nothing Gold Can Stay," a poem by Robert Frost, the first two lines of which read "Nature's first green is gold, / Her hardest hue to hold." This hexagram is the chrysalis holding the new form before it emerges into the joy of being alive on Earth. *Chrysalis* comes from the Greek *khrusos,* meaning "gold," referring to the color of the nascent pupa. It is spring in all its glory. I got this information when I asked the I Ching a question regarding the nature of life and how things are created.

The Changing Lines

Line One—The Self

The pillar upon which all is built. It is said that faith is the pillar of the firmament. Pay attention to what is giving you support. Here we see a column rise from the mucky swamp. This is Mount Ararat, where Noah's ark was able to find dry land and come out of the chaotic waters. The ground on which you stand has a core foundation that has allowed something to come to fruition. Try to give it room to grow. The maypole arises from the friction of the demons and angels playing tug of war with your emotions; find what remains in the center to rise into clarity.

▸ Transforms into Shadow 8.1

Line Two—The Other

Stability wavers as commitment falters and communication falls into disarray. Before freaking out over why something is falling apart, first focus on repairing the foundation before the whole edifice topples to the ground. Commitment is easy when everything goes your way, but if you are willing to cease your efforts as soon as circumstances change, your carefully spun pot soon crumbles into shapeless mud.

▸ Transforms into Shadow 60.2

Line Three—The Union

Spring energy can bring spring fever and throw people into impulsive behavior. Do not get so lost in the fertilizing energy that you lose your direction. It is always fun to go after romance, but keep your responsibilities a priority to prevent an eclipse of the heart where fantasy obscures reality.

▶ Transforms into Shadow 63.3

Line Four—The Earth

Things have gotten to a point of stability with others. Disagreements start to fade into the background, and unification can take place. The material is there to feed everyone, so grow it with generosity and abundance for all without hoarding or suspicion entering the scene.

▶ Transforms into Shadow 17.4

Line Five—The Conflict

Your tiny seedling has grown into a tree that now can provide life-giving fruit to everyone. You are now able to enjoy the fruits of your labors, which are meant to be shared and enjoyed in merriment and conviviality.

▶ Transforms into Shadow 24.5

Line Six—Heaven

Your carefully nurtured project or relationship has fallen to the ground. There has been a separation, and your foundation is shaken. Do not overly grieve the loss, for all things return to the earth when their time has come. Your salty tears can't water a garden. Let the rain nourish the earth and leave the salt water for the sea.

▶ Transforms into Shadow 42.6

All Lines Changing—Hexagram 50

From the fertile earth of hexagram 2, an earthenware pot has taken shape and has been fired in the hot kiln of trial and tribulation, taking us to the vessel portrayed in hexagram 50. The efforts of solidification of form in hexagram 3, when charged with change in every line, have made the shape of the *ding,* or sacred cooking pot. The plant that has grown from the soil can be harvested and placed to simmer in the pot. This vessel can now contain the food to feed and nourish your spirit thanks to all your patience in creating a stable shape. You can be sure you will have plenty to eat all winter.

Sometimes playing stupid opens your eyes to the truth.

ANTHONY LICCIONE

Hexagram 4
The Child
Meng

Oracle Script:
Covered Over in a Blanket

"The Revelation"
Ignorance Is Bliss
The Veil

Tarot Card: Fool

Hexagram 4 shows up when we don't even know how very little we know. Veils of ignorance are real and must be shed for the light to reach our eyes. Once all the protective coverings have dropped from our face, we can engage with the world as it really is instead of from our emotional response to it. This is the hexagram of the mysteries and the Book of Revelation; here all the truth is revealed once you understand how deeply ignorant you are. Admitting your own limits can be a vastly expanding experience. Once you arrive here, you are able to learn and see things from eyes that are uncovered and unobscured.

In addition to all its religious significance, the I Ching uses this hexagram as a response if you are asking a question that is inappropriate or if you have asked the same question over and over without listening to the answer it already gave you. This hexagram can be a chastising slap on the wrist.

This hexagram embodies the Book of Revelation, where symbolically the individual comes out of ignorance as the truth slowly becomes visible and the unconscious mind rises to the surface to come into gnosis. Once the covering is removed from something, the light can expose or reveal all aspects; a revelation is a disrobing, a coming out of childish foolishness into mature adulthood and wisdom. The process of the apocalypse is played out in this hexagram, which tells the story of understanding what ignorance is and how it affects humanity. This understanding begins with first recognizing what you do not know and progresses to a sympathetic awareness of the inherent state of humanity living in a world of darkness and fear.

Guru: Humility can only be arrived at by initiates if they first admit how little they could possibly know from their limited perspective. Miraculously, once you can deeply understand that you are by nature unable to be aware of all the infinite possibilities, you come into a state of joyful folly at how absurd you were to think otherwise.

Personal Example: I receive hexagram 4 consistently if I overask questions and the I Ching refuses to give me more answers. The meaning of this hexagram is also related to something not quite done developing yet, or not done cooking, like a fetus in a womb. I received it in response to someone asking if she were pregnant several times, and it turned out she indeed carried a baby in her womb. Each time a client inquires repeatedly about a subject, we invariably arrive at hexagram 4. This hexagram has also come up with clients who feel shame concerning a subject. The hexagram suggests Adam and Eve hiding in the Garden of Eden from God because they were ashamed they had disobeyed the rules. Make sure you are not hiding something from yourself because you are ashamed of it.

The Changing Lines

Line One—The Self
Your need to be protected is preventing the freedom of your own expression. The very thing that will make you feel more at ease is restricted

and confined due to past loss and failure. Free and liberate yourself once more and be as an innocent child.

▶ Transforms into Shadow 41.1

Line Two—The Other

Sometimes it is important to cover things over. Not everything has to be ripped apart to expose its tender underbelly. A child does not need to know the horrors of everything. In some circumstances, it is better to keep something under wraps for the good of all. Be discreet when innocence is involved.

▶ Transforms into Shadow 23.2

Line Three—The Union

Trying to keep secrets with some people could be dangerous if their commitments to someone or something else place you in jeopardy. Some secrets are yours to keep, but others do not belong to you. When you keep your own secrets, the potential fallout is less than when you keep the secrets of others. Make sure there are no conflicts, and only keep secrets that involve your personal affairs.

▶ Transforms into Shadow 18.3

Line Four—The Earth

Accept that people will make the wrong choices; next time, present them with a better choice. Ignorance means someone didn't know any better, and we have all been there, so compassion is in order when such a situation develops. Make sure you give second chances, but don't fool-ishly acquiesce to constantly repeated patterns.

▶ Transforms into Shadow 64.4

Line Five—The Conflict

There is nothing like learning from your own ignorance to inspire you to teach others who are in the same boat. Once the veil is removed from your eyes, assist those around you to clear their vision as well. Someone who realizes the folly of his or her ways enough to attempt to assist others suffering the same mind-set achieves great virtue through repentance.

▶ Transforms into Shadow 59.5

Line Six—Heaven

If you are tempted to beat a teaching or message into someone who is not getting it, you may not be a good teacher. Take care how you handle those who are acting out of ignorance: you don't know everything either. Defend against violence, but don't use violence against ignorance as a means to control it. Lack of education is a failure of responsibility of the powers that be, not a failure of the ignorant.

▶ Transforms into Shadow 7.6

All Lines Changing—Hexagram 49

Some secrets when covered over for too long may require revolutionary action to prompt a change or expose the secret. If you leave things under wraps indefinitely, someone may come along to reveal what you were trying to hide—like a sudden gust that lifts up a skirt. Better to reveal your own dirty little secrets than wait too long and leave them for someone else to notice.

Hexagram 5
The Growth
Xu

Oracle Script:
Waiting for a Break in the Weather

"Precipitation Cycles"
Out of Your Control
Be Ready When the Time Comes

Tarot Card: Seven of Pentacles

Working the earth to sustain yourself requires great toil. Even if you do everything just right, Nature might not do what you think she should to support your harvest. Those who work through and understand the cycles of nature know they must be patient and prepared. True wisdom can be found in that approach. Many modern people are used to instant gratification. They expect to be fed immediately when they walk into a restaurant. But those who cultivate the earth understand the labor involved.

The Seven of Pentacles, which represents this hexagram, is called by some the Lord of Failure. The Lord of Failure is also a nickname for Jesus because he was able to beat death and rise again: he prevailed over failure. There is an occult secret to this hexagram, which is the mystery of the grain gods. These dying and resurrecting gods

He drew me up from the pit of destruction, out of the miry bog, and set my feet upon a rock, making my steps secure. He put a new song in my mouth.

PSALM 40:2–3

perish in the winter but rise again in the spring. These lessons involve being able to go the distance and rise again, even through scarcity and death. The image in the Rider-Waite Tarot of a man leaning over his tools, waiting for his garden to grow, is a perfect picture for this lesson. All food grown from the earth is given, as manna: we need only nurture it and we are fed.

Fair ladies, you drop manna in the way of starved people.
WILLIAM SHAKESPEARE, *THE MERCHANT OF VENICE*

Guru: This hexagram can be a lesson in waiting for spirit to provide you with spiritual nourishment instead of actively seeking it. Rather than taking action, cultivate your environment and prepare for something to emerge, but do so with a certainty that it will happen and with an awareness of how nature operates—not through blind faith and ignorance. Doing this will surely bring success. The key in this situation is not to anxiously await something but rather to occupy your time by productively nourishing until the moment arrives. If time is spent forever in disarray, worrying over the next event, we will lose, instead of gain, the gift.

Personal Example: This hexagram appears when clients have done a lot of work and are eager for their reward. In answer to the question, "When is it coming?" I often receive hexagram 5, which essentially says: when it's good and ready. It's a bit mean but also a reminder that not everything works on your schedule; some things run on nature's schedule. One client asked a question regarding when his next job would arrive, and the I Ching's response was hexagram 5, as if to say, "It will arrive in due time; in the meantime make all your preparations." This response calls for patience and faith in cycles when you have done the work needed.

The Changing Lines

Line One—The Self
Focusing on the task at hand and working hard toward preparing for an eventuality has power in affording confidence and comfort through

sheer force of labor. Predictions of the weather are poor substitutes for standing outside in the elements with your flesh and bones. You can feel the rain coming a mile away if you try.

▶ Transforms into Shadow 48.1

Line Two—The Other

If you set a lightning rod into the ground, you will attract a strike. A flexible blade of grass is much less likely to be struck down by the gathering storm, which blows right on by, seeking something more reactive.

▶ Transforms into Shadow 63.2

Line Three—The Union

A foolish farmer believes the gossip that the sky is falling and destroys his crop in expectation of a failure, while the wise one watches the weather before coming to any conclusion, much less taking an impetuous action. Gathering clouds are not enough to act upon.

▶ Transforms into Shadow 60.3

Line Four—The Earth

If you are trapped in a storm cellar waiting for the hurricane to pass and all you do is imagine the damage, your prison extends farther than the walls of earth that surround you.

▶ Transforms into Shadow 43.4

Line Five—The Conflict

Seeking shelter from the storm is a natural instinct. To run and seek cover could be wise. Some individuals, whom others might call crazy, choose to dance in the rain and call the thunder into their hearts—strange practices that seem like madness. Can you see the beauty in the decision to disregard safety in favor of feeling alive?

▶ Transforms into Shadow 11.5

Line Six—Heaven

Just because a storm left you in the mud doesn't mean you have to sit in it and wallow like a pig. Free yourself from the force of its suction through concentrated effort. Quicksand captures what panics and sinks you deeper in its embrace. Release your flailing despair, and you might find that you float to the surface.

▶ Transforms into Shadow 9.6

All Lines Changing—Hexagram 35
After all storms at sea the dawn arrives. Be transformed by the renewing of your mind even after a brutal barrage of negative charges that mired you in negativity; it is never too late for a fresh perspective.

Wise men speak because they have something to say; fools because they have to say something.

PLATO

Hexagram 6

The Conflict

Song

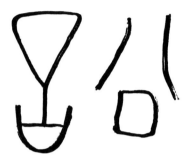

Oracle Script:
The Argument

"Friction Is the Driving Force of the Universe"
Differing Viewpoints
Stating a Complaint

Tarot Card: Lovers

Hexagram 6 arrives when there is trouble in paradise. Either you are already having an argument, a situation has occurred in which you must state your case, or this situation is about to happen. Hexagram 6 leads us into a time when we must come into contention. It describes two oppositional forces making contact with each other. This is a beneficial and necessary thing on Earth and in heaven. Oppositional forces *must* interact, for this is the way that growth occurs. If everything were always easy, nothing would happen. There are different ways oppositional forces can contend with each other so that both of them benefit and grow, and there are also times when one dominates and even destroys the other. Every relationship of our lives will come to know such times. If you view these times as opportunities to grow and mature, you can make some real headway. When arguments are aimed toward diplomacy and growth, all of civilization benefits. Keep your focus on the goal of growth rather than destruction, and you may come into the value of hexagram 6 rather than its detriment, which is bickering. Negativity must be expressed to achieve intimacy; here we see the methodology of such communications brought to the forefront.

The deep meaning of this hexagram is best represented by the symbol of the caduceus. The caduceus is a staff with two snakes intertwined around it. The serpents are the two oppositional forces. The places where their bodies cross over each other represent the moment when they came into confrontation and contention with each other, and these points are what permit them to rise up along the staff. It is friction that moves all things. This hexagram is connected to hexagram 43, the internal struggle of the mind, but here we externalize it in our dealings with others through discourse and debate. Look into Socratic dialogue methods for assistance in such matters.

When the debate is lost, slander becomes the tool of the loser.

SOCRATES

Guru: Diplomacy requires wisdom. If we do not learn how to negotiate with family members, friends, and acquaintances, our relationships disintegrate. On a national scale, disagreements lead to war. Being able to mediate between people and problem solve was King Solomon's role in the Bible. People sought his advice because he was one of the few people who had this ability, which speaks volumes about the difficulty most people have in achieving this important life skill. First, realize that this is a universally challenging task, and you are not alone in finding it difficult; second, develop some skills in this area to help in all aspects of your dealings with others. Imagine if we were all such wise judges as Solomon!

Personal Example: I had an exceptional instance of this hexagram regarding a male client. He sat down and asked about a surgery he was going to have and then said nothing more about it. We drew hexagram 6, which in many books reads as "a lover's complaint"; the image is interpreted by some as a penis and a mouth. So I asked him if he was having penis surgery, and he responded that yes he was. I asked him if the reason for the surgery was due to a complaint from a lover, and indeed it was. He and his girlfriend had argued over it, and she won, which resulted in him modifying his body. So here the image and title of the hexagram were exactly specific to his situation. This hexagram also occurs frequently for court cases and litigation.

The Changing Lines

Line One—The Self

Focusing on other people's attacks upon you is as foolish as thinking you can grasp a storm cloud. If it is already over, permit the weather to change and move on. Don't hold a grudge.

▸ Transforms into Shadow 10.1

Line Two—The Other

When we fall into disagreements with the other, sometimes simply sacrificing a personal need for acknowledgment in favor of finding the truth can resolve the entire situation before it escalates. If you are speaking with another person out of a desire to get sympathy or to emotionally manipulate the situation, you are not speaking from your heart and being vulnerable; you are trying to influence the situation in your favor—and here truth is lost. Follow the truth even if it doesn't go your way.

▸ Transforms into Shadow 12.2

Line Three—The Union

If we are resilient we can more readily flex our way through a passageway than if we are resistant. If you are clinging to the threshold in fear, resisting change, release your grip, even if that first step is a doozy. Be willing to meet the challenge and investigate it rather than dreading it as something you don't want to do. By permitting ourselves to go through transformational experiences, we are transformed.

▸ Transforms into Shadow 44.3

Line Four—The Earth

Even if you win an argument through force, it is a loss because you have lost the other's respect and loyalty to you through your disrespectful and uncaring, arrogant dominance. Truth requires no dominance, and if you are so frustrated that you raise your voice, reexamine your own ability to promote education rather than your need to be heard and validated.

▸ Transforms into Shadow 59.4

Line Five—The Conflict

When witnessing others in conflict, use strategy and diplomacy to assist them in settling their differences. It's easier to resolve problems when you are not on the hot seat. Advocating for others is a blessing and a virtue for you can offer an objective view that hovers above emotional entanglements like a flying bird. The value of gaining perspective is that the contention can be released and rectified.

▸ Transforms into Shadow 64.5

Line Six—Heaven

If you are victorious in all your battles, perhaps you are powerful indeed. But you may find yourself without any friends. Make sure you choose your battles wisely and make choices that de-escalate others if something is not worth fighting about. Actively choose peace when there is no need to confront.

▸ Transforms into Shadow 47.6

All Lines Changing—Hexagram 36

If an argument becomes destructive, or too much force is used, one of the participants might receive an injury. When this happens there will be a withdrawal so as to recover and avoid future fallout. If the injury sustained is great enough, the withdrawal will be permanent, and you will have gained an enemy as well as the responsibility to face the consequences of your actions. Destruction should always be a last resort, and only to defend the value of life; aggressive destruction in contention ruins all.

Hexagram 7
The Leader
Shi

Oracle Script:
The Leader of the Pack

"Governing the Vessel"
Strange Attractor
Discipline through Inspiration

Tarot Card: Emperor

Hexagram 7 represents an individual who has somehow been able to trust her own heart regardless of the opinions of others. She holds her truth as a sword before her, and no dark demon can convince her otherwise. Hexagram 7 is a place where we find a balance between severity and mercy so that the greater good can be served. The Emperor understands that to serve the greater good, he must engage in evil and also perform acts of evil to protect what is valuable, while at the same time hold his discernment lest he become corrupted. This is the general or one who has been placed in charge of leading an army, not just because he was appointed to this position but because he earned it. Here people are willing to follow out of love, trust, and devotion to the leader based upon his merit and character.

Running taught me valuable lessons. In cross-country competition, training counted more than intrinsic ability, and I could compensate for a lack of natural aptitude with diligence and discipline. I applied this in everything I did.

NELSON MANDELA

In China one man was responsible for uniting all the tribes under one nation. His name was Qin Shi Huang. He was considered the first emperor of China because he made all of the provinces come together through force of his will. The famous army of terra-cotta soldiers were buried with him in his tomb. The ability of a single, alpha human to unite many and accomplish something great is an important ability that we all contain within us. Those who can unite many are forces of nature and inspire us to go beyond ourselves and what we think is possible. Imagine the impact of some indivduals through time on the hearts and minds of millions of humans. Truly, there is greatness in what a single person can achieve in his or her lifetime upon Earth. Do not forget about these individuals when you feel like you can't even get out of bed in the morning. Your innate capacity is greater than you think.

If your actions inspire others to dream more, learn more, do more, and become more, you are a leader.

JOHN QUINCY ADAMS

Guru: If you are going to be a general and lead a legion of armies, you first better make sure that you are up to the task. The guru lesson of this hexagram is self-discipline and constantly working on your character so that you become worthy of leading by example rather than just blindly rushing forward. Here we see the benefit of a daily personal discipline or devotional action or practice that makes us better able to lead because we ourselves are doing the job. The best generals who lead armies to victory were once soldiers.

Personal Example: In an interesting play on words, I received this hexagram once for a client who was of Indian descent. Her question to the oracle was, "Who am I?" The response was hexagram 7, with no changing lines. The words read "leader of armies" on the title of the hexagram, and the client started to freak out. "What?" she exclaimed. "That is impossible! My last name is in the Hindi language, and it translates exactly to 'leader of armies.'" The I Ching responded to her identity question with her ancestral identifier, her last name. She was, in fact, also a leader in her job, managing a large group of people.

The Changing Lines

Line One—The Self

If you have really big muscles, you might think that you can lift anything. But the wind laughs at you while it sweeps you off your feet. Be realistic about your abilities, and if you have been placed in a position of responsibility due to your achievements, don't blow it through buffoonery. Maintain your discipline, and keep up the good work.

▸ Transforms into Shadow 19.1

Line Two—The Other

When you want someone to get his or her life together—and maybe you want to share your life with that person—show the other how you do it, instead of telling them what to do. Leading by example has more efficacy than tyranny. When people are bossed around, they get resentful, but when they are motivated to action through inspiration, they are devoted.

▸ Transforms into Shadow 2.2

Line Three—The Union

Mutiny can happen to even the most competent leaders. It is important to understand what turns the hearts of others against you. If your people feel that they are not receiving acknowledgment or honor for their ideas, they will seek to steal what you have gained through hard work. The mutinous are seeking glory, validation, and participation. The best way to stave off a mutiny is to validate and praise your people every day. If they are not starved for attention, they won't bite the hand that feeds them.

▸ Transforms into Shadow 46.3

Line Four—The Earth

A good leader knows when to throw in the towel. If a retreat is in order for the greater good, do not wait too long and suffer losses due to pride. Always make choices for the good of the group and not just the end result. If you as a leader are unable to see past your own perspective and perform in a selfish manner, all your hard work to achieve leadership will be destroyed through unnecessary losses.

▸ Transforms into Shadow 40.4

Line Five—The Conflict

A position of high leadership comes with great responsibilities, and the leader, more than anyone else, cannot quit. Better to ensure that you are passionate about leading and are ready to go down with the ship than to turn tail and be a deserter when the going gets rough. If others depend upon you, try to be dependable.

▸ Transforms into Shadow 29.5

Line Six—Heaven

Leaders perform poorly when most of their schemes and ambitions reside in their own imagination. Remaining firmly grounded in what is possible—recognizing what can be done and how long it will take—is essential for good leadership. If a scheme is too grandiose and unmanageable and lacks the resources or food to sustain it, the leader sets up everyone, including him- or herself, for a fall. These types of failures are the saddest because they were caused entirely by delusions of grandeur. Keep your goals simple and achievable; goals that all involved have the capacity to handle.

▸ Transforms into Shadow 4.6

All Lines Changing—Hexagram 13

A leader loses her sense of self within the group so that the group may move as one. A true soldier is an alpha, complete and contained within himself, but a general can be the entire group as well as himself and, in this way, merge the minds of all to one common purpose. When a leader acts for the whole, the herd moves forward as one, all connected to one another, as if marching to some distant drum. A leader's mind becomes the one mind and expands into all.

It is an absolute human certainty that no one can know his own beauty or perceive a sense of his own worth until it has been reflected back to him in the mirror of another loving, caring human being.

JOHN JOSEPH POWELL,
THE SECRET OF STAYING IN LOVE

Hexagram 8

The Union

Bi

Oracle Script:
Kindred Spirts

"Coagula"
Team Work
The Ones We Stick To

Tarot Card: Six of Cups

Hexagram 8 represents the people we find ourselves surrounded with in our lives. These are the groups we are slotted into and categorized as, in addition to cliques of friends and our spiritually bonded kindred spirits. Birds of a feather flock together, and when we find kindred souls, we make constellations. These groups may change throughout our lives: some drift from one grouping to the next, while others remain in small tightly knit groups for their whole life. We tend to repeat patterns throughout our lives, orbiting with similar groups, even if the faces of the people change. It is important for us to notice whom we gravitate toward, for this helps us understand who we are. The people in these groups form our tribe, which become vitally important because they provide us with support. Hexagram 8 is not just about the people around us but includes the people who help support us and whom we assist in their times of need. They are companions and coworkers on up to villages and cities. Groups of people depend on and need to trust one another for civilization to be free of terror.

The image of the Chinese word *bi* for this hexagram shows two people standing next to each other, or one is watching over the other. These are the people who are nearby. The word *bi* in Chinese means "someone in proximity," or whoever is around, as in standing next to you. This image suggests the lyric from a song by Stephen Stills: "If you can't be with the one you love, honey, love the one you're with."

> *It is literally true that you can succeed best and quickest by helping others to succeed.*
>
> NAPOLEON HILL

Guru: Here we learn the lesson that we all need somebody to lean on. People are valuable for us in our lives, and one of the primary functions of the group is support. If we are self-supporting, then we must provide support for others. By supporting others, we not only ensure, through karma, that we will therefore be supported in our time of need, but we also make humanity better as a whole by assisting individuals in need. No soul should fall between the cracks of life, when this can easily be avoided by offering a helping hand. We are all mirrors of one another and at different times both give and receive support.

Personal Example: A client once asked if he had support for a project he was involved in because he felt very isolated and alone. The I Ching responded with hexagram 8, which was a strong indicator that indeed he was supported, even though he was not feeling it. After thinking about it for a moment, I asked him if he had fans who gave him feedback for the project or who bought his product, and he said yes, lots. He came to realize the support he was getting was in the form of people far away and not those nearby, such as friends and family. So I suggested that he go to the fans who supported him to be near them, which he did. He later said that he was then able to feel the support directly, once he placed himself near it.

The Changing Lines

Line One—The Self

Trust is based on how true and reliable something is. When you touch a tree and feel its bark, you trust that it exists. If you reach out and expect to touch something but find nothing there, you become suspicious and afraid. Trusting others comes with truth found through time and action. Impulsive behavior and thoughtless acts can cover what is truly eternal and can stand the test of time. Only through repeated efforts over time can we arrive at what is sincere in ourselves and others.

▸ Transforms into Shadow 3.1

Line Two—The Other

When you give to someone who supports you just to ensure that he or she will continue to do you favors then the giving becomes contrived. Sincere offerings are made from devotion and not from expectation of future gains.

▸ Transforms into Shadow 29.2

Line Three—The Union

Union with others presents risks. Avoiding all risk is impossible, but if alliances are formed through improper means, they can lead to improper things. Keep alliances simple and unfettered and for the good of all. What goes around comes around, and manipulation can catch up to everyone in the group before the end of the cycle has been reached, impeding the unfolding of organic events in their proper time.

▸ Transforms into Shadow 39.3

Line Four—The Earth

Alliances formed with someone in a position of leadership can benefit not just those in the alliance but also all the members of the group that the leader serves. To benefit the most, assist leaders who support large groups of people.

▸ Transforms into Shadow 45.4

Line Five—The Conflict

Nobody is perfect. Alliances based on perfection are as sure to crumble as the vain Tower of Babel. This is the same type of vanity described in hexagram 27 between Cain and Abel. Cain is so concerned with the perfection of his offering that he attacks his brother out of wounded pride. The work that Cain made with his hands to reach perfection is like the striving to erect a wondrous monument to show and celebrate the talents of man without acknowledging that they would be nothing without spirit. The perfection of an alliance pales in comparison to the spirit that formed it. You can put as much work as you want into something, but if you ignore the spirit behind it, it is done in vain as it will amount to nothing. Go deeper in your relationships, past the surface appearances; see the spirit within, and the roots you form will last through harsh winters of cycling errors.

▶ Transforms into Shadow 2.5

Line Six—Heaven
All things change in time, and alliances change as people change and grow. People who stay near to one another through the cycles of the seasons have a better chance of growing together, like two trees rooted side by side, their roots intertwined. But if they grow away from each other, their roots will stray to other places to look for nourishment.

▶ Transforms into Shadow 20.6

All Lines Changing—Hexagram 14
As the group and our relationship to it change, we find ourselves needing to be more self-reliant. The ability to survive with others is important, but the ability to survive on your own is crucial. Having friendships and alliances is how humans survive, but it is what you do when you are alone that defines who you are.

Hexagram 9
The Raising
Xiao Chu

Oracle Script:
Collecting the Rain

"Rearing the Cattle"
Inch by Inch, Row by Row
Cultivation

Tarot Card: Queen of Pentacles

Hexagram 9 forms a pair with hexagram 26. Both of these describe a concept of restraint or being restrained in order to build or accumulate something. These two hexagrams discover how to build power through nonaction and play a key role in spiritual work as well as learning how to restrain the physical and emotional self. One who is unable to restrain something will never be able to domesticate an animal to do important work, for the animal prefers to live in the moment, running wild in a field. As humans, we must consider things past the current moment on occasion, such as storing grains to eat in winter and containing anger so that it does not destroy a relationship. Hexagram 9 describes a small or earthy restraint that is needed to function here upon Earth. It is built a little at a time and accumulated through repetition. If we carelessly shoot off our power all the time, we may be spent

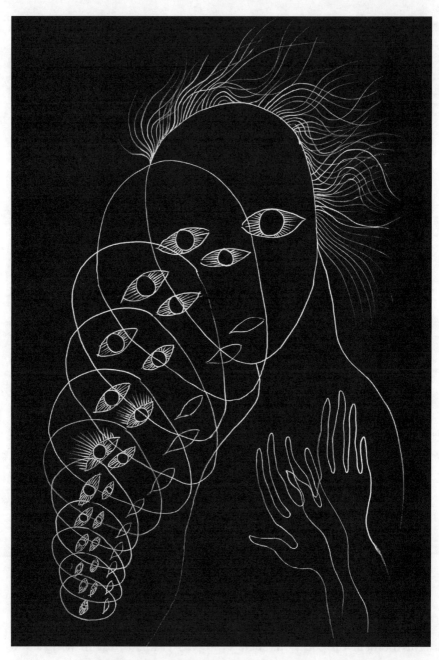

Till the gods to destruction go;
Thou too shalt soon, if thy tongue is not stilled,
Be fettered, thou forger of ill.

FROM THE POETIC EDDAS

when we most need our energy. Even though rain falls, it does not fall every day, and so some of it must be stored in a rain barrel, or we will find that we have nothing to drink.

Hexagram 9 expresses the long view over time, the need to apportion ourselves, our time and energy, in our domestic affairs. If we have a child, we know that raising the child will be spread over quite some time, so we must plan accordingly. Daily food rationing will serve us better than having a feast that lasts only one evening. Through restraining the child's impulses, we teach the child how to live in society with others.

> For want of self-restraint, many men are engaged all their
> lives in fighting with difficulties of their own making.
>
> SAMUEL SMILES

Guru: In hexagram 9 we see the story of the ant and the grasshopper. The ants work hard to store for the winter as they know that small actions build great rewards. The grasshopper, on the other hand, has not taken any small actions to plant seeds to provide for his future—and when it arrives he finds that there is nothing to support him in his time of need. If we can know what we will need through a period of unfolding or to accomplish a project or goal, we are less likely to spend all our capital on one impulse, and then suffer potential dire consequences when we lack sufficient resources to cover needs. Addressing needs is something that can be done preventively as well as in the moment. An indulgence that is restrained until it is earned carries more power than instant gratification. Enjoyment is gained through what is waited for in peaceful patience.

Personal Example: A client asked me if she could tell her boyfriend what she really thought of his behavior, and she received this hexagram unchanging. The message was to restrain her own ideas and wait to see what happened through time and to track the pattern of what was really occurring instead of just her own opinion of it. She contacted me and said that she was so grateful she restrained her emotions in favor of observation for she discovered that her accusations were assumptions and not valid in reality. A small amount of patience served to save the relationship from a volatile escalation based on misperception and prejudice.

The Changing Lines

Line One—The Self

Self-restraint is called for when joining together with those more powerful than ourselves. You might have an opinion about how things should go, but when you give up your power to one who you are trusting to be an authority, maybe you should listen to what he or she has to say. If you vastly disagree, make a choice to find another leader.

▸ Transforms into Shadow 57.1

Line Two—The Other

Family ties can feel like burdens because of the ongoing responsibility and how relationships can consume our time and attention. But is there really something more important than this?

▸ Transforms into Shadow 37.2

Line Three—The Union

Relationships must be nurtured and supported. If left unattended for too long, the relationship can come apart, like a neglected vehicle that loses a wheel. When a breakdown in communication happens, everything must be stopped and attention paid to the relationship: the car needs to be repaired lest it wind up abandoned on the side of the road—with the parties disembarking and heading in different directions. If the car seems to be having trouble traveling down the road, best to fix it before driving any farther.

▸ Transforms into Shadow 61.3

Line Four—The Earth

We redeem ourselves through self-restraint and respecting ourselves and others. It's all right to defend the self but not at the cost of the other. Do just enough to get the job done. If in your need to be righteous, to be vindicated and acknowledged, you cease to consider the life and well-being of another, you have surpassed self-defense and entered into aggression. Giving respect even when not receiving it is virtuous. When we restrain ourselves enough to let another rise above us, we are redeemed.

▸ Transforms into Shadow 1.4

Line Five—The Conflict

A soldier who gives his life to serve a cause exhibits the highest form of self-restraint through service to others, but perhaps he is martyred for nothing, since causes are human constructs. Make sure your restraint is not wasted on something that serves no purpose and has no quality to endure through time.

▸ Transforms into Shadow 26.5

Line Six—Heaven

If you restrain yourself too much, you may lose the power to act, and stagnation will result. You lose concern for yourself and are unable to act in your own self-interest. Water stored in a rain barrel cannot be used if, over time, dead leaves, dust, and insects drift into it. Grain stored must be eaten before it rots. Hoarding serves no one, so make sure what is restrained is also let free in time.

▸ Transforms into Shadow 5.6

All Lines Changing—Hexagram 16

In cases where self-restraint has gone too far, it will inevitably change into its oppositional energy, pleasure seeking. Indulgence follows famine, so be cautious about how much you restrain yourself, or you will suffer an internal rebellion—living to excess despite your best intentions.

She the refuge, peaceful and merciful undoubtedly,
She pervades over all, is universal form certainly,
Her lotus feet worshipped by universe—all Glory,
On your appeal "Protect me Durga" saves entirely.

MUNINDRA MISRA,
CHANTS OF HINDU GODS
AND GODDESSES IN ENGLISH RHYME

Hexagram 10
The Tiger
Lu

Oracle Script:
Fed by a Beast

"The Power Path"
Make Your Way in the World
Instinct

Tarot Card: Hermit

In hexagram 10 we learn how to make our way in the world. Here we are navigators, and we must rely on our own devices and decisions to find our destiny. Destiny appears only to the one who seeks a way to realize his purpose in the world. Many sleep through opportunities to reach for the stars. The stars are always there, waiting to guide people forward, but destiny will never find those who slumber. If we are courageous enough to take risks and break our habituated patterns that give us a false sense of security and well-being, we discover a new world we never knew existed. As our awareness grows past our structured domestication, we find ourselves on an exciting roller-coaster ride, going forward with our own momentum. Life is made of these daily decisions: to take a risk and grow or remain the same. Only growth can expand us enough so that we can reach the arms of Destiny, waiting to embrace us.

As long as we are persistent in our pursuit of our deepest destiny, we will continue to grow. We cannot choose the day or time when we will fully bloom. It happens in its own time.

DENIS WAITLEY

This is the hexagram of Durga, who rides a tiger in Hindu mythology. She is a goddess and one of the forms of Shakti. The earth goddess Cybele, the Magna Mater, or Great Mother, is frequently shown riding on the back of a lion. The Harlot of Babylon also rides a beast. These images illustrate using the power of nature. You contain nature within you, and when you master your nature, as Durga has, you have the powers of creation at your disposal.

Guru: The main interpretation of *lu,* the Chinese word for this hexagram, is "to tread," but it is also like a footprint or impression of something. Lu is both a verb and a noun in this sense. Our destiny is imprinted upon us from our birth, but we must tread upon its road to realize it. It is contained within our flesh; we may feel it as an instinct, driving us to look for opportunities, to express ourselves and realize our destiny. In hexagram 10, where we choose to tread, what steps we choose to take, determines the extent to which we fulfill our destiny. The guru of hexagram 10 tells us to walk upon the path, not just think about, talk about, or imagine the path.

Personal Example: I think of this hexagram like beating all the traffic by following behind a speeding ambulance and riding in its wake. When I was confused as to what to do next to realize my purpose, the I Ching answered with this hexagram. At the time I took it to mean that I should look for a powerful symbol to follow. In some translations this symbol is a tiger. We are instructed to follow behind a dangerous, powerful animal but make sure we are not bitten by it. Later that day I received an email that included a picture of a tiger, and so I followed that path, which took me through a powerful synchronistic series of events and brought a significant goal of mine to completion.

The Changing Lines

Line One—The Self

It takes courage to speak your mind, especially with a powerful leader who has more authority than you. When you must speak up about an issue that concerns the good of all, diplomatic phrasing can prevent it from becoming a clash of wills. Giving respect to all involved while bringing up grievances ensures that alliances will not be damaged.

▶ Transforms into Shadow 6.1

Line Two—The Other

Taking risks will have less emotional impact when we release our expectations. When we are free of prejudice, we suffer less from the consequences: if the risky venture is a failure, there is no loss, and if it is a success, it becomes a delightful surprise. When false hopes are dashed, we incur damage, which drives the spirit deeper into the earth. Hope and fear are not needed to act and sometimes influence the action due to expectation. Better to drop them both.

▶ Transforms into Shadow 25.2

Line Three—The Union

When you can recognize a huge risk in an action you may choose to take, it is important to be aware of the consequences. To know fully the danger involved and deny it the proper attention will result in a fall should failure ensue from the action. Precautions taken when great risk is involved can lessen the impact of a fall. If you place a mattress on the ground before jumping off a roof, you have a better chance of saving life and limb.

▶ Transforms into Shadow 1.3

Line Four—The Earth

If everything fails from a significant risk you took, don't forget that a friend in need is a friend indeed. We may find ourselves in situations of dire consequences through our choices, and it is during these times that asking for help is not only appropriate but also necessary to help us survive our risky behavior. But if you find yourself in this position continually, your friends might get tired of your requests and ask you to take responsibility for yourself.

▶ Transforms into Shadow 61.4

Line Five—The Conflict

If you choose to engage in significant risks, do not look around for someone to blame when you fail and find yourself in a stew of your own making. Be ready for what occurs and place the blame upon yourself for engaging in the risky action; that way you can move on to a solution to your dilemma. Take responsibility and avoid writhing in self-pity, looking around for someone to blame just so you can feel better about your failure.

▶ Transforms into Shadow 38.5

Line Six—Heaven

If one must engage in risky action, it can be more enjoyable with friends. Burdens are lighter when shared as a group instead of shouldering it in heavy isolation. When we find a group with which to share risks, we can be in a fellowship rather than on a hero's journey. Much glory can be found by the hero, but joy and laughter comes when we fondly share and remember with our fellow travelers even the most severe failures.

▶ Transforms into Shadow 58.6

All Lines Changing—Hexagram 15

When someone lives a life of great risk, he or she will eventually come to a place of needing others. This shift from courage in the face of danger to humbly accepting help from another can happen rapidly and fluctuate. We might think of ourselves as undefeatable, until the pendulum swings and we are humiliated. Being humbled after falling from a lofty position of self-sufficiency need not be embarrassing, as long as we can conquer our pride.

Hexagram 11
The Peace
Tai

Oracle Script:
Making Bridges

"Straddle Both Sides"
Harmonize
Grow through Including Others

Tarot Card: Justice

To achieve justice, which is the balancing of the scales and not punishment, as one might think, we must first have tolerance. Tolerance does not mean nonaction or enduring injustice; it means understanding and knowledge. I don't have to like something to tolerate it, but I *must* tolerate it because it is a part of everything. Personal feelings are not part of tolerance. Tolerance occurs when we accept reality as it is. When we both accept and tolerate, we come to understand and appreciate the work that needs to be done to resolve an issue rather than simply despising the situation or the people involved. Once the decision is made to work on an issue, emotions are disconnected from the event and a reconciliation can begin. This reconciliation permits people to reason their way to an appropriate action and encourages creative spirits to join the effort to rectify the situation.

All dunces, all punished, let's all spit on one another and—
hurry! To the little-ease! Each tries to spit first, that's all.
I'll tell you a big secret, mon cher. Don't wait for the Last
Judgment. It takes place every day.

ALBERT CAMUS, *THE FALL*

Tolerance also allows for discrimination to determine what events are irreconcilable and beyond repair. If something is intolerant it remains under the skin and poisons the system. The whole body rebels against an intolerable object, sacrificing itself in the need to kill the intruder. This is the defensive immune response that fights off all our diseases. Achieving peace and justice does not mean that there is no more conflict but instead that everyone has become tolerant of one another; we are able to coexist and achieve a balance, maintaining equivalencies.

The Chinese word *tai,* associated with this hexagram, means "large, great, extensive, extreme, greatest exalted, honorable, superior, good, excellent, safe, peaceful." When something is "great" in China it means that it is large enough to include many things. It is also sometimes used for describing something literally as big, as in "fat." When applied to people, it often connotes a leader or great person who is larger than themselves and includes the many. It was also used to show a God who is larger than human. Tolerance is what permits greatness, through an ability to include more than just yourself. A great leader will always follow the whole and not the one.

Guru: Here we learn a universal law of nature. Although humans tend to focus on things they perceive to be either fair or unfair, nature shows no such discrimination or judgment. All nature sees is balance. The true and never-ending law is that nature will seek equilibrium. The reason we seek vengeance on what is perceived as unfair is only nature seeking equilibrium through us. We are so unaware of this driving force that we often succumb to punishing those who have wronged us. If we right a wrong through revenge, we also are wrong, ironically. The larger force of nature works to achieve equilibrium, regardless of what we feel about a situation. To overcome our deep instinct for reciprocity, we must observe nature, which provides an example for the best way to balance the scales of justice, coming into peace by balancing through opposition.

Personal Example: A client had been betrayed by her boyfriend: she discovered he had been cheating on her. She drew hexagram 11, which didn't seem to make any sense because it read as harmony and people coming to peace. But over time it happened that her boyfriend, through the laws of karma, received justice for his actions. He was cheated in nearly every area of his life. He had a lawsuit (literal justice) filed against him in his work, and all his friends left him in the lurch. The hexagram was the I Ching's way of showing her that the situation would take care of itself; she need not seek vengeance, for justice would find him.

The Changing Lines

Line One—The Self
To come into harmony requires effort. To climb a mountain, one must take the first step. Beginnings are especially important, because without them, nothing will follow. If more harmony is desired, you must learn, through practice, how to play the music. Coming out of an imbalance will need some equal and opposite measures to tip the scales.

  ▸ Transforms into Shadow 45.1

Line Two—The Other
If your focus is singular, many things will be lost. In any life, there is what was, there is something right now, and there is something far down the road. If we focus too much on any one of these—past, present, or future—or on whatever it is we are obsessing about, we starve other aspects of our existence. Try to balance your focus, for when it becomes a pinpoint on something specific, you become polarized. When the scale tips and we become extremely imbalanced, other areas of our life are neglected. Seek balanced focus of attention and awareness to avoid such mishaps.

  ▸ Transforms into Shadow 36.2

Line Three—The Union
Preparation is what leads to harmony. Preparation for discord ensures that the song continues even when a false note is played; the song is not discarded due to imperfection. Expectation of all possibilities is what can build an orchestra. Learn from error and accept it in others, in nature, and in the universe. Not every song needs perfection to make it a work of art; it only requires sincerity.

  ▸ Transforms into Shadow 19.3

Line Four—The Earth

Surrendering ideas of being more powerful than another will open opportunities for the other to shine, thus making stronger the whole and the alliance. If giving others the power to be themselves threatens you, maybe you are a little too controlling. Allow yourself and others to benefit by not lording over them in false arrogance.

▶ Transforms into Shadow 34.4

Line Five—The Conflict

It is the way of nature to maintain equilibrium; this is a universal force. The force of peace in humanity does not vary greatly from this natural force. Allow it to emerge within every situation, and you will become a natural human instead of one in conflict with the truth of nature, which is seeking equilibrium—harmony and peace.

▶ Transforms into Shadow 5.5

Line Six—Heaven

Having an ability for harmony means deciding to remain dedicated to peace when war threatens. If when faced with war, one adopts an angry face, then all is war, but if one's face can remain peaceful while warlike ones shout into it, some hope remains.

▶ Transforms into Shadow 26.6

All Lines Changing—Hexagram 12

Part of understanding the nature of harmony includes periods of discord. Without conflict all songs would be boring and too sugar sweet. Pay attention to the discordians and value their presence as much as the pretty tunes, for what they have to offer you is a range of frequency seldom found in a one-hit wonder. Integrate the off notes so that the harmony of the whole remains cyclical, then true peace can never be threatened.

Let today mark a new beginning for you. Give yourself permission to say NO without feeling guilty, mean, or selfish. Anybody who gets upset and/or expects you to say YES all of the time clearly doesn't have your best interest at heart. Always remember: You have a right to say NO without having to explain yourself. Be at peace with your decisions.

STEPHANIE LAHART

Hexagram 12
The Separation
Pi

Oracle Script:
Learn How to Say No

"Boundary Guardians Make Walls"
The Last Straw
Line in the Sand

Tarot Card: Ten of Swords

Very few people enjoy hearing the word *no*. Rejection and the feelings associated with it are some of the worst, most negative feelings humans can experience. Many fall into negativity, into depression, when they are rejected. But rejection need not be so dire. Learning to handle both negative and positive energies is required for life on Earth. Enjoy times when hexagram 12 comes into your life and learn to feel the negative and embrace your no and the no of others. Sometimes others give us a boundary and tell us no or reject us, and sometimes the shoe is on the other foot. When you have to deliver or receive negative energy, explore strategies to disassociate from emotional attachments and encourage acceptance. Respect the no boundaries of others, and if they refuse to communicate with you, take it in stride, just as you would hope they do when you need some space. Although many experience rejection as a kind of death, no doesn't mean an ending; it just means no. When we've reached the limit of what we can take, it is time to say no. When your belly is full, you need to stop eating; this is okay and healthy.

The Chinese name for this hexagram is *pi*, which shows a mouth and a negative sign, which means saying no. Some view the pictogram as the stalk of a plant cut off, meaning growth is halted or arrested.

> *Death never takes the wise man by surprise: he is always ready to leave.*
>
> JEAN DE LA FONTAINE, *FABLES*, BOOK VIII, FABLE 1

> *This melancholic state is so powerful that, according to scientists and doctors, it can attract demons to the body, even to such an extent that one can get into mental confusion or get visions.*
>
> CORNELIUS AGRIPPA

> *I came into the unknown*
> *and stayed there unknowing*
> *rising beyond all science.*
>
> *I did not know the door*
> *but when I found the way,*
> *unknowing where I was,*
> *I learned enormous things,*
> *but what I felt I cannot say,*
> *for I remained unknowing,*
> *rising beyond all science.*
>
> ST. JOHN OF THE CROSS

Guru: Negative emotions can hold us back if we do not acknowledge and honor them instead of feeling guilt and shame. It's okay to say no, and it's okay for others to say no. Sit with it and come into your feelings around it. Negative energy in ourselves and others is perfectly acceptable and natural. We don't need to remove anything as a result; we can accept it, process it, and even utilize it to generate energy in a productive fashion. If we depend on and need a positive response or validation from others or the environment, we will fall to negative energy repeatedly until we can supply our own antidote to it to balance it out. Acknowledge your needs and provide for them yourself when another will not provide them for you.

Personal Example: Hexagram 12 appears when we need to draw a boundary or someone has to draw a boundary with us. Often if a client inquires about another person who has rejected him, this hexagram appears, which indicates it is time for him to back off. Respect the boundaries of yourself and others when this hexagram appears, and take a step back rather than push forward. This hexagram also appears when the I Ching is trying to communicate a simple no in answer to your question.

The Changing Lines

Line One—The Self
When things come to a halt or standstill, they begin to ferment and decompose like a swamp. This can create listlessness and disassociation. Depression and sadness are caused by still waters that need to flow and circulate. When we need to get moving again after a time of congestion, it helps to have a source of inspiration. This can spring up like a fountain to drain the swamp and provide the fresh air needed to get us out of the doldrums and reinvigorate our passions to move forward again.
▶ Transforms into Shadow 25.1

Line Two—The Other
It is far less frustrating when we ourselves halt our progress than when we are at the mercy of another. If someone you rely upon and need and trust is not cooperating in an agreement or is cutting off communication, devise a strategy to handle the situation rather than react emotionally and become overwhelmed. Maybe you had some justifiable expectations that have thrown you into confusion because they were not met. Shift your focus onto something you do have control over and can produce on your own until the other changes his or her mind or the situation comes to a conclusion. Feelings of bitterness, envy, and

resentment will fill us when we are not met with integrity by others, but these too can pass if you simply let them flow through you and work on building something of your own in the meantime.

▸ Transforms into Shadow 6.2

Line Three—The Union

Ignorance is more than just not knowing; it is also ignoring. If something is rejected and ignored, it will weaken through a lack of nourishment. Being cut off from others will starve us from what we need for life. It is true that we can supply this to ourselves by joining with the source of all and turning inward, but we can also choose the people in our lives who will be open and sharing with us and ignore those who are ignoring us. Turn your attention to where it is reflected back to you instead of diverted into the shadows.

▸ Transforms into Shadow 33.3

Line Four—The Earth

We can have healthy boundaries and say no without isolating ourselves and others; everyone is able to do this. Leaders have to say no a lot; otherwise they are liable to fall under an inferior influence that might not be in the best interest of all. Some might resent this kind of leadership and rebel, as a teenager rebels against the rules set by the parents, but perhaps they can see that the rules are there for their own safety and not punishment. Getting others to abide by your rules requires that you yourself follow them lest you be resented as a hypocritical tyrant.

▸ Transforms into Shadow 20.4

Line Five—The Conflict

Encountering the boundary of another and getting rejected can trap us in a pity party, experiencing feelings of unworthiness and neediness. We all must stew in this pot now and then: it is an unavoidable reaction to the obstacles we face in life. But for life to continue, we must limit our time spent in such places. Forgive yourself and others for falling into these negative energies. Go ahead: have a good cry about everything and feel the depths of your despair, and give yourself a big embrace. Just make sure you get out of bed the next day.

▸ Transforms into Shadow 35.5

Line Six—Heaven

Some periods of stagnation are only temporary and are bound to occur in every situation, possibly multiple times before the end of the day. Learn to recognize the causes of these blockages so that you can work through them or wait them out, and when they are over, rejoice in gratitude as you experience the opposite of flow and movement. Some days we lie in bed, and some days we run through the fields. Life needs a bit of both, and one can follow the other in a sequence. Follow these cycles and notice how they resolve, one into the other.

▸ Transforms into Shadow 45.6

All Lines Changing—Hexagram 11

Because nature seeks equilibrium, periods of stagnation and rejection will soon be balanced by the powers of the great scales. If you find yourself all gummed up and unable to move, trust in nature to bring you opportunities to move again, offering balance to your current state. Make sure you recognize the opportunities, and if you miss them, learn from these mistakes to be ready when the next one rolls around. Just because we were rejected doesn't mean we can't still be friends with the one being difficult: sometimes we are the obstinate one but don't want to be isolated because of it.

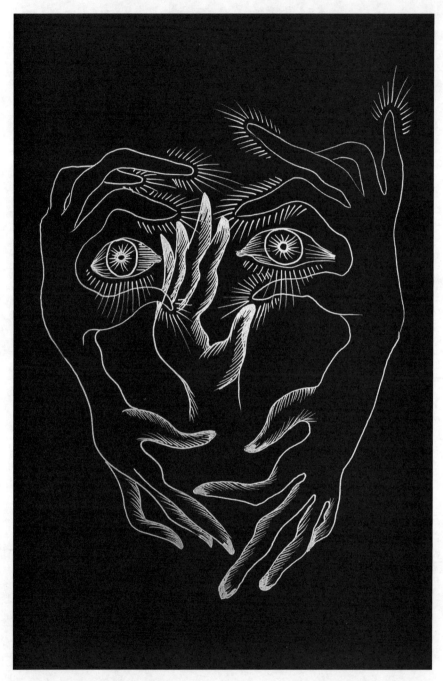

Remember, upon the conduct of each depends the fate of all.

ALEXANDER THE GREAT

Hexagram 13
The Fellowship
Tong Ren

Oracle Script:
We Are All Made in the Same Image

"Move as One"
All for One and One for All
Kinship

Tarot Card: Three of Pentacles

This hexagram is akin to the three musketeers as it denotes not only a tightly bonded friendship but also a deep spiritual kinship on an inherently human level. Hexagram 13 is like *The Fellowship of the Ring* by J. R. R. Tolkien from the Lord of the Rings trilogy in which people come together with a shared goal in their minds and hearts that they are all devoted to. Hexagram 13 is the moment in a musical concert when all the crowd is jumping in unison to the beat and everyone knows all the words and joins in, singing from their hearts. To be a part of something larger than the self makes the self as large as the sum of all who join together. Even one you consider an enemy has something in common with you. This hexagram represents the notion that all humans are created equal under heaven.

In Christianity there is an axiom that became very popular that reads: *Ubi tres, ibi Ecclesia* (Where three are, there is a church). This concept is communicated through a well-known scripture quotation from the Book of Matthew and can be applied to a deeper understanding of this hexagram.

> *"Again, I tell you truly that if two of you on the earth agree about anything you ask for, it will be done for you by My Father in heaven. For where two or three gather together in My name, there am I with them." Then Peter came to Jesus and asked, "Lord, how many times shall I forgive my brother who sins against me?"*
>
> MATTHEW 18:20

The name of this hexagram, *tong ren,* means "joining or being together with men." According to historical scholar Ralph D. Sawyer, it is similar to Sunzi's *tong dao,* "unity in the dao."[1] The word *tong* comes from the Cantonese *t'ong,* which means "assembly hall" and is very much like the gathering place in the Book of Matthew. Tong ren is also used in a famous Chinese proverb: *Yi shi tong ren,* which translates as "Treat people as if they were the same as you."

Guru: From the guru aspect of the I Ching, this hexagram represents moving in unison with all your parts and demons. This is about having every part of your consciousness focused on the same goal, moving toward that goal with every part of you—mind, body, and spirit. To perform an exercise well, you must unite mind and body to execute the move correctly. Only the athlete whose mind, body, and spirit are all focused on the goal will break the record. When you come into the flow and move together with yourself, as if you were a flock of birds flying in tandem, true beauty is achieved. On a deeper level, this hexagram represents a unification of differences within the psyche.

Personal Example: I received this hexagram unchanging when I lost my place to live and I needed to move but could not find a place. That same day a friend of mine found herself in the same position and randomly contacted me. It was clear, as a result of receiving this hexagram, that we were to team up together and become roommates, which turned into a very helpful situation through following the oracle's advice. Helping each other made us more powerful, and we were able to achieve our goals. The meaning of this hexagram was also conveyed to me through a synchronicity with the My Little Pony children's TV cartoon series called *Friendship Is Magic* that made me realize the magic that happens when friends help each other.

The Changing Lines

Line One—The Self

You keep no secrets from yourself, so how can you keep secrets with or from others? All are the same inside the darkest place. Use discernment and your gut instinct when choosing who you should trust, and understand the differences between false promises and integrity. Trust is built over time with others, but when trust is given to yourself, you need not fear the truth of what others are displaying, for inner virtues are displayed across the face.

▸ Transforms into Shadow 33.1

Line Two—The Other

Each of us has his or her own desire, and so our wills can clash. In any fellowship, even when all are for one, each will have his or her own idea of how something should be done. Learn to negotiate, compromise, and meet one another somewhere in the middle when difficult decisions have to be made. Unison requires communication and feelings for the other, even when we are certain we know the direction to take. If we fall into disagreement our deepest truths and desires go unexpressed and unexecuted as the integrity of the group collapses. Don't be afraid to listen to all points of view before choosing the way to proceed.

▸ Transforms into Shadow 1.2

Line Three—The Union

Being suspicious of others and hiding your dislike of them can cause them to separate from you. Try dissolving negative feelings, emotions, and attachments. Do not use weapons of war to solve problems that can be resolved through discussion and honest inquiry. If you distrust a companion, discuss the situation with him or her. These conversations are difficult and create discomfort, but if we don't manage uncomfortable conversations, we endanger productive alliances because of unresolved conflicts.

▸ Transforms into Shadow 25.3

Line Four—The Earth

A wall has been built to protect or launch an attack on others. Though it may seem sad, if you climb to the top of the wall you can see clearly why there is no real problem. Although we build walls between ourselves and others, those walls provide us with the most intense breakthroughs we could hope for. The buildup is what generates energy for propelling forward. Build as many walls as you like, but don't forget to scale them upon completion. We naturally build walls, but if we can see over them, we will break them down and find that we have elevated ourselves to a new level in the process, through learning about obstacles.

▸ Transforms into Shadow 37.4

Line Five—The Conflict

Even the worst of times will eventually change into its opposite; disputes with others can resolve over time. Sometimes differences with others are just a way to provide different perspectives and diversity. If we think that a fight means the end of the relationship, we are missing an opportunity for growth. The strongest would never gain in strength if the going was always easy. Learn how to reconfigure conflicts and oppositions with others into sportsmanlike contests and games that can show the worth of both sides. The victor will be made easy for all to see after a test of mastery.

▸ Transforms into Shadow 30.5

Line Six—Heaven

The stranger in the strange land need not remain so for long if he knows how to break the ice. People you don't know can become your friends. Even though you are not with your beloved, you can love the ones you are with nonetheless. They might not be your best friends, but all humans are a fellow in some capacity. There is a bottom line that connects us all, and it is inescapable. You don't need a heart connection for fellowship; it is inherent in our being on Earth together. If you don't like the same things, you can recognize that you both love to breathe the air and feel your heart beat in your chest.

▶ Transforms into Shadow 49.6

All Lines Changing—Hexagram 7

If all the lines are changing in hexagram 13, you need to lead the group of fellows as a general would lead the troops of an army. The guru says, if all lines are changing, get yourself in order, stop listening to others, and take charge of yourself through responsibility and discipline. The best way to make people follow your direction is not to bark orders in their direction but to believe in yourself and become an amazing person. Then people will automatically look to your directions based on the merits of your choices. The sun doesn't need to shout that it is making light; everyone can see this with his or her own two eyes.

The essence of independence has been to think and act according to standards from within, not without.

ALEISTER CROWLEY

 # Hexagram 14
The Messiah
Da Yu

Oracle Script:
Standing on the Shoulders of Giants

"Self-Respect"
Self-Worth
Self-Satisfaction

Tarot Card: Nine of Cups

This is a person of substance: to be substantial means to act and not be a spectator. Hexagram 14 represents people who can stand up all by themselves and stand on their own two feet. In the image one person is raised up by others. Here we see a leader, or one who is self-contained and needs no other, and yet is supported by others. This hexagram contains the concept of the messiah because it represents the deepest places of the self. Self-respect, self-worth, and self-reliance are all key factors here. If you have drawn hexagram 14, you will be on your own, and what a gift that is. We have all we need inside ourselves and do not have to worry about someone else stepping in: you got this! After we have traveled through hexagram 13, which is a group of people, we may find ourselves in a position of needing to return to the self and our own resources; periods of friendship can only come again when we are strong in the self. This is often thought of as a prosperity hexagram, with some intimations of wealth and abundance, but most do not understand that these are references to the unending value of the inherent self. Rather than seeing value in the golden eggs, take a good gander at the goose.

In China this hexagram is thought by many scholars to represent Yu the Great, a legendary ruler of ancient China, born in 2200 BCE. The suffix *da-* means "great" and can be seen in several other hexagrams in the I Ching. Da Yu was a descendant of the Yellow Emperor Huangdi and was said to live in the ancient city of Xian. Yu the Great is also the primary figure of hexagram 39. There are many who have tied his story to the story of Noah and the Flood because one of Da Yu's tasks was to repair the world after a huge deluge.

> *Insist on yourself; never imitate. Your own gift you can present every moment with the cumulative force of a whole life's cultivation; but of the adopted talent of another you have only an extemporaneous half possession. That which each can do best, none but his Maker can teach him.*
>
> RALPH WALDO EMERSON, "SELF-RELIANCE"

Guru: When we value ourselves, there is no end to what we can produce. A deep recognition of our innate talents is so much better than any single fish we catch through our labors. We must see how we ourselves hold the key to being the fisherman. Until then, we will struggle with codependency and unhealthy reliances and seek validation or use emotional manipulation to secure our place in the hearts of the people. In hexagram 14, the spiritual lesson is to form a foundation of self-love deep within you that is not dependent on any exterior quality, for this is the source of our abundance in all our many experiences throughout our lives.

Personal Example: I was in dire financial straits and asked the I Ching, "Who can I ask for help with money?" Hexagram 14 was the response. It indicated to me not to ask anyone for help with money but, instead, to figure it out myself. Hmmm, not really what I wanted to hear but, in fact, exactly what I needed to hear, for when I heeded the advice, I resolved the issue all by myself. I paid close attention to the directive that wealth is contained within me and that I myself hold what is valuable. I used my own talents and arts to make the money and did not have to beg, borrow, or steal; instead, I created wealth by valuing my own creations.

The Changing Lines

Line One—The Self

When we are great and self-reliant, we have a strong ego. This is necessary for greatness. As hexagram 36 points out, the danger here is arrogance. To maintain health with a strong self and independence we must not let it go to our heads. To be strong in self and keep arrogance at bay gives us truly great abilities that can be maintained over time and not lost due to foolish illusions that we exist in a vacuum, needing nothing and nobody. Even great people stand on the shoulders of giants.

▸ Transforms into Shadow 50.1

Line Two—The Other

Although others can support you, and this is very important and needed, what usually carries you from place to place are your own two feet. Look at your physical body, it is your vessel of transport during your lifetime. Some have many challenges with their bodily vehicle—disabilities, diseases, and genetic factors. According to the legend, Da Yu had a terrible limp and lived in great pain because of a leg injury, so his fleshy vehicle was at a seeming disadvantage. But that did not stop him from carrying on what he had to do regardless of his handicap. Some people with a perfectly functioning body do much less than those with severe challenges. Be grateful for your body, no matter what shape it is in, and honor it by taking good care of its needs.

▸ Transforms into Shadow 30.2

Line Three—The Union

When we find that we are super amazing and strong and capable, we will certainly be called upon to assist others. Why do we become strong and powerful if it is not to help others achieve the same? The one who helps himself may gain power, but the one who shares power becomes a legend and can approach what it means to be a messiah. The one who aids the many is the alpha who lifts the omega. My teacher Kelvin DeWolfe told me his philosophy, which is in alignment with this: get strong to make others stronger.

▶ Transforms into Shadow 38.3

Line Four—The Earth

If you want to make yourself great because you admire others who are great, there is no fault in this; it is called inspiration. But there is a fine line between inspiration and envy. We can achieve a lot and then look around only to find that there are many others who are at the same level or who have surpassed us. Those who become great may find that others envy them, and they can become the victims of gossip or worse. If we get distracted at this point in our journey we lose the self, and what made us great can be compromised. Always focus on yourself and let others mind their own business.

▶ Transforms into Shadow 26.4

Line Five—The Conflict

Your character is what makes you great. Character is built through hard work. This hard work can come as a result of our own choices and efforts or as the result of outside forces. When we are forced to create our character, it is usually due to hardship. Though it is not the most enjoyable way to come to greatness, a character forged in the fires of hell can withstand almost anything. Diamonds aren't made out of flowers and butterflies but through extreme heat and pressure.

▶ Transforms into Shadow 1.5

Line Six—Heaven

Being independent is a blessing. When we need nothing, everything is a gift. When we find we need certain things, other things are overlooked or not appreciated, but when everything is a bonus, this is abundance indeed. Recognize and count every blessing you have as a result of all your hard work and character building. That is the big payoff: when we see our own value after a day's hard work.

▶ Transforms into Shadow 34.6

All Lines Changing—Hexagram 8

When we have achieved our goal, we are ready to join with others. Hexagram 8 is slightly different from hexagram 13 in that the people who come to us in hexagram 8 are sent by providence to assist us in a task, as we are to assist them. After great achievements, other great people will find you, and you must undergo the difficult task of knitting together gigantic egos into a great union. This group will then attract many others who have not achieved great things but who seek to emulate you and rise to your level. This supergroup becomes the avengers, undefeatable because of their strength.

When the high horse's legs break, you will crawl on your belly like a snake.

Maja D'Aoust

Hexagram 15
The Golden One
Qian

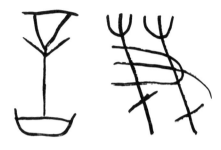

Oracle Script:
Humbled

"The Golden Middle"
Moderation
The Path of the Tao

Tarot Card: Temperance

Often hexagram 15 will be drawn when we have gotten a bit off balance and have to return to the center. This hexagram comes after hexagram 14, so if you have become too much in the self, you may need to make some adjustments to return to humility. This is the hexagram of mediation, of the golden mean and the humble center. If the I Ching has led you here, it is asking you to be realistic and pare down your expectations away from extremes, both positive and negative. Perhaps you have become excessive or deficient in one area and you need to even out. Coming back to the middle value requires that we first know where the deviation and imbalance has occurred. This also harkens to a more esoteric Taoist alchemical concept that the center or middle way lies between two opposites. Far from being a warning, this hexagram indicates that with slight adjustments, you can easily get back on track.

In China this hexagram mentions a specific kind of mythological creature called the Jian, or Qian, bird. This bird has one eye and one wing and requires a partner or a mate to fly and see correctly. The symbolism of this bird, as it relates to the hexagram of humility, is to remind us that we are stronger together even though we, in ourselves, can be strong. The Qian bird and its partner often represent a married couple. According to some, the tales of this bird are the source for our modern proverb "kill two birds with one stone."

Guru: The spiritual lesson of this hexagram is one of the main keys to the whole of Taoist philosophy. Hexagram 15 is the golden ratio and the mathematical proportion that all of nature follows. This hexagram shows us how to follow the way of nature so that we tread the path of the golden mean, becoming our true nature. When we become our true nature, we naturally find our innate purpose and fulfill our existence or purpose on Earth as a human, living in nature. Simply learning that you live within a mathematical proportion of balance can help you tremendously as you navigate this plane of existence.

Personal Example: This hexagram often shows up for clients who are either in a period of indulgence or excess or are denying themselves something. Alcoholics or addicts who are binging will receive this hexagram to urge them to get back on course. When you have done too much or too little of something, hexagram 15 pops up to guide you toward temperance and moderation.

The Changing Lines

Line One—The Self
Being modest does not require an advertisement. If you have to tell someone you are humble, maybe you are missing the point. Being is in the being not in the talking. More is said in what is not said when it comes to finding the humble portion of the conversation. When we talk about what the topic is instead of talking about ourselves, there are more gains to be made on the golden highway.
▸ Transforms into Shadow 36.1

Line Two—The Other
One might assume that to promote oneself one needs the sheer force of arrogance and a ego with no humility, but this is hardly the case. It is quite possible to present and promote the labors of the self without being overly egotistical. If your work is beneficial to others, it is actually your responsibility to put yourself out there. If shyness is preventing you from doing this, it may be humiliation not humility that is crippling you. Shame is not needed to be humble.
▸ Transforms into Shadow 46.2

Line Three—The Union
When we get attention from others for things we have accomplished, we might find it embarrassing. If this attention comes in the form of others trying to humiliate or troll us, we must devise a strategy to handle these attacks while remaining humble: we do not need to justify ourselves or defend our egos. We have a self-evident right to be our shining self, and that needs no justification; do not take the bait.
▸ Transforms into Shadow 2.3

Line Four—The Earth
When you contain the middle in your being, it can't be plucked from your hands. Real actions done with humility will never be lost; they are virtues forever stored within your soul and spirit. The more real-life actions we perform in this fashion accumulate to make a big life of the middle way. Even small deviations cannot harm us when the majority of our actions have been moderate, undertaken according to the golden mean.
▸ Transforms into Shadow 62.4

Line Five—The Conflict
If you are so humble that shyness starts to creep in and you are ashamed of your needs, this could prevent you from reaching your destiny. The whole point of walking the middle path is to attain the rights to your hard-won destiny. Don't steal it from yourself by refusing to be assertive enough, now and then. Occasionally the middle path requires extremes, which are fine as long as we return to the middle. But if extreme measures are never taken, how in the heck do we even know where the

middle is? It takes experimenting to figure it out. Don't be afraid to put yourself forward, especially when you carry something valuable for others. Speaking up for your heart is a virtue, as much as being quiet as a mouse is; both are needed at different times.

▸ Transforms into Shadow 39.5

Line Six—Heaven

Sometimes humility and moderation are achieved simply by sitting still and contemplating something. We don't always need to rush into action. If you are struggling to balance your life or accomplish something, just hang on a minute and see if anyone can offer you assistance before you rush out and try to do it all by yourself. Your Jian bird mate could swoop in and help you fly to greater heights.

▸ Transforms into Shadow 52.6

All Lines Changing—Hexagram 10

When moderation has reached its peak, and you have come into the fruition of nonaction, it will invariably be followed by a time when you need to start making decisions and taking risks again. Remember the beneficial lessons that humility has taught you and make wiser choices this time in the risks you take. The whole point of walking the path is to find our way to destiny, one way or another, and hexagram 10 demands that we stay focused on that goal and continue taking steps toward it and not letting opportunity pass us by.

Hexagram 16
The Pleasure
Yu

Oracle Script:
Larger than Life

"Preparations for Living"
Ease through Practice
Spontaneous

Tarot Card: Knight of Wands

True freedom arrives when we are able to act in an uninhibited fashion. Inhibitions are dropped when we feel comfortable and confident. Confidence can be gained through repeated trials that convince us that we are good at something or have the capacity to deal with things when the time comes. One might watch a rock star playing an amazing piece of music effortlessly on a guitar and not realize and appreciate the decades of practice that went into being able to achieve such a performance. These performances are nerve-racking until we feel comfortable, and then they become ecstatic pleasure in its highest form. We can move freely when we have lived a life that has prepared us to be confident with our actions and flow with everything in a natural manner.

I felt my lungs inflate with the onrush of scenery—air, mountains, trees, people. I thought, "This is what it is to be happy."

SYLVIA PLATH, *THE BELL JAR*

"Purposelessness," "empty-mindedness" or "no art" are frequent terms used to denote the ultimate achievement of a martial artist. According to zen, the spirit is by nature formless and no "things" are to be harbored in it. When anything is harbored there, psychic energy loses its balance, native activity becomes cramped, and the spirit no longer flows with the stream. When the energy is tipped out of balance, it is unable to cope with the ever-changing situations. But when there prevails a state of fluidity, the spirit harbors nothing in it, nor is it tipped out of balance. It transcends both subject and object and responds with an empty mind to whatever is happening.

BRUCE LEE

Guru: The spiritual lesson in this hexagram is discipline or practice. When we work really hard, then we can take pleasure in our work. When something is mastered, it becomes a joy and pleasure, not work, which we are ready for at any instant because we have spent so long preparing for it. All of life can become this instead of just a specific task. When we make life itself a practice that we must master, we can enjoy the spontaneity of being prepared for each moment as it unfolds: here we are truly in the flow and at one with our nature.

The dedication of the fruits of one's work to God is a spiritual exercise of vital importance; especially to those who are compelled by their duties to lead very active lives. It is known as karma yoga; the way to union with God through God-dedicated action.

CHRISTOPHER ISHERWOOD, *HOW TO KNOW GOD: THE YOGA APHORISMS OF PATANJALI*

Personal Example: Maybe the cutest thing ever is that I drew this hexagram for a client who was asking about raising funds to free an elephant from captivity in Thailand. The actual image of the hexagram is an elephant, and it is usually interpreted as packing up provisions for the future on an elephant, which you will ride off into freedom. The elephant the client wanted to free had lived nearly her entire life in captivity. The client had had a spiritual experience while riding on her back and felt moved to try to free her so that she could spend the rest of her life in dignity and freedom. A perfect reflection of the reality seen in the pictogram carved so many thousands of years ago.

The Changing Lines

Line One—The Self

Making preparations requires some contemplation. The whole point of being prepared means that we won't need to suffer from a poor choice based on impulse so as to get pleasure quickly. If we are able to prepare for pleasure, it can go much deeper than instant gratification and turn into a lasting tantric ecstasy. The difference between the two is practice, dedication, and preparation.

▶ Transforms into Shadow 51.1

Line Two—The Other

When we can act in the moment it means that we are able to drop our defensive walls. In order to feel comfortable, part of that means we are not afraid. When there is no fear, joy can enter, so the art of pleasure is largely learning how to fearlessly open the heart. In Chinese medicine philosophy, the heart can become clogged by phlegm or stagnation, which is attributed to fear, anxiety, and constriction. Called "phlegm misting the heart orifices," this condition blocks the perception of the spirit, or *shen,* that lives inside the heart organ. When the phlegm of fear is cleared, through prior preparations and training, the heart can spontaneously receive clear perceptions in every moment, allowing it to feel in an unfettered fashion.

▶ Transforms into Shadow 40.2

Line Three—The Union

When we spend a good deal of time preparing for something, this can hamper spontaneity. We want so badly to use the skills we have spent so long developing that our timing may be off. We must cultivate patience as well as preparedness to maximize results. Otherwise, we may find ourselves out of step with the times, or our mastery may make us overconfident and we may try to force something to happen.

▶ Transforms into Shadow 62.3

Line Four—The Earth

Having a symbol or vision of something is important while making preparations. It will keep us on track and help us get ready. We can simulate something and make an image of it that can inspire us to get ready when it appears in the future. In the fashioning of these images, we strive to hold something in our mind until it comes to pass. By doing this, we steady our will so that we can persevere through the time and space needed to make it happen.

▶ Transforms into Shadow 2.4

Line Five—The Conflict

There is a fine line between having a vision and making an image to inspire us and forming a projection. Projections come usually out of fears or anxieties, and they can have a powerful influence on our preparations. Stick to inspiration to move you. Don't fret if you get a bit nervous anticipating the performance of something you have practiced so long to achieve; that nervousness will fade as soon as you fully engage in the action.

▶ Transforms into Shadow 45.5

Line Six—Heaven

Too much pleasure will throw us back into reality. If we have become too indulgent in our visions of an ideal, it won't be too long before reality catches up with us and disciplines us again. To avoid this, make sure there are healthy limits on the ecstasies we are seeking, and keep them in their proper time and place. You still have to do your laundry, or you won't have any clothes to wear to your performance.

▶ Transforms into Shadow 35.6

All Lines Changing—Hexagram 9

We can only indulge in pleasure for so long before we must practice some restraint lest we fall into disrepair. When all the lines are changing, it's time to come out of a desire for pleasure and do some hard work and self-care for the health of body and mind. Perhaps we partied a bit too much, and now it's time to get back to work!

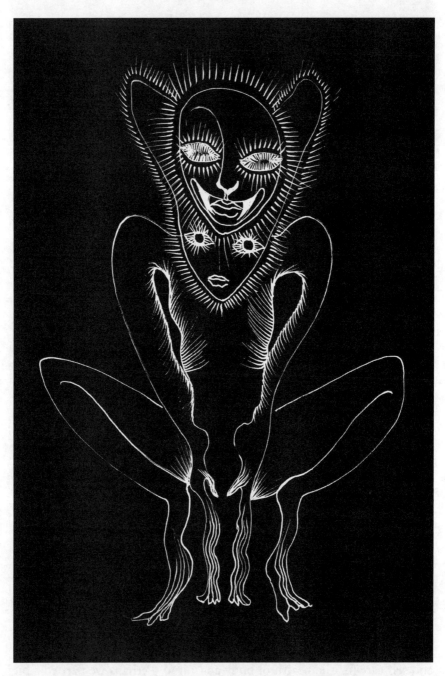

Let yourself be silently drawn by the strange pull of what you really love. It will not lead you astray.

RUMI

Hexagram 17
The Followers of the Way
Sui

Oracle Script:
Followers of the Way

"On the Path"
The Initiate
Stairway to Heaven

Tarot Card: Wheel of Fortune

Here we are drawn or almost pushed forward by some inexplicable force. We are clearly being led. There is a trail of bread crumbs laid out before us, and we can see it very clearly. The path is not something someone can find; it is shown to you. When we choose to follow the way, each brick in the road will light up, but only as our foot steps upon it. There will be no future knowing, as we have reached a test in our journey to see if we can be led or if we will attempt to steer the ship. You must release control on the path and simply follow the next step that spirit makes clear to you. You won't be told where it is going, and this will cause you fear. In hexagram 17 we learn how to trust and give ourselves over to the will of God and not impose our will. Providence will find us, and synchronicities will happen. Our only task is to flow with them and not force the direction of the river.

In many of the Chinese texts, hexagram 17 is compared to a hunter and its prey, which are drawn together through desire or happenstance. But 17 is also about the spontaneous chase that follows the encounter. We must be cautious and pay attention to what we are following, or we could end up tracking something that will influence us badly. In following the stream of events, look before you leap and make sure the river isn't headed into a waterfall. Often, if we are blindly following, we may find ourselves waking up in a cult. To follow the way and the path of providence, seek out signposts that your guide is trying to show you. If there is danger ahead, you will probably be able to see it coming, so look! Although surrender is called for with this hexagram, you must know it is the path and not a rabbit hole. The way to see the path is to follow the lantern of your conscience, which is a few steps ahead of you and showing you the way to proceed. You must listen to and watch very closely your heart's guidance to avoid following the path of desire and hunger.

> To hear the voice of the silence is to understand that from within comes the only true guidance. . . . For within you is the light of the world—the only light that can be shed upon the Path.
>
> MABEL COLLINS, "LIGHT ON THE PATH"

Running after rings
See the pattern in the things
Thought myself so cool and clever
Discerned the path that stretched forever
Leading me to destiny
With confidence and certainty
Tracking as a hunter to a deer
Footsteps that were made so clear
Truth was found in hunger pangs
Propelling forward by my fangs
Till my body forced
By its fatigue

Brought itself
down to its knees
Upon a pause
My labored breath
Caught itself in emptiness
Silent in a golden gleam
A wink appeared behind the scenes
Your form was there between the trees
Folly became realized
And my heart was magnetized
I laughed so hard I couldn't speak
Strength was found when I was weak
I veered direction, went off course
Thorns and brambles pierced me to my source
A name echoed inside my ear
Dripping through the sweat of fear
Dark and lost I fell into the mud
Felt the Earth become my blood
Penetrated a harmonic chord
As a corpse collapsing on a sword
You took me into your embrace
With a smile upon your face
I had descended from the chase
Found a diamond in its place

MAJA D'AOUST

Guru: To be led is a special skill that will be required of all who wish to hold the great spirit within them. If we are unable to trust in spirit and instead think we know what to do, we will miss the opportunities spirit lays at our feet because they won't be what our desire has fantasized. A camel walking through the desert won't make it very far if it refuses to drink water along the way, and we won't make it to our destiny if we deny what providence provides us because we are finicky or know-it-alls. Spirit knows what you need and shall place it right in front of your nose. Learn how to recognize it, and your passage will be much easier, like hopping from stone to stone across a river, instead of drowning in the rapids.

Personal Example: When I have asked the I Ching a sneaky question about the future to see how something might turn out, I have often gotten hexagram 17, which instructed me to take each thing as it comes and purposefully advised me to not concern myself with the future at all. When I ask advice about a relationship and draw hexagram 17, the advice is to take each next thing as it comes, not concern myself with success or failure, allow things to unfold according to providence, and just enjoy the stroll.

The Changing Lines

Line One—The Self
We can be following something diligently and passionately, with all of our attention focused upon it, and then at the last moment swerve in another direction. Such is the nature of the ever-changing Tao!

▶ Transforms into Shadow 45.1

Line Two—The Other
Paths will be set out before your feet, but you still have to navigate. This is a "choose your own adventure" journey, with several options presented to you in some cases. One might appeal to your inner child, while the other will lead you into maturity and wisdom. The childish appeals to all universally, but few, indeed, will choose the austere path of the sage into the wilderness. Choose wisely which influences and paths to follow.

▶ Transforms into Shadow 58.2

Line Three—The Union
To choose a path that will invariably lead to your maturity as a result of some in-depth transformation can be very daunting. If we decide to follow the path of someone who is revolutionary to our way of thinking, we can at least be sure that this will cause growth directly as a result of the sheer differences in worldviews. But how wonderful to experience the variety of life, as long as we are safe from threat and are willing to undergo a new state of mind and be resilient in the face of change.

▶ Transforms into Shadow 49.3

Line Four—The Earth

When other people flatter us, we may assume that they have our best interests at heart, and so we may follow their lead. Do not be tricked into deception by kind words; we are still in charge of ourselves and our choices. Even if someone else leads us astray, we can't fool ourselves into thinking we are not responsible for our actions. Hold on to responsibility and self even while following another's lead, and all will turn out well in the end.

▸ Transforms into Shadow 3.4

Line Five—The Conflict

A brand-new path emerges out of nowhere quite suddenly, and we have to make a choice whether to follow it. Try the new and amazing opportunity, which could be risky, or stick with the tried-and-true path that we were following? Even if we don't choose the shocking new option, we must still pay attention to what it awakens within us, for our response to such things can be very telling of the hidden desires that lurk within the depths of our hearts.

▸ Transforms into Shadow 51.5

Line Six—Heaven

When we consistently choose the correct and best path that spirit lays before us, others will notice that we are following the way and suddenly follow us. Do not be tricked into thinking that the others are following you, as they may lead you to believe; spirit is guiding you all. You can see this clearly, so now you have the added responsibility of continuing to follow the spirit and not lead them astray.

▸ Transforms into Shadow 25.6

All Lines Changing—Hexagram 18

When we have been following the path of our choice for quite some time and have been led by spirit, we must return eventually to ourselves and check in. Following spirit can rest heavy on the self as you may have put aside some of your wants and needs. Parts of you may rebel—suppressed desires rising to the surface that need to be examined. Look for any corruptions or neglected areas before continuing along the journey to ensure that you are not sacrificing too much of yourself in order to follow the spiritual path. Resume when you are well rested and healed of any maladies that may have accumulated along the way.

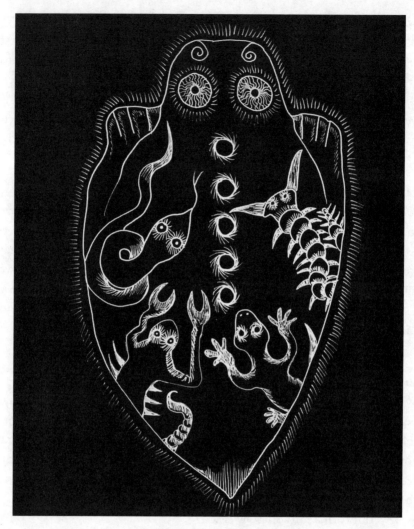

The Sick Rose

O Rose thou art sick.
The invisible worm,
That flies in the night
In the howling storm:

Has found out thy bed
Of crimson joy;
And his dark secret love
Does thy life destroy.

WILLIAM BLAKE

Hexagram 18
The Corruption
Gu

Oracle Script:
Can of Worms

"Decomposition"
Repair What Is Rotten
Fight to the Death

Tarot Card: Death

I began an intimate relationship with hexagram 18 while investigating the Chinese concept known as *gu* poison during my Taoist medicine studies. In Chinese medicine, gu is considered a parasitic infection that blocks the perception mechanisms of the mind and heart and eats away at the bright spirits known as the *shen*. I discovered through my research that gu can't be avoided on Earth as it essentially represents the forces of decay and death that penetrate all living things. We contain these forces in our bodies and organ systems, and they can pull us down into the grave if not kept in check, although, ultimately, they do pull us into the grave given enough time regardless of our attentions to them. Only the Taoist alchemists claimed to find a way to escape their grasp. Metaphorically, gu can symbolize corruption of the flesh on all levels, such as real physical diseases, moral and ethical repercussions for evil behaviors, or being possessed by something other than our true essence. To battle the forces of gu, which poison our bodies, minds, and spirits, we must shine our light upon it, transmuting it through fire and heat into something indestructible. The good news is that once we have mastered the powers of gu, we become immortal and incorruptible.

There is a special medicine and healing aspect of gu. The ancient Chinese shamans, or wu, had a cauldron in which they would place some venomous creatures. These creatures would fight among one another until only one was left. This creature, the victor, was known as the golden worm, sometimes translated as the golden silkworm. This worm was considered to be immune to any poison because it had not been killed by any of them. Gu suggests the idea of developing immunity to poison. This concept had a far-reaching influence in China and was depicted in the popular kung fu film *The Five Deadly Venoms*.

Gu was also thought to be transferred to other people and handed down to children from their parents and was even, according to some scholars, inherent in the original ancestors of all, rather like the concept of original sin. These gu gifts can be considered to be the thoughts that can poison us. They can affect our lives even if we ourselves are free from sin; they are unavoidable when we interact with other human beings. Things decay here on Earth; decomposition and renewal are parts of the natural cycles and processes that we all undergo as creatures of nature.

When the last sacramental words are said;
And beneath grass and flowers that lovely face
Moulders among the dead.

Then, O Belovèd, whisper to the worm
That crawls up to devour you with a kiss,
That I still guard in memory the dear form
Of love that comes to this!

CHARLES BAUDELAIRE,
FROM "THE CORPSE"

Guru: To find an example of a human being trying to be like the golden worm mentioned above, we need look no further than the case of Mithridates VI of Pontus, also known as Eupator Dionysus. Mithridates spent seven years living alone in the forest. While there he cultivated an immunity to poisons by ingesting small amounts of them, an ancient practice of the alchemists. His strategy, that of placing inside himself everything we are told to avoid, worked very well. It was said that he could not be killed, even by the most deadly poison. When he attempted to commit suicide to avoid getting captured, he was unable to do so because he had made himself indestructible. According to the legend he had to get a friend to stab him with a sword. The recipe for his antidote was reputed to to have been discovered in his cupboard, handwritten by him. The potion, called mithridatium, had more than sixty-five ingredients and was prescribed as an antidote for poisoning.

Personal Example: I received a desperate text in the wee hours of the morning from my dear friend seeking my help. He was in India at the time and was violently ill. He was at the hospital when he sent the text, and I could see he was in trouble. The doctors there were not assisting him, and he feared for his life. I asked the I Ching what was wrong, and the response was hexagram 18. I instinctively knew he had gotten parasites. I gave him a list of remedies and actions to take and how to proceed to navigate the infection. In going over his exposure possibilities, he realized he had ingested an unwashed piece of fruit from a nefarious source that had probably been the culprit, but in India it could have been so many different situations it was hard to tell. After we realized this was, indeed, what was causing his illness, he was able to take appropriate measures and made a full recovery.

The Changing Lines

Line One—The Self

Everything gets corrupted. If you expect something to be pure as the virgin snow, chances are you will be brutally disappointed and reel away in horror, even though you yourself are not without your own poisons. Don't throw something away just because it is broken. The virtue of the ability to fix things is known as repentance, and although repair requires labor, the restoration of a broken thing represents the beauty of life everlasting. Reinvigorate something that has enough value to make it worthwhile to invest in its repairs.

▸ Transforms into Shadow 26.1

Line Two—The Other

Needs are one of our largest forms of corruption. You might do things you never thought you would if you have nothing to eat. Learn the lesson of unmet needs in self and others to forgive the seemingly evil actions of those who have found themselves unable to meet their own needs, which has caused a corruption in their heart due to contempt at being abandoned and unwanted. Whatever you need from this world, make sure your spirit forgives you for all involved whether you are successful or find yourself in failure.

▸ Transforms into Shadow 52.2

Line Three—The Union

Once things have been rotting for quite some time, we can rest assured they will take time to heal. Many go to a doctor only when they are desperate, after a disease has been growing for years, and then give up when they discover there is no quick fix to end their pain. Be prepared for the length of time required to heal and repair. Rome wasn't built in a day, and it will take more than a day to restore your situation to its former glory.

▸ Transforms into Shadow 4.3

Line Four—The Earth

We will become corrupted easily when we don't have a direct connection to our own sense of feeling and communication with our conscience. We are easily influenced when we are off center. Listen to others, but never forget to check in with how you feel, and feel confident in your own compass. Make sure you are informed enough to make your own decision even when you listen to advice.

▸ Transforms into Shadow 50.4

Line Five—The Conflict

Some corruptions we inherit from humanity. We may, for example, have been born in a racist town. Though the fault isn't our own, we must, nonetheless, deal with and take responsibility for the corruption we find around us. Taking a stand can be dangerous and may require strategy to be effective. Be ready for a long slow labor to raise awareness, bring about repentance, and engender forgiveness and love in those around you.

▸ Transforms into Shadow 57.5

Line Six—Heaven

Sometimes humanity is so corrupted at its core, the best course of action is to focus on heaven to prevent our own corruption. As long as we keep ourselves pure and don't fall into the unfortunate behavior of those around us, we will be victorious in keeping corruption at bay by keeping it out of our own person through personal responsible action.

▸ Transforms into Shadow 46.6

All Lines Changing—Hexagram 17

When we have repented of our own corruption, and the corruption of those around us, we must set out on an expedition to root it out in the world. We needn't search far and wide to see where we can be of service; we need only follow the path in front of us and trust it will take us where we need to go, where the medicine we have made within ourselves to combat poison can be given to those who truly need it. They will be found along the way our feet may travel.

Do not be conformed to this world, but be transformed by the renewing of your mind. Then you will be able to discern what is the good, pleasing, and perfect will of God.

ROMANS 12:2

Hexagram 19
The New
Lin

Oracle Script:
A Novel Approach

"With the Eyes of a Child"
A Clean Slate
Like a Virgin

Tarot Card: Page of Wands

One of the most important powers of creation is the ability to begin again, fresh and new. Without the ability to make and create a new thing, we are trapped in death and dying and what is old. Imagine if you were doomed to repeat the same thing all day every day for all of your existence. This is said to be the fate of the gods: being perfect, there was nothing left for them to do. All growth has occurred, and so nothing ever changes; they are frozen. The secret of hexagram 19 is the power of a new day, a new beginning. It is the ability to do something you may have done a thousand times before in a new way, with fresh eyes, free from past prejudices. Hexagram 19 is the ability to view your spouse as if he or she were a stranger, to see your spouse with delight, rather than taking anything for granted. Getting stuck in the past leaves no room to grow. If we want to be forgiven for past errors, we have to forgive those with whom we wish to spend our time.

Ridding ourselves of the past and of memories is a formidable task, but this is contained in the fountainhead of Shiva, the destroyer of time. The lesson of hexagram 19 is to be in the present. It is the tip of the arrow head shooting through space, and every moment it has passed through becomes destroyed because the only thing that there is belongs to what is before it in each and every moment. This hexagram belongs to the now and the state of mind that becomes consumed by the ever-unfolding moment we find ourselves projecting through. This is the divine masculine, the creative destructive energy that burns the last moment so that the next new second can come into being. When we find ourselves stuck in the past and afloat among our memories, unable to come into the power of Shiva, we must make a fountain of our mind, to keep the energy circulating, lest we become a swampy dwelling place for unsavory creatures.

> *The idea that at each successive moment he was deeper into the Sahara than he had been the moment before, that he was leaving behind all familiar things, this constant consideration kept him in a state of pleasurable agitation.*
>
> PAUL BOWLES, *THE SHELTERING SKY*

Guru: When you think you have mastered something, that thought can actually stop you from learning. When you think you know who someone is, you place that person in a box or make him or her into a statue made of stone. The smarter you think you are, the more limited you make your mind. Better to have the mind of the fool who sees things for what they are, with no prior knowledge of them. After you have educated yourself on something, make sure you forget everything and then allow yourself to have a pure experience, unadulterated by what you expected to happen. In this way, you align with nature and include everything in your perceptions instead of what you thought you would find. This is the secret to the beginner's mind.

Personal Example: My clients and I almost always receive this hexagram when it is time to start over or view something from a different perspective. The image of the hexagram shows the eye of providence looking down on the situation, so you should be objective in viewing something instead of just seeing your own position. Clear out your assumptions so that you can see everything. Don't be afraid to scrap every idea you ever had about something. It is never dangerous to take something as it is rather than forming a bunch of opinions about it. You might be pleasantly surprised and see something you never noticed before, even with something you look at every day.

The Changing Lines

Line One—The Self
When you are able to approach things free and clear of prejudice, you will find that others approach you, seeking guidance. This happens because they know you will give them the benefit of the doubt; they trust you and feel safe in your presence. Leading others requires the ability to see them anew each day, without judging them based on past successes or failures and not allowing the past to color the new day. When the past dominates, the leader is not clear and grounded in reality and is at a disadvantage.
  ▸ Transforms into Shadow 7.1

Line Two—The Other
The way we approach those close to us is vitally important to the relationship. If you are constantly negative or accusational, the relationship will become strained. Approaching fresh and clear without a burden of grudges honors the present and provides opportunities for forgiveness and for new things to grow and emerge from the situation.
  ▸ Transforms into Shadow 19.2

Line Three—The Union
Being able to harmonize with others is a great skill to have, and not all of us are born with this talent. If you find yourself lacking in social graces, you need not worry but instead educate yourself on some common manners so that you can learn to approach people with respect and humility. When you don't step on anyone's toes, more people will want to dance with you. Take some dance classes.
  ▸ Transforms into Shadow 11.3

Line Four—The Earth

When approaching others, we do not need to put on a mask or hide our true self. It is perfectly acceptable to be honest and forthcoming and still manage to be respectful. You can approach someone in a novel manner, with all your judgments are removed regardless of the other's missteps, and focus on growth instead of punishment if a slight has occurred. When we make this type of approach, we can expect partnership proposals and alliances to head in our direction because we take people at face value and honor them, while still acknowledging indiscretions that have occurred.

▸ Transforms into Shadow 54.4

Line Five—The Conflict

Just because we approach people with a fresh and clear attitude does not mean we need to accept bad behavior. It is okay to make boundaries, to say no, and to decide with whom you wish to consort. While everyone deserves the benefit of the doubt and fair treatment, you still get to be in charge of who you spend your time with. Everything has its limitations, and when you reach yours, be able to recognize them. When you do, you will be able to sense when others are fed up with you also and with this self-knowledge can better navigate the situations presented to you.

▸ Transforms into Shadow 60.5

Line Six—Heaven

When no one will listen to us even when we are clear and approach with a sincere and open heart, it can be tempting to try to escalate our intensity. This rarely works. But in some cases we may have no choice because we need others to listen to us simply because we know the truth in the situation and everyone else has fallen under a spell of ignorance. In such cases where you are certain of some special knowledge, it becomes your duty to approach others with it, even if they may be unreceptive. Make sure there is no attitude in your presentation, and keep it simple.

▸ Transforms into Shadow 41.6

All Lines Changing—Hexagram 33

Sometimes it is time to approach, and sometimes it is time to withdraw. After the approach has been completed, we may find that we wish to pull back and reconfigure ourselves. A retreat may be in order after a difficult approach; we may need some time to rest and think things over. After you have laid it out on the table, pull back and give the other room for the next move; feel content and confident in what you have offered. Don't worry about playing the fool so much that it makes you become paranoid; just wait to see how it all plays out.

For contemplation is both the highest form of activity (since the intellect is the highest thing in us, and the objects that it apprehends are the highest things that can be known), and also it is the most continuous, because we are more capable of continuous contemplation than we are of any practical activity.

ARISTOTLE

Hexagram 20
The Observer
Guan

Oracle Script:
Bird's-Eye View

"Lofty Vantage"
Contemplation
Oversee

Tarot Card: Judgment

This hexagram is the Bennu bird of ancient Egypt. In the image of the hexagram we see a bird flying high with large eyes that can see all things below them. The Bennu bird was affiliated with herons and the phoenix and was said to be self-created and regenerative, independent in and of itself. When hexagram 20 shows up for us, it is a time for us to contemplate. We have to break out of our landlocked views and take to the skies of our higher intelligence to get an overview of the situation that is not just based on our own personal experience. It is time to go transpersonal. Read some philosophy to see what the greatest minds have thought about what you are facing. Connect to the whole of humanity through your issue and contemplate how your issue or your suffering connects and ties you to the history and immediacy of all of humanity. Can you make your problem so big that is it also everyone else's problem? Or see how everyone has your problem, not just yourself? The power of the archetype is that we are made larger through our capacity to understand that our experiences are shared by all humans. It is here that we can grow large, indeed, and soar through the skies of time and space. In this place we are as eternal as the phoenix; we are as immortal as the deathless ones.

This is a hexagram of the divine feminine in that it provides us with an all-inclusive mind. Nothing is discarded, and all things come into view with no limitations. Often the goddess Hathor is shown with an interesting face that is spread to the sides and kind of wide. She looks like this because she is a goddess of the horizon that spreads the length of the sky. If we can broaden our horizon and see it as the flying bird views it, we expand in a new direction. Here we are asked to stretch. This is the function of yoga in its esoteric sense: you might think you can only go so far, but maybe try to inch your way a little farther. If you can stretch your mind to include everything, you may achieve an *aha!* moment. Now you are really getting somewhere. Push your limits and boundaries as large as the overreaching sky.

I am the Bennu
The soul of Ra
And the guide to the gods
In the tuat
Let it be so done
Unto me
That I may enter like a hawk
And that I may come forth like Bennu
The rising star

THE EGYPTIAN BOOK OF THE DEAD

Oh, bird of my soul, fly away now, For I possess a
hundred fortified towers.

RUMI

Guru: In ancient times, augury was the practice of watching the omens of the birds and looking to the skies. There are many forms of divination, one of which you are using now, but the best oracle is Nature herself. When we look to the skies and watch the birds, we can be taken to their heights; we can fly with the eagles. To get the mind close to the things that are the closest to heaven is the highest form of contemplation, so contemplating the birds is to be next to the highest places. In alchemy and occult lore, this is known as the language of the birds and is the highest mindedness available. Even the Catholic Church has professional bird-watchers who still partake in this sacred ancient art.

> *Time is the substance from which I am made. Time is a river which carries me along, but I am the river; it is a tiger that devours me, but I am the tiger; it is a fire that consumes me, but I am the fire.*
>
> JORGE LUIS BORGES, "A NEW REFUTATION OF TIME"

Personal Example: One day I traveled with my boyfriend to a river that was banked with reeds and felt very Egyptian. While at the river, I did my daily reading and received hexagram 20. A great blue heron flew over my head so close that I was able to look into the pupil of its eye as it flew past. We sat with our mouths open in awe at the visitation. As we were getting ready to leave at the end of the day, the heron came back from the direction it had headed off into and graced us with another fly-by, and as I turned my head to watch it, I realized it was going into the setting sun; earlier it had flown off in the direction of the rising sun. I felt I had come as close as possible to seeing through the eyes of the phoenix, the great heron who follows the path of the sun as it travels its journey across the sky.

The Changing Lines

Line One—The Self
Being able to take the long view down the road is said to be lacking in our current society. Many indigenous people can see for generations ahead and generations behind. Modern cultures tend to see things only as far as the self. When you connect the self to your lineage, you see further because what is you extends through time and space. It's hard to see consequences for seven generations when you can't even see the results of

your own actions. Expanding our view in this way is of great benefit to humanity and results in behaviors like planting trees and tending Earth.

▶ Transforms into Shadow 42.1

Line Two—The Other

When we can see clearly, things are clear. There is no overshadow of prejudice when we follow the path of the sun, for the light is always ahead of us, preventing our own thoughts and opinions from obscuring things. When you can see people and see their problems, think of what can clear their view. You need not impose any moral or opinion upon them. In this way, everyone is free to fly unhampered.

▶ Transforms into Shadow 59.2

Line Three—The Union

Being able to see down the road is a special skill that many do not have. Some Buddhist driving practices encourage drivers to not only focus on the car right in front but also to fix the gaze in the distance, when appropriate. By being able to see near and far, our vision expands, and we can see traffic jams that might be coming and so divert our path to avoid such pitfalls. Navigating requires vision and the ability to hold a vision. To progress on a journey, you will need your eyes to see the way through. In relationships also, we must focus on the now but also see where it is going, and in this way determine what direction best suits all involved. If you have a child who someday will go to college, you can start a savings account; this is looking ahead.

▶ Transforms into Shadow 53.3

Line Four—The Earth

Just being able to see obstacles ahead won't dissolve them. We eventually come upon them and then have to deal with them. If we see an omen that warns us of a storm ahead, that knowledge alone is not enough; we still need to make preparations before it arrives. If there is a substantial roadblock ahead, begin to think upon ways to approach it beforehand, and then when you reach it, implement your plan. If you know someone can be difficult about particular things, develop strategies to improve communication ahead of time.

▶ Transforms into Shadow 12.4

Line Five—The Conflict

Sometimes the hardest thing to have objective vision about is ourselves. To apply the unbiased observer upon ourselves using our own eyes means transcendence of the self. To rise above the self while being in the self means we must be able to occupy two locations at once. This split of our person shall require us to ascend and discard the self for a moment; we break the shell of our ego and leave the nest as a fledgling. Soar above and beyond the self on occasion, and you can view yourself in totality, even though your own eyes can never leave your head.

▶ Transforms into Shadow 23.5

Line Six—Heaven

The purpose of an elevated contemplation is not to place the self above others but rather to see so as to be helpful. If others can't see from the lofty heights we are able to obtain, tell them a story of what you witnessed; this might bring them closer to heaven than if you chastise them for being so low to the ground. I doubt anyone was ever scared into flying, but inspiration is a wind that catches many wings.

▶ Transforms into Shadow 8.6

All Lines Changing—Hexagram 34

When we come into the highest form of contemplation and soar the skies, it is time to come back down to Earth into human form. Now it will take strength to integrate what we have learned into practical living. In hexagram 34 we must take our power and make it useful. Power of the mind is made useful through practical things. Nikola Tesla was a genius, but he would not have amounted to much if he never made any of his inventions that people still find so useful and practical today. Have more than ideas: make them real.

It's enough for me to be sure that you and I exist at this moment.

GABRIEL GARCÍA MÁRQUEZ,
ONE HUNDRED YEARS OF SOLITUDE

Hexagram 21
The Difficulty
Shi He

Oracle Script:
Discernment

"Excalibur"
The Truth
Differentiation

Tarot Card: Ace of Swords

This is the hexagram of coming into knowledge of the truth and being able to discern between two oppositional forces. Here we come into knowing the difference between things, and we are able to know what is true and what is not true for ourselves. This is the sword held by Justice; in her other hand she holds the scales. There are polarizing forces of duality, and there are things in the middle, and the sword knows which is which. In the myth of King Arthur, Arthur must pull the sword from the stone. Most can't accomplish this task, which goes to show what a rare talent discernment is. Most of the populace relies on outside sources to tell them the truth, but feeling it on your own is a superpower. The truth is stone cold and hardened into solid form; you can't bend it to suit your will. Universal truths remain eternal, and time can't change them. The origins of the name Arthur are under dispute, but some scholars connect it to the Greek *arktos* and the word *arctic*. These words are said to come from the constellation of the bear where the north polestar, Polaris, resides. Thus, Arthur is linked with the north, a compass setting that is esoterically connected with the ability to connect to your internal compass, which points to the truth. This is the sword of Excalibur, which when held above the head represents an intellect that follows and guides to the perennial philosophy of the wisdom of the ages. The sibyl oracles of Greece and Rome were often depicted with a sword to represent their connection to this truth in unbiased and transpersonal form.

The mind in occult symbolism is often shown as a sword or metal that can cut through things. A mind that is functioning properly adheres to logic, reason, and the science of discernment. The scientific method was brought to us via an ancient occult technique of discernment (to the chagrin of many scientists who are unaware of this). René Descartes engaged in a Socratic daimonic dialogue with what he called the evil demon in his mind, which helped him to arrive at the currently held scientific method. To know what objective truth is, we must investigate with an open mind, which means fluttering to both extremes, to both sides of an issue, to the bitter end. There must be no bias toward any outcome lest our narrow-minded view prevent us from perceiving the truth that is right before our eyes. The true scientific method must include all possibilities for the proper revelation to take place; otherwise, it is prone to corruption and a personal or political agenda.

> *Somewhere in the world today there is a woman for whom the Sword is forged. Somewhere there is one who has heard the trumpets of the New Age and who will respond. She will respond, this new woman, to the high clamor of those star-trumpets; she will come as a perilous flame and a devious song, a voice in the judgment halls, a banner before armies. She will come girt with the Sword of Freedom. Before her, kings and priests will tremble, cities and empires will fall, and she will be called BABALON, The Scarlet Woman. She will be lustful and proud, subtle and deadly, forthright*

and invincible as a naked blade. Women will respond to her war cry, throwing off their chains, men will respond to her challenge, forsaking foolish ways. She will shine as the ruddy Evening Star in the lurid sunset of Gotterdamerung. She will shine again as a Morning Star when the night has passed and a new dawn breaks over the garden of Pan. To you, oh unknown woman, is The Sword of Freedom pledged.

JACK PARSONS,
FREEDOM IS A TWO-EDGED SWORD

Guru: The proper use of the mind for the spiritual adept is to cut through illusion. In Tibetan Buddhism are many swords and objects used for cutting through *samsara*. The function of our mind, though few of us engage it in this fashion, is to discern and cut through to the truth about existence and reality by heightening our perceptual capacity through practice and discipline. When the mind is used like the sword of the bodhisattva Manjushri, or the *kartika* or ritual knife of a *dakini,* an enlightened female being, it can be a weapon against all deception and falsity—for what darkness of ignorance can stand against the flashing light reflected from a diamond mind that cuts like steel? These weapons are used to cut away all the attachments we might accumulate along our journey through life. Often the mind picks up things, which cling to it, or it clings to things, and these must be cleared away on a daily basis. Our knives must be kept sharp and our wits made keen.

Personal Example: It is usually very rude when the I Ching answers with this hexagram because it is calling on the querent to make a choice for him- or herself. It's saying, "You already know the answer." Not what anyone wants to hear, but, in fact, this hexagram is confirming what you thought was correct. I also receive hexagram 21 when some serious mental work needs to be done to sort through my thoughts about something, so this line is about the inner debate and talking to yourself you may need to do if you are having a hard time arriving at a decision. I know if I get this line I need to make a list of pros and cons and arrive at my answer.

The Changing Lines

Line One—The Self

Finding your own sword is one of the most exciting things that can happen. Even though you are here asking an oracle, if you can feel and understand within yourself the function of both the question and the answer and hear an echo resonate throughout your whole being—a *boom Shiva!*—then you will come to know how truth *feels*. This is a blessing of life and removes all the confusion, doubt, and suffering you may be feeling. It is the dawn that brings light to your hidden lands of thought. You will know when it happens because you will feel like a he-man or a she-woman and will shout, "I have the power!"—as you raise your sword above your head.

▸ Transforms into Shadow 35.1

Line Two—The Other

The only way we can learn to tell the difference between things is through experience. We are going to have to get into evil to know what evil is: you can't avoid this. You don't have to analyze everything as either good or bad or judge it too much. You can feel your way through and learn which is which for yourself as you go along. But if you choose not to embark on this journey, how on earth are you going to learn? The sword of your mind comes in handy here, helping you to take on the quest. Taking on the quest means getting to know the dragons at the crossroads. At every direction we choose to go, there will be a dragon guarding the entry to present us with an oppositional force, testing our resolve to take that path. If we want to keep to our decision, we will confront the dragon; if not, we may just remain in the same place.

▸ Transforms into Shadow 38.2

Line Three—The Union

Clarity of realization comes when we can heighten our perception and awareness to include a lot of things outside our usual methods of perceiving to arrive at certainty. Ways we get to knowledge are easiest when they are direct. Have you ever experienced not knowing your food was rotten until you took a big bite of it? But sure enough, the eating of it removed any trace of doubt. We don't need a weather report if we go outside and stand in the rain. Learning things the hard way, hands-on learning, can lead to certainty. When you have an experience of smelling poop, the next time you smell it, you know it is poop. How could you broaden to know with certainty things that are beyond your sensory experience?

▸ Transforms into Shadow 30.3

Line Four—The Earth

There will be times, even after we have found our sword of truth and pulled it from the stone, that we fall back into a pit of doubt and confusion. Some issues are complicated beyond our capacity to know. While at first you may doubt your compass because it was off or you thought you made a mistake in your judgment, it could be that more than one thing is true here. This is the line of holding two opposing views simultaneously. You were not incorrect in your judgment, but as it turns out, something else, also true, is occurring here. Do not let yourself be cut in two trying to figure it out; go into primal mode, as you learn to follow instinct as well as mind. When things confound the sword of your mind, it is time to descend into the depths where your animal lives.

▸ Transforms into Shadow 27.4

Line Five—The Conflict

Just because we know the truth does not mean we need to wield it as punishment over those who have not yet arrived at it. The truth is to be carried with us and shared, not plunged righteously into the hearts of the corrupted to show them how depraved and benighted they are. The temptation to accuse the ignorant as guilty is our mistake only. You have to make your own decisions, but unless you are a judge in a court of law, you don't get to impose your assessments on anyone else. Try communicating with them as you would like someone to explain something to you—instead of ramming it into them regardless of whether they like it. Some people aren't ready for the truth: you can only tell them and then let them decide for themselves.

▸ Transforms into Shadow 25.5

Line Six—Heaven

The truth can be very upsetting. You will find that some truths cause everything to collapse. This is a destructive action, causing our castles of sand to fall away under the wave of truth that hits them. There is nothing to be done at these times but allow it to happen and brace for the fallout. Trying to hide a truth that destroys illusion will not last long and will only prolong the decay and rot of what needs to come down for rehabilitation and rebuilding. Tear off the lies like an old bandage covering a wound that needs redressing. Get ready for a shakedown. The truth is rising!

▸ Transforms into Shadow 51.6

All Lines Changing—Hexagram 48

When we find our own personal sword of truth, if we follow it long enough it will lead us back to the Lady of the Lake, who is the well. The well is the source of all truth and the mysteries of the universe. Your sword is both a dowsing rod and a magnetic compass that will lead you here, its ultimate destination. First, you will find your truth, and then you will find *the* truth. Do not hesitate to drink these waters when you come upon them, even if it means abandoning all the beliefs you hitherto held dear to yourself, like a clinging, unyielding armor.

Hexagram 22
The Grace
Bi

Oracle Script:
The Redemption

"The Mercy Seat"
Amazing Grace
Forgiveness

Tarot Card: Six of Pentacles

When you hit the absolute bottom of the barrel, and there is no way to go farther down, we find, in the depths of hell, a secret hidden in the folds of fire. Here, in hexagram 22, we learn what it means to be humble in the face of a powerful mercy that cares nothing at all about what our worth and value is. It sees that life itself is valuable, regardless of our opinions of ourselves. We have lost everything—our integrity, our will to live, our self-esteem—but there is a spirit that says we are a beautiful diamond, deserving and worthy of love. This is the hexagram of the unconditional that few humans can obtain within their own hearts, but it matters not, for it is a universal force independent of our thoughts, fears, and actions. No matter what you have ever done, the worst deed you have ever performed, it is all burned away in the face of

Always forgive your enemies—nothing annoys them so much.

OSCAR WILDE

the unconditional love of everlasting mercy, which belongs to one and all. Coming into the knowledge of your innate worth as a human being is truly humbling for we learn that all our deepest anxieties are mere trivialities of little or no importance when compared to the beauty of life. You might think you are beautiful, but I promise you, your whole essence, your being—body, mind, and soul—is a sight to behold, as lovely as a shining star.

This is the hexagram of the *kaporet,* the mercy seat of the Ark of the Covenant. It is the point where suffering has reached a peak of misery, and so the oppositional force of grief is drawn down to Earth in the form of divine grace. This is the dove of the Holy Spirit, which descends only in response to the pull of gravity, bringing it down from its lofty heights. If we are able to hold grace even in the midst of our suffering, we embody the mercy seat of the covenant, while still in this life and in this body. This is the great equalizer, which is a force of nature itself, seeking equilibrium. In the kabbalah and ancient esoteric Jewish sources, this concept is known as Shekinah, which represents the indwelling of the Holy Spirit, its descent and presence within matter and the flesh. If we are to make a place for grace to enter, to make a dwelling for it to live, we may experience living mercy of grace upon the face of Earth. For some this dwelling was in temples or churches, in physical structures that humans could construct. Christ was seen as revolutionary because he attempted to reveal to people that Shekinah dwelled within their own hearts.

Teach me to feel another's woe,
To hide the fault I see;
That mercy I to others show,
That mercy show to me.

ALEXANDER POPE,
FROM "THE UNIVERSAL PRAYER"

Guru: When we come up against the hard wall of defeat and failure—the total loss of our own strength and ability to understand, a failing of everything—a hope appears, as if out of nowhere, to relieve us of our suffering and misery. This is grace. When we discover a mercy that was kept just for us in the depths of hell, when we see a thing come through when all light was extinguished, we learn of the presence of a divinity that shall not permit us to be consumed. It may come at the end of everything, even in the form of death, but it is mercy, nonetheless. And when this comes, we realize there is a larger force guiding and watching us. We realize how foolish we are and how little we know and are humbled and made small in the face of the great. We can become great when we give this mercy and forgiveness to one we may feel is not deserving of it. It is here we learn the meaning of humility.

> *Someone who has acted carelessly, but later becomes careful and attentive, is as beautiful as the bright moon emerging from the clouds.*
>
> NAGARJUNA

Personal Example: I overwhelmingly receive hexagram 22 for myself and clients when someone needs to forgive something or someone. If a client is asking about a relationship or something she is angry or upset about, and she draws hexagram 22, she needs to forgive both herself and the other. I always get the song "Let It Go" from the Disney movie *Frozen* stuck in my head when I think of this hexagram.

The Changing Lines

Line One—The Self

To keep grace and mercy within the self, you will need to walk on your own two feet. If you need mercy, if you need someone else to give it to you, you may be in danger of falling into codependent tendencies, forever reliant on someone else. But the one who has enough mercy to give it to themselves does not need to be scared to set out on a journey on foot without backup. If you have been brought to your knees to beg for mercy from another, the best way to stand up is to use your own feet.

▸ Transforms into Shadow 52.1

Line Two—The Other

To speak with grace means that we need some restraint. That doesn't mean we have to lie, however; raw emotional communication, which can seem honest, can also veer from the truth in favor of self-indulgence.

If we can have patience first, our words will be much more graceful in the end due to the power of contemplation, the power of the pregnant pause.

▶ Transforms into Shadow 26.2

Line Three—The Union

When we are lifted into an embodiment of grace and beauty, it can go to our heads, and we may be taken by our base desires again. Even when we have the best intentions, being placed upon a pedestal has its own issues. Stick close to the ground even when raised up, or bring your desires into a place of grace. Keep forgiveness in your heart, as your attractive qualities draw the fools in your direction.

▶ Transforms into Shadow 27.3

Line Four—The Earth

We can obtain such an embodiment of the presence of mercy within ourselves that we can break through into enlightenment, as the Holy Spirit enters us. Such a moment should be shared with others to heal and rejoice. When your light shines the brightest, it is important to show it to others—not to show off, but to spread it like a forest fire into the hearts of all in the Pentecostal fashion of lighting the torches of all around you because you have become filled to the brim with awareness of divine mercy. When you have been forgiven then you can forgive others because you can afford it.

▶ Transforms into Shadow 30.4

Line Five—The Conflict

We can't always be in the spotlight, and sometimes, even though we carry the grace and light of our hearts within us, we might not be recognized by others. Maybe we find that we are in a subservient position with no power. Holding the gold of heaven doesn't mean you are rich on Earth, and this paradox can cause us some grief. But serve as best you can to the ties that bind you, and if others are undervaluing you, make sure you don't fall into believing them. Keep your inherent dignity firmly within your chest, even while scrubbing the floors.

▶ Transforms into Shadow 37.5

Line Six—Heaven

When people see others shine, some very low things can arise—namely envy and jealousy. A bright light can attract a lot of shadows. If you find yourself in such an environment, you can lie low and hide your brightness, while not forsaking it within yourself. Dedicate yourself to your divine grace no matter where you find yourself. Do not make your realizations dependent on your environment and keep your truth regardless. The time will come for you to shine again; wait it out.

▸ Transforms into Shadow 36.6

All Lines Changing—Hexagram 47

When we are completely relieved of all our suffering and come into a state of grace, we may attract suffering to us again because of the law of oppositional attraction—all tides turn after exaltation. If we do find ourselves suffering again, keep close in your heart the feeling of grace, and you can be sure you will not tarry in these places for long. Once the feeling of mercy has been experienced, we will never again fall as hard or as low as we did before, so try to land somewhere in the middle.

Hexagram 23
The Cleansing
Bo

Oracle Script:
Disrobing

"Protective Armor"
Shed the Seed Husk
Removal of Fear

Tarot Card: Knight of Swords

In hexagram 23 we see a recapitulation of hexagram 4 and the apocalypse. Here we are forced to drop our protective coverings and return to the naked state of innocence that we arrive at in hexagram 25. In the story of Adam and Eve the Bible makes a strange statement regarding their skin. According to the Bible, God only gives Adam and Eve their skin after they try to hide their nakedness. Somehow, Adam and Eve were without skin before they became ashamed and humiliated (or lacked humility). This a fascinating distinction that is mostly lost and relates directly to this hexagram. The pictogram of 23 shows a knife for removing the skin from dead animals. This knife is to remove the dead parts of ourselves so that we can become transparent and completely without shame or even the concept of humiliation. Adam and Eve were hiding and then were

*And the day came when the risk to remain tight in a bud was
more painful than the risk it took to blossom.*

ELIZABETH APPELL

given a hide to cover over themselves. In the apocalypse, this hide or cover is revealed and everything is see-through. In 23 each layer is peeled off like an onion until we return to our original state of innocence.

We are not to imagine that prior to the "garments of skin" made by God for Adam and Eve, they were utterly naked. On the contrary, their original garb, like that of Aaron in the Tabernacle, consisted of light, in consonance with the purity of their earthly paradise. In Hebrew the words for light *and* skin *are homonyms, both pronounced 'or but spelled differently,* light *with an* alef *and* skin *with an* ayin. *That linguistic kinship enabled the* Zohar *to soar: by sinning, Adam and Eve had their garments of celestial light replaced by "garments of skin," which merely protected but no longer illuminated. Indeed, it was not their exterior but their interior which had mutated. Beyond paradise, there was neither comfort nor security nor wisdom (Zohar, II, 229a-b). The ethereal light that made everything humanly comprehendible had dimmed.*

Some three-and-a-half centuries later, another kabbalist, Isaiah Horowitz, the author of a meta-halakhic work of grand scope and power, made the Zohar's *explosive distinction between garments of light and garments of skin the linchpin of his mystical worldview. Our garments are our cognitive limitations. Bereft of the light of Eden, we no longer see the interconnectedness of heaven and earth or spirit and matter. . . . The expulsion made everything so much more obscure and impenetrable.*

ISMAR SCHORSCH, "THE GARMENTS OF ADAM AND EVE"

Guru: We are only seeds. All life-forms start as seeds or embryos or eggs, and birth happens when the shell is broken by a life-giving force. In a recapitulation of our beginning, our conception, growth, and birth, we too must vigorously break through our shell. Nature begins all of life covered in protective shells, to be birthed into vulnerability over and over again. We shall do this many times during our lives, with death the ultimate shedding and breakthrough. The coverings and removal of coverings becomes physical, mental, and spiritual. How many layers can you shed while you are here? How many have you shed already?

Personal Example: I often receive hexagram 23 for inquiries that concern someone confronted with or experiencing a primal response to put up a wall of defense. Either there is something in the external environment that is negative and causing them to repel, or there is some internal barrier that needs to be shed or removed. One client asked about her current relationship, and hexagram 23 responded that she needed to drop her protective armor and open to it without being afraid of the outcome.

The Changing Lines

Line One—The Self
Before we lean on others, we need to stand on solid ground ourselves. Finding that island of firmament in the deep seas of change is part of our task in this life. Other people can help support us, but the foundation of what is stable inside us can't be substituted. Using others as a support is not meant to replace our own common sense or heart. Love from another person can't replace self-love. There is only one thing that can provide that. Once we nourish ourselves, we can then look to others for additional, not primary, assistance. It is this clear distinction that will prevent you from falling into ruin when all your support systems fail or are unavailable. Self-reliance first, then seek the aid of others.
▸ Transforms into Shadow 27.1

Line Two—The Other
The apocalypse has ripped off your clothes, like walking through a fire wearing polyester. When everything you knew is shed, and you stand naked in the rain, it's time for a rain dance. You did everything you could to avoid being revealed, but now that the massive wave of alteration has happened, you can breathe a sigh of relief and do whatever dance you want. Maybe even sing too.
▸ Transforms into Shadow 4.2

Line Three—The Union
When everyone is following his or her own path, it may be hard to know which way to go. But not really. Let the ones who are leaving separate as a natural occurrence, and then look around to see who remains, still holding your hand. You may find the loss unsettling and even think you have to chase after them, but letting things go is a good way to see what

is true. Sit and wait until the dust settles and trust in what remains.

▸ Transforms into Shadow 52.3

Line Four—The Earth

Well, there goes that. When everything is stripped away by forces outside your control, and the whole thing crumbles and falls apart, it might be tempting to react to the loss with grief and sadness. Handling failure in our truest form of self without fear can happen when we truly accept our naked bodies. You don't need to dress anything up. When bad things happen, it's no one's fault. Some things really are what they are. Just sit there and see events in the light of awareness. After all the old skin has been shed, down to your toes, a new day will dawn. Though it feels like the end of the world, this line is Venus, standing in her shell, arising from the ocean after being born from the discarded remnant of Uranus. Lovely things can come from the ending of an empire.

▸ Transforms into Shadow 35.4

Line Five—The Conflict

When our true self emerges and we are fully free from our shackles, everyone else might not be, so we may still come under fire. Because our character proved rock solid to another once, someone may come to our aid, now that we are in need of it. An advocate or ally steps in when other negative forces attack, and we are saved in a last-minute reprieve.

▸ Transforms into Shadow 20.5

Line Six—Heaven

Some seeds are eaten before they can set down roots and grow; some seeds cling to their husks, refuse to grow, and rot. The seed that took its time falling to the ground, remains uneaten, and willingly sheds its husk grows into a new tree. Because we are willing and the earth is receptive, a fertile time of growth can begin for us here.

▸ Transforms into Shadow 2.6

All Lines Changing—Hexagram 43

Now that we have come to the end of stripping away all that is no longer useful, we must give ourselves a new name, and so we find ourselves at the location of Israel. The things we were holding on to have been forcibly removed from our hands, wrestled away by the angels, so that we can see the coins nestled deep within our palms.

One can ascend to a higher development only by bringing rhythm and repetition into one's life. Rhythm holds sway in all nature.

RUDOLF STEINER, *SELF-TRANSFORMATION: SELECTED LECTURES*

Hexagram 24
The Return
Fu

Oracle Script:
Recapitulation

"The Eternal Return"
Back from Whence You Came
Ouroborus

Tarot Card: Two of Wands

Many feel that the metaphor of samsara, expressing the circular, cyclical nature of existence, is only a symbolic representation, but it is also very physical. You are currently standing on a large sphere that is rotating and circling the sun. If you keep finding yourself back at the beginning of something, don't forget that you are literally traveling in spiraling circles through outer space. Maybe our human capacity to repeat behaviors is a consequence of our very real physical experience of the circles we are traveling through. In many occult works, sooner or later one will come across the ouroborus: the serpent consuming its own tail. Here we meet with the cyclic nature of all that is alive and the patterns through which things travel. If we have returned to something, it is because we eventually return to everything. The old saying "what goes around comes around" is not some mere adage but rather a universal law due to the spiraling nature of the golden mean. Planets travel in orbits just as electrons do. Can you see the cycle in which you are orbiting? If you can't, just wait awhile until you arrive back upon the head of the serpent.

The ancient alchemists discovered that things are spherical. A theory came about known as the harmony of the spheres, which examined some of this phenomenon in detail. The repeating nature of our physical existence is symbolically represented in karma, reincarnation, the circle of the zodiac, the repeating seasons, and the orbits of everything. All the way up and all the way down are orbiting circles that never end. People say you can change habits, but everything comes back around, so how do we come out of habitually traveling round and round? Realization and observant awareness of the circles could be the first step.

Guru: To become aware of your own patterns and cycles is one thing, but can you also see how everything has a pattern? The trained eye can see the patterns from the outside; the reflective self can see them on the inside. Can you merge the two viewpoints? What is the reality of self and other, nature and nurture through the lens of repeating circles? The one who can raise her awareness to the level of seeing the circles (through the spheres, which are their eyes) may just come into wisdom.

Personal Example: I had a repeat client for about four years. She had gone through several relationships during this time. She found herself at the end of another relationship. She asked, "Why does this keep happening to me?" Hexagram 24 was the I Ching's response. When she considered the answer deeply, she realized her current breakup had occurred in the exact same way as all her other relationships during the time of our sessions. I pointed out her pattern, and her awareness of it increased greatly.

The Changing Lines

Line One—The Self

Much like the addict who needs to willingly choose to go to rehab, not be coerced into doing it, we must choose to return to something. If it is not our own choice, we will probably rebel against it. Every return happens when we are ready for it. If you don't want to go visit your family, you probably won't. But if you miss them, you will find joy in the experience. We can even be presented with something over and over again and keep refusing it. Chances are, if there is something we have to confront for a karmic lesson, it will keep showing up until we choose to meet it head on. Otherwise, it's another trip around the merry-go-round.

▸ Transforms into Shadow 2.1

Line Two—The Other

You can never go home again. Just because we return to something doesn't mean that it will be the same as the first time we experienced it. Each time we experience the same thing, it is different. Try a new approach in your return this time. See it as the new thing it is, even if you have walked that road before. The way to make something new, even though it is old, is to notice that every moment is new and not take anything for granted. Take on beginner's mind, even with someone you see every day; maybe start with yourself.

▸ Transforms into Shadow 19.2

Line Three—The Union

Unless we are nostalgic, a forced return is never fun. Maybe you had to move back in with your parents because you ran out of money. Going back is always depressing if we see it as a defeat, but maybe fate gave it to us to help us hole up and recover from something that just didn't work out. Make the best of your return and gather your resources until it is time to set out again.

▸ Transforms into Shadow 36.3

Line Four—The Earth

When we are astounded by the actions of others, such as a betrayal, it can be tempting to fall into the misery of events beyond our control. When we view it more as an opportunity to return to ourselves and our own path, it could be a blessing in disguise that slaps us out of a codependent stupor. What parts of yourself had you been ignoring in favor of someone or something else? Return to yourself now and accept what fate can teach you about your own character rather than spending too much time marveling at the flaws in another.

▸ Transforms into Shadow 51.4

Line Five—The Conflict

Now we can start fresh all over again. It is all right if something didn't go as planned. Start over now and enjoy this new beginning. It is hard to start from scratch, especially if we have mastered something else, like an accomplished guitarist who now must learn to play the piano. Accept this new endeavor, and don't be shy about starting from the ground up.

▶ Transforms into Shadow 3.5

Line Six—Heaven

When the time comes to start again, don't miss the head and go back to the tail of the snake. Leap forward now, or you might miss your chance to grab the ring as you go by on the merry-go-round and then have to go through an entire cycle before you get that opportunity again. Luckily, everything lost is returned, so it is just a matter of time before the opportunity presents itself again. But why wait when all you have to do now is reach out your hand? Seek to nourish the new time and don't fall back into the old.

▶ Transforms into Shadow 27.6

All Lines Changing—Hexagram 44

We will be tempted over and over again to maintain old habits and patterns. This will never stop. If we think we have conquered it, we will meet it again and wonder why. Simply do not engage with it, but do not be surprised when the thing just won't go away. Do not worry over habits and behaviors you see repeatedly in your lifetime. To make and instigate change requires that we be in the world but not of it. See these habits coming toward you, and make changes as you go. When something keeps happening over and over, just make sure that, the next time you see it coming, you make a different choice.

Hexagram 25
The Exorcist
Kan

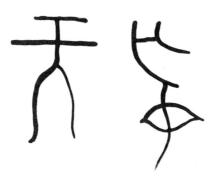

Oracle Script:
Adam Kadmon

"Return to Eden"
Pure
Shameless

Tarot Card: Nine of Pentacles

When we find ourselves to be truly innocent and natural, we become free. This is liberation, an escape from prison. We then see that this is inherently true for all humanity and does not belong to us alone, independent of any particulars. All our thoughts, terrifying and unjust though some of them may be, do not negate our innate innocence. Through humility we come to this realization, and it is a hard one in the face of the horrors of humanity. This is the true meaning of liberty, to be free from a distorted belief that we or any other human is guilty and deserves something we would never wish to endure ourselves. Solutions for punishments for crimes need not include judgments of shame. They require correction, repentance, and repair. When we bind nothing and no one, all the titans

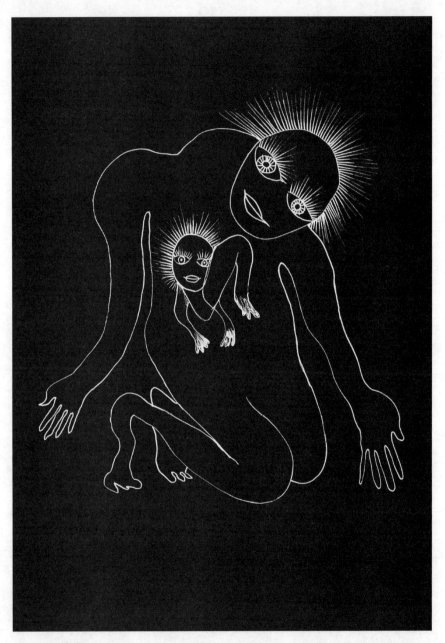

The tortures of the accused did not equal mine; she was sustained by innocence, but the fangs of remorse tore my bosom, and would not forego their hold.

MARY SHELLEY, *FRANKENSTEIN*

that have been ensnared in the depths of Earth are let go into their true forms.

This is the hexagram of the immaculate conception of Mary when she became free from all sin, including original sin. This happened not because of some special favor bestowed upon her or some unique quality of hers but was entirely due to her own realization that she was whole and perfect, exactly the way she was. When we liberate our mind from all thoughts that we are somehow evil, we inherit our birthright, valuing our life and our humanity. True beauty is inherent in all; we need only have the eyes to see it.

Holy Mother we do believe,
That without sin Thou didst conceive;
May we now in Thee believing,
Also sin without conceiving.

A. P. HERBERT

Guru: The return to the Garden of Eden comes when we understand that we left it of our own free will. Shame and guilt are what keep us from eternity, and once those are shed, we see ourselves as bright and shining new babes. Innocence does not leave us when we grow into adulthood; it is only thought to become distorted or somehow disinherited, when in fact it is our birthright. When we learn of our own innocence, we stop punishing not only ourselves but also all people, and the delusion of samsara can be penetrated.

Personal Example: I received a specific line of this hexagram when I was deathly ill with pneumonia. It seemed to indicate that the illness was caused due to some form of corruption, as I had also gotten hexagram 18 for the same illness, and when I inquired as to the cure, I got this response. I realized that the I Ching was not addressing the illness but rather the guilt, shame, and loss of pride and strength I was suffering because I viewed myself as weak and flawed for having fallen ill. Here the I Ching was trying to assure me that there was no shame in being ill. Realizing this made me feel better, and I recovered.

The Changing Lines

Line One—The Self

Human beings, like mountains, are a natural phenomenon. We are in nature, and nature is in us. Just as there is no judging the stars, there is no judging ourselves. Everything we do comes from and exists within nature; there is nothing we can do to escape this, unless we become supernatural or subnatural. If you accept your nature, you will learn what all of nature is.

▶ Transforms into Shadow 12.1

Line Two—The Other

Things in nature exist in the stream of events. All things have their time and place within a larger matrix or structure. If you do what you can in the time that presents itself, you will always be within the stream. If you get off course, all you need to do is jump back in; in time you will catch up, even if something gets lost or misplaced along the way. Missteps will constantly occur, but we always have now, and that can never be lost.

▶ Transforms into Shadow 10.2

Line Three—The Union

Bad things can happen to good people. And good things can happen to bad people. This is a hard fact of life to reckon with but has remained true through the millennia. Try not to feel too judged by the heavens when bad luck happens to you, and don't judge when good luck attends those who you feel don't deserve it.

▶ Transforms into Shadow 13.3

Line Four—The Earth

Somewhere, hidden within our very flesh and bones, is our nature, the secret of our destiny. When we are pure in our actions, we line up with this nature and find that we are able to express ourselves in an authentic manner. Like an otter who finds pure joy swimming in a river, as it was meant to do, we too must trust that we have an allotted task to perform here, in the time and place we find ourselves.

▶ Transforms into Shadow 42.4

Line Five—The Conflict

Some diseases arise from our mind, creating a state of discomfort, a state outside our being. It is hard to find a medicine for this state as it can never be resolved materially. The only cure for this severe discomfort is to comfort the inner state of the self with its true nature, which is joy and innocence.

▸ Transforms into Shadow 21.5

Line Six—Heaven

You might think that because you are in a state of purity and innocence then the world, or at least others, will recognize and honor this. When this does not come to pass, you may be thrown into emotional disarray, convinced that you are not innocent and that the other's judgments of you are correct. This is where we fall into a state of doubt about our own worth and validity and seek the validation of the other so as to maintain or somehow prove our innocence, which is our inherent birthright. All else is only confusion due to exterior circumstance.

▸ Transforms into Shadow 17.6

All Lines Changing—Hexagram 46

After we have cleared ourselves from all thoughts, we free ourselves to rise. Following our liberation into innocence, we come into our true nature, which is to ascend toward the heavens like a mountain. The nature of the human is to strive and continue forward, going forever up and skyward from Earth. The mountain teaches us humility, as it rises to the greatest heights attainable while remaining of the Earth.

The Fremen were supreme in that quality the ancients called *"spannungsbogen"*—which is the self-imposed delay between desire for a thing and the act of reaching out to grasp that thing.

FRANK HERBERT, *DUNE*

Hexagram 26
The Restraint
Kun

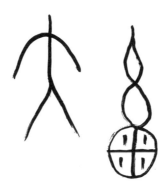

Oracle Script:
The Golden Girdle

"Gravity"
Pressure Makes Diamonds
Within the Limits

Tarot Card: Chariot

Here the animal or great beast that led us in hexagram 10 must be restrained and subdued to keep chaos at a minimum. This is the hexagram of Fenrir, the wolf in Norse mythology who requires the restraint of the golden mean to prohibit him from destroying everything we have worked so hard to build. A moment of unrestrained emotional energy can be as destructive as a bull in a china shop, if we allow our bestial impulses to roam wantonly. Sometimes we need to let the beast lead, and sometimes we need to put the reins on. When properly subdued and cared for, this energy can be at our disposal and be turned into power that can pull our chariot. We still must feed our creature and let it out when appropriate, but if you pull hexagram 26, you may need to restrain your emotions so that you don't wreck something.

We can also be restrained from the outside by forces that are larger than us. Hexagram 26 is for those times when we are restrained by forces beyond our control, and we must then be extra cautious about our emotional response to being placed in these kinds of circumstances lest we create more problems by causing damage within and without, instead of just enduring the stress the forces are exerting upon us.

> *And if thought and emotion can persist in this way so long after the brain that sent them forth has crumpled into dust, how vitally important it must be to control their very birth in the heart, and guard them with the keenest possible restraint.*
>
> ALGERNON BLACKWOOD

Guru: The lesson we learn in hexagram 26 is that we can strategically withhold ourselves to get better results. Rather than being to our detriment, this restraint can assist us in obtaining maturity if we can learn to control our emotional expressions for the greater good so that destruction does not result. In 25 we are liberated in our innocence, but in 26 we can dial it down and keep chaos from taking over everything.

Personal Example: A client who was furious at a friend's betrayal received this hexagram in response to how she should handle the situation. Needless to say, this was very disconcerting to her because she really wanted to let it rip and lay into the offending party with the full force of her passionate emotional response. She later learned that the betrayal had been a misunderstanding, and if she had done what she desired, she might have ruined the relationship beyond repair. But because she restrained herself, the friendship survived.

The Changing Lines

Line One—The Self
Sometimes restraint can save your life. Knowing when to stop and hold back is an important survival skill. If you don't know how to contain your impulse when it is most important, you could suffer from some fairly severe consequences. Try to examine what you can contain so that

you can act without haste and feel out the proper action in the proper time.

▸ Transforms into Shadow 18.1

Line Two—The Other

When we get mad that exterior forces are restraining us from acting, we should instead look around to see if it is not a blessing in disguise. Sometimes the hand of providence can practically reach down from heaven and pin us to our seats to make sure that we do not cause a catastrophe by being childishly rash in our actions. If something outside is stopping you, be grateful for the time to examine it, and make sure you have not made any errors before going forward. If your car stops suddenly on the road, it is probably because something is broken. Stop and fix it.

▸ Transforms into Shadow 22.2

Line Three—The Union

There is self-restraint, and then there is restraint placed upon us by others. This can be hard to accept if we don't trust and respect them. But even if there is not a close and intimate relationship, if we are being restrained by others, we could still stand to benefit from their actions, even if it is through the cultivation of inner strength.

▸ Transforms into Shadow 41.3

Line Four—The Earth

Aggressive emotions are needed from time to time, and we will never make it if we aren't able to express ourselves aggressively sometimes. But if we are able to temper and train our strong emotions from the start, we will be better able to prevent all-out wars and fistfights that could result from escalation. To use the force of the beast without the frenzy is what really gets the job done.

▸ Transforms into Shadow 14.4

Line Five—The Conflict

Every animal in nature has defenses. There is a reason for horns, tusks, claws, and teeth. Without them we would be far too vulnerable to exist in nature. But if an animal goes crazy and tries to attack everything that comes across its path, it is likely to find itself alone and isolated. Not even a mate wants to approach such an animal who has become stuck in attack mode.

▶ Transforms into Shadow 9.5

Line Six—Heaven
When we are in a balanced state of restraint, not too severe and not too mild, the chariot can run smoothly, and our animal natures are at their best, pulling cart and rider over the most unreasonable obstacles to obtain the goal. Coming into accord with our nature can place the powerful force of our emotions at our own disposal. This is the line of Kuan Yin riding the dragon across the sea.

▶ Transforms into Shadow 11.6

All Lines Changing—Hexagram 45
When we have mastered our emotional nature, we can join together with others in confidence that we will not destroy relationships as a result of reactionary fears releasing inappropriate aggression and drama at the wrong time. People join together in crowds and follow leaders when everyone feels safe and not threatened as well as protected by someone who is capable of keeping the order because they themselves are in order.

Hexagram 27
The Nourishment
Yi

Oracle Script:
Tiger's Mouth

"The Manna"
Give Us This Day Our Daily Bread
God Bless the Child Who Got His Own

Tarot Card: King of Pentacles

We come to hexagram 27 when we are hungry. When everything is empty, and we need to be nourished, our instincts will give us a hunger and a desire for something to fill ourselves. This is a consequence of nature. Hexagram 27 is known as the tiger's mouth and has a jawbone affiliated with it. This is a hexagram of Cain and Abel and is related to our offerings and how we choose to feed ourselves, through growing crops and eating the flesh of animals. Cain used a jawbone to murder his brother Abel for offering the meat of an animal instead of the fruits of his labors. It is the hexagram of the scapegoat and of blaming and punishing others rather than taking responsibility for ourselves. The things that go in and out of our open mouths during the course of our lives are mostly our choice, but hunger and

Thy words are like a cloud of wingèd snakes; And yet I pity those they torture not.

PERCY SHELLEY, *PROMETHEUS UNBOUND*

desire can cause us to lose conscious control and make choices and take actions we wouldn't have done in a more sober moment. When we eat our own scapegoat, we take liability into ourselves and grow a character in the void of emptiness and longing. The name Abel comes from the Hebrew verb *habal,* which means to "act emptily or become vain," and from the Hebrew noun *hebel,* which means "vapor, breath, or something close to nothing." The word *vain* reflects the fact that Abel was a thing created only to be destroyed, much like a straw dog or sacrificial animal made of grain. The vapor or breath suggests "here today, gone tomorrow."

> *Grace fills empty spaces, but it can only enter where there is a void to receive it. We must continually suspend the work of the imagination in filling the void within ourselves.*
> *. . . In no matter what circumstances, if the imagination is stopped from pouring itself out, we have a void (the poor in spirit). In no matter what circumstances . . . imagination can fill the void. This is why the average human beings can become prisoners, slaves, prostitutes, and pass thru no matter what suffering without being purified.*
> SIMONE WEIL, *GRAVITY AND GRACE*

We need more than just food for our bodies; we need food for our minds and souls as well. Otherwise we seek what others have to fill our empty places. Feed your character, and you can provide food for all.

Guru: Manna is something that is given to us by God. We are not dependent upon others for it, and other people don't need us for it. Everyone can get their own manna and exactly enough for themselves; still we covet what the other has. Though we have been provided with everything we need, we still seek validation or worth from the other. But you can't get self-worth from someone paying you something or giving you attention; valuing the gem inside your own soul is what gives you worth and value. Hunger is desire; we are so hungry and seek each other to fill our empty and vacuous souls. When we seek fulfillment from one another, we are like vampires; when we seek to be filled from God, we are renewed and reborn.

Personal Example: I was very ill and was afraid I was not going to get better. I asked the I Ching what I should do to recover from the illness. With this hexagram, the I Ching told me that I needed to take in nutrients and nourish myself in every way possible because I had become depleted. I have found that each time I am depleted, I get this response and advice for recovery. I have had many clients who need to watch their diet receive this hexagram in response, as well as the need for self-care and keeping away from stress. This hexagram can also mean that we need to watch what we say, our language and phrasing.

The Changing Lines

Line One—The Self

Jealousy has stricken you. You have everything you need but see that another has taken something from you. This is the line of the victim and requires self-care to avoid blame. Feed yourself before others are fed, and you won't look at their meal with a drooling mouth. Find your goal and go after that, then you will not be led astray to wander in the desert because of others. There are places we can get nourishment to prevent holding grudges against another for not looking after us. We are not our brother's keeper; we are our own keeper. Building character is what can feed us the most because we will not be consumed by envy and seeking after what another has but will instead look only for what we can get and provide.

▸ Transforms into Shadow 23.1

Line Two—The Other

This is the codependency line. Being dependent on another for your livelihood and basic needs breeds resentment and is difficult to sustain over time because one's own destiny is thwarted and forsaken. Normally a person either provides his own means of nourishment or is supported in a proper way by those whose have a duty to provide for him. If, for some reason, perhaps through no fault of our own, we cannot provide for ourselves, this means we will be dependent on others for our very life. This is a very disempowering state to find ourselves in but can still provide us with a deep humility and encourage growth if we can avoid bitterness. Keep your self-worth intact during such times and do not devalue yourself or others to the point of justifying anything that would cause dehumanization to occur through making someone your enemy.

▶ Transforms into Shadow 41.2

Line Three—The Union

If we seek only to gratify our needs and desires, we will find ourselves in a state of instant gratification. Although this may seem rewarding at the time, deeper parts of us—namely our soul—go into a state of starvation. If we can learn to go without something, this is where our character is built. If we get everything we ever need, we may find that we become a spoiled brat with needy expectations. Delay the gratification of your desires in a healthy way to ensure that you do not become addicted to pleasures or indulge in the physical world to the point where you become lost in seeking Earth, missing deeper parts of life that can't be found in food and drink and money.

▶ Transforms into Shadow 22.3

Line Four—The Earth

What do you depend on for nourishment? What is supporting your basic needs? We all need to look into these underlying factors in our lives so that we may seek them when our hunger arises. Knowledge of the self ensures that we will be able to seek proper support for our needs. Do not ignore your needs; if you do, you will find yourself desperate and hungry with no way to feed yourself. Address your survival needs and the needs of others, and be realistic about what this will entail. It is beautiful to need things and to need one another. Do not turn it into something that you view with disgust or as weakness, or the fruits of your labors shall turn bitter and rot.

▶ Transforms into Shadow 21.4

Line Five—The Conflict

When we are unable to meet our needs from our exterior environment, this can be a blessing, for it drives us within to seek our own source or well. Here we are augmented through the blessings of our labors, for they feed us when the harvest of our character arrives. Through the steady building of our inner strength, we find that we can support ourselves, and from this strength we inspire others to do the same. A blessing indeed is when we share the offerings of our sacrifices and have a bountiful cornucopia from which to draw.

▸ Transforms into Shadow 42.5

Line Six—Heaven

Total independence from needs seems unlikely; however, when we can find the source of manna, we see that relying on providence rather than the work of our hands gives us faith, trust, love, and the free flow of entering the stream of life. It can be nerve-racking to avoid actively seeking security and trust that we will be provided for, but when we trust that we shall be given what we need rather than what we desire we enter into the life of the sage and true master who knows that spirit provides when we ourselves cannot. Surrender to this truth and find abundance where before there was a wasteland.

▸ Transforms into Shadow 24.6

All Lines Changing—Hexagram 28

When we have reached the fullness of being nourished that occurs with hexagram 27, we might find that next comes the flood. Now that everything has been taken care of, suddenly we find ourselves back in a crisis. Turn now to what is not dependent on ourselves and what is out of our control. There is only so much we can do to provide, and sometimes nature puts a wrench in the wheels of our progress. Turn your attention now to those outside your circle who may have been affected by the uncontrollable crisis and who need your support and help with repairs.

Hexagram 28
The Collapse
Da Gou

Oracle Script:
The Path to Greatness

"Walk the Lonesome Valley"
Across the Great Divide
The Undying Tree

Tarot Card: Ace of Wands

Inside the Ark of the Covenant, one of the treasures kept sacred is the rod of Aaron. A deep and vast mythology surrounds this staff. According to Hebrew legend, when Adam found himself dying, he ordered one of his sons to sneak back into the Garden of Eden and get him a branch from the Tree of Life so that he might not have to die. This same branch was rumored then to be passed down through generations, entering the hands of Aaron, and also rumored to be the staff of Moses himself. When Moses was trying to heal the ill Israelites, he raised a serpent upon the staff to show them that they need not die if they would only release their complaints. This symbol became immortalized in the caduceus, which is the universal sign of medicine and doctors today. This rod and branch would continue to produce flowers

Relaxing with the present moment, relaxing with hopelessness, relaxing with death, not resisting the fact that things end, that things pass, that things have no lasting substance, that everything is changing all the time.

PEMA CHÖDRÖN, *WHEN THINGS FALL APART:
HEART ADVICE FOR DIFFICULT TIMES*

for all eternity, even though it had long been separated from its tree. It is said that we are like this branch: although separated from everlasting life in our human form, we also contain the power of regeneration, which we have mostly forgotten. Alchemists in China and around the world attempt this passage from mortal life to return to the Garden of Eden. In hexagram 28 the image is of a giant man, akin to the giant that is Adam Kadmon, who makes the passage through the valley to return to the garden. This crisis is breached through the rod of Aaron, the caduceus, and the knowledge that even when things fall apart in death, still there can be new life. For Adam his progeny were his everlasting life, not the tree branch his son retrieved.

> *And as concerning the Ark: God saved* NOAH *in the Ark. And God held converse with* ABRAHAM *in the wood of* MANBAR, *that is to say the wood that cannot be destroyed; and He saved* ISSAC *by means of the ram which was caught in the thicket; and He made* JACOB *rich by means of three rods of woods which he laid in running water; and through the top of his staff* JACOB *was blessed. And He said unto* MOSES, *"Make a tabernacle of wood which cannot be destroyed, in the similitude of* ZION, *the Tabernacle of the Covenant."* . . . *Hearken ye now unto me, and I will show you plainly how God had ordained salvation through the wood of His Cross, in the Tabernacle of His Law, from the beginning to the end. Salvation came unto* ADAM *through the wood. For* ADAM'S *first transgression came through the wood, and from the beginning God ordained salvation for him through the wood.*
>
> E. A. WALLIS BUDGE, TRANSLATOR,
> *THE KEBRA NAGAST*

Guru: The power of spring is the life everlasting. In Chinese medicine and philosophy, the spring power is contained within the liver. The liver is also said to rule the element wood. And so, Aaron's rod within our flesh is located in our liver, and the wood element controls and protects the earth that is our flesh. This hexagram can also contain a secret of keeping your health that is often overlooked, which is to nourish and protect your liver as it holds the key to your caduceus. If you get hexagram 28, make sure that stress isn't causing your anger to rise up, for anger is the negative emotion expressed when the liver is out of balance. If you find that under pressure your temper breaks, you must care for your wood so that it does not burn up.

Personal Example: One interpretation of this hexagram is of a wooden beam that holds up a house. I received this hexagram for a client who was asking about purchasing a home. The I Ching advised him that the house had serious issues with its load-bearing beams, which seemed to indicate that the roof would collapse. In fact, when the client performed his inspection, he found that the wood was rotten and the entire roof needed to be redone. In this case, it was a literal wooden beam in a structure that needed to be replaced.

The Changing Lines

Line One—The Self
Spirit kin find each other like families and clans. When we have a tribe or grouping that is part of our destiny, we can be sure that they will find us, and if we can lay a foundation from our bloodlines, both material and spiritual, we create a net that will catch us when we fall. We lose this net when we become suspicious and distrust the net we have laid so carefully. Like acrobats, we are only as safe as our safety net, so make sure your net is strong when you make it.
  ▸ Transforms into Shadow 43.1

Line Two—The Other
Even old trees bear fruit. The Tree of Life is never-ending in its bounty. Just because you may think your time has passed or you are feeling old and your life no longer has meaning, you still hold life within your bones, which can make your blood like new. Try a little bit of bloodletting or open a window to let in some fresh air. You can still put fresh flowers into an ancient Egyptian earthenware vase.
  ▸ Transforms into Shadow 31.2

Line Three—The Union
Feeling all used up can cause complaints. Complaints cause us to feel depleted and all used up. Take a look at what you are complaining about

and see if you can focus your mind on something else. It may be true that you have some ailments due to the passing of time, but these might not need to become the focus of your awareness. Care for yourself and be responsible, but don't fret about decay. Live your life. Sometimes life is the best antidote to feelings of death and decay. Don't forget to spend as much time caring for yourself as you do sitting around complaining.

▶ Transforms into Shadow 47.3

Line Four—The Earth

Just when you've reached rock bottom of a crisis and think you are dead, a window opens, letting in the fresh air of renewal. We find the headwaters of a spring, a new well, an almighty source of water. The secret to life everlasting is self-reliance in moments when we face death, and the knowledge that even if death is real, it is only a passage into a new space and time and so it need not consume the vital essence of our spirit. Do not be fooled by threats of death, for death itself is no threat to an immortal spirit. This is hard to see when staring into the abyss but true nonetheless.

▶ Transforms into Shadow 48.4

Line Five—The Conflict

When real death does occur, it is a terrible time for all. The power of death can consume all the life around it and spread deep into your psyche, planting seeds of fear and illness, worry and anxiety. How silly a thing, really, that death can stop all life around it. Do not give such power to a natural thing. It would be as if you were so afraid that you might be struck by a car that you never left your house. Even a single old woman who thinks she is no longer attractive can get a young husband. Never give up.

▶ Transforms into Shadow 32.5

Line Six—Heaven

It is naive to think you will be spared misery on your path. If you know misery is coming, you can prepare your character to endure it and become resilient. While some people bemoan negative occurences and view them as punishment for their personal existence, we can refuse to take such things personally and instead see how all things happen in cycles and in balance with nature. We then grow to be giants and can cross the valley of judgment in just a few mighty strides while others crawl the whole distance on their belly, bellyaching the entire time.

▸ Transforms into Shadow 44.6

All Lines Changing—Hexagram 27

When we come to the end of the lonesome valley, we enter the promised land and the Garden of Eden, where manna falls from heaven itself. After a long struggle and crisis, we reach the other side. This is where the fruits fall at our feet, and we can again be nourished and cared for by providence because we have proved ourselves strong enough to undergo challenges.

Hexagram 29
The Danger
Kun

Oracle Script:
Repeating Pit

"Purgatory"
Practice Makes Perfect
Abbadon

Tarot Card: Five of Swords

In this very special hexagram is hidden an important secret for navigating life. This archetype represents, on many levels, how to overcome fear and obstacles that we may meet in the course we take through the river of life, including the biggest obstacle of all, death. On first inspection, this hexagram advises us that, to overcome fear, we must confront it over and over and over again. The story tells of a repetition or rehearsal that allows for more freedom of movement through many many defeats rather than through being victorious. This can also be viewed in terms of the everlasting life that comes through repeated lives, regenerating through reincarnation until enlightenment and wisdom are achieved. Much like the film *Groundhog Day,* the message of hexagram 29 is to go at something over and over and not give up until you have mastered

If you fell down yesterday, stand up today.

H. G. WELLS

the ability to confront and conquer something that instills fear in your heart. It also brings the message of rehearsing and the discipline it takes to do something difficult. It is doubtful that someone can just be naive and approach a dangerous situation, but if one gets to know and learn about the situation, taking precautions and being strategic, suddenly a seemingly insurmountable obstacle becomes manageable, and we are no longer afraid and can soar through it with little to no resistance. Mostly we are afraid and resist based on past failures, and then we stop trying. This is a sure way to failure, and it is how fear blocks success through an inability or unwillingness to try, try again. The point where we stop trying is where fear enters and death occurs. If we train to die properly without fear, we can ensure that our consciousness can flow through death, as a boat along a river, without coming up against a wall. The ghost river is purgatory, where souls get stuck because they cannot move past a point where they failed or died. With no fear of death, we do not get stuck in the ghost river and can flow on to the next destination of our soul. Make peace with everything, and then nothing will snag or fetter you on your journey.

The story of the fall of Lucifer from heaven has a message regarding the pit of the abyss. From above, the angel Lucifer peers downward into the darkness of samsara, a purgatorial pit that is Abaddon. Lucifer cannot look away and becomes transfixed, obsessed. He makes a judgment that it is horrible and awful and recoils from it in fear and hatred. He feels the fear and hatred so strongly that the emotions act like a magnet and draw him down into the pit through the nature of oppositional attraction. Here, Lucifer finds himself trapped within the very thing he fears and wishes to abandon due entirely to his repulsion to it. Do not be so transfixed by death that you draw it into every day of your life, over and over again, through your mind.

> *we are all*
> *museums of fear.*
> CHARLES BUKOWSKI,
> FROM "POEM FOR NOBODY"

Perceive ye not that we are worms, designed
To form the angelic butterfly, that goes

To judgment, leaving all defence behind?
Why doth your mind take such exalted pose,
Since ye, disabled, are as insects, mean
As worm which never transformation knows?

DANTE ALIGHIERI, *PURGATORIO*

Guru: Some people become alive through facing death. The way to knowledge is often through contrast, and this is the power of negative energy. Without the negation of something, we do not know how it is upheld. The second side of something brings us the full view of gnosis of the thing. It is very true that you do not know what you have until it is gone, because in those moments the feelings you have for the missing thing erupt from your heart like lava flowing out of the earth. The true way to know love is through death so that you find the passageway that flows through it, connecting you to love even in its absence and destruction. We may have to learn this lesson by constantly repeating this confrontation until we can trust that love is eternal and is separated by nothing; we learn to avoid the pitfalls of misunderstandings because we have *respect for life*. When you understand what went into that cow you just ate for dinner because you raised and cared for it yourself, you will feel much differently about your meal. Rather than simply taking your meal for granted, you will come to know the meaning of sacrifice through the contrast of the knowledge of suffering. You might, after that experience, switch to a salad because you can better understand what the animal has given you through its absence from Earth.

Personal Example: Hexagram 29 is drawn when the querent is obsessed with something she is unable to escape, and it usually has a repeating factor involved. Often the client will have a repeating pattern in relationships; even when she switches partners, she finds herself in the same predicament over and over again. Or the client may have the exact same problem with a boss no matter how many times he switches jobs. When we are in 29, we must confront and resolve some fear or unpleasantness we are experiencing, or we will meet it over and over again until we make a different choice and stop re-creating the situation. Recognizing what we are afraid of so that we cease to make the same mistake is the only ladder out of the pit. I have also often received this hexagram for people who are experiencing PTSD and are unable to stop reliving a death or fear experience.

The Changing Lines

Line One—The Self

When we keep entering into the pit over and over again, but still blame everything but ourselves, chances are we will fail to see what we are responsible for in the situation. Perhaps a small boundary or limitation placed upon ourselves to avoid certain things can prevent our arrival at this same location on the next rounding of the wheel. If we take it upon ourselves to initiate some discipline for what continues to find us, perhaps it will just leave us alone. If you don't go to the bar, you increase your chances of not getting drunk.

▶ Transforms into Shadow 60.1

Line Two—The Other

Fear of risks are escalated when we have taken falls and hits in the past. It paints the color black over our eyes, which influences our view of new and unrelated occurrences. It is hard to get back up on the horse when you broke your leg the last time you rode. If instead of being afraid to remount your horse you could instill within yourself a healthy respect of what is involved in being with the animal, you could shift the whole situation merely by being aware of the potential obstacles. But you will still be able to enjoy a beautiful ride into the sunset even though there is a capacity for injury; the two can exist simultaneously.

▶ Transforms into Shadow 8.2

Line Three—The Union

When we are smack dab in the middle of the pit of darkness, the abyss, we might be tempted to abandon all hope. But if we have made a foundation within ourselves, a rock or pillar to which we can cling during such times, we can trust in ourselves that we can simply wait it out until someone drops us a line or a window appears through which we can simply climb back out of the pit. The more fear we generate while within the darkness, the more damage we do to ourselves in addition to the dank environment. Keep still inside and be patient through the test.

▶ Transforms into Shadow 48.3

Line Four—The Earth

Even a pit can have a party in it if we mind our attitude and sense of humor. The worst times are made tolerable through merriment. Even if this place is some form of purgatory, by God, there are good times to be had regardless. Try to find the silver lining in the darkness, and it will make a golden thread through which you may navigate your way back through the labyrinth into the sunshine again. Just because things are dark and you can't see doesn't mean your funny bone is broken. Make the best of it with what you've got. Play some games or tap your feet.

▸ Transforms into Shadow 47.4

Line Five—The Conflict

When we finally crawl out of the pit and are standing on its edge, it could be tempting to turn around and stare right back into it. But don't turn around. Don't be like Lot's wife, pining over what is done, or you risk turning into a pillar of salt. Discipline yourself to move forward into the new time and don't get caught back up in what you just came out of. Figure out a more practical way to move forward and learn from past failures to avoid making the same mistakes. Make a firm decision to depart this dark place once and for all!

▸ Transforms into Shadow 7.5

Line Six—Heaven

Here we are trapped in a pit that has a staircase leading out of it, but we have forgotten how to see it, much like the elephant who thinks it can't break free from the tiny rope tethering it. You have the power to remove all your illusions now; you have only to become aware of them. Make valiant efforts to discern between your thoughts and reality to avoid fooling yourself into believing what is only a projection of your fear. Try to become a fool who knows nothing at all; this is your best bet for liberation. Erase and clear everything you thought you knew.

▸ Transforms into Shadow 59.6

All Lines Changing—Hexagram 30

After a long time spent in the dark, we emerge eventually into the light of day. As the shadows of the pit subside, we are reinvigorated by the fire of life and appreciate and are sincerely grateful for everything we have. That first meal after a long starvation tastes better than anything we have ever eaten.

Hexagram 30
The Light
Li

Oracle Script:
The Burning Bird

"Clarity"
Baptism by Fire
Independence through Union

Tarot Card: Queen of Swords

Hexagram 30 is often called the hexagram of enlightenment, or clarity of mind, that allows our perceptions to see far more than we ever could have imagined through a deeper understanding. The image presented is of a bright burning bird of fire or gold who is caught within a net. I received a meditation upon this meaning indicating that it is depicting the awareness of our consciousness trapped within the matrix of matter. The matter itself obscures and prevents our perceptions from rising unless we create enough light of awareness to see through the mesh encapsulating us. Like an epiphany, theophany, or spontaneous spark, here we become made aware of some greater knowledge that can potentially spread to others. Like a phoenix, we are reborn. This is the hexagram of the Pentecost, for when Mary took in the fire of the Holy

We see in order to move; we move in order to see.

WILLIAM GIBSON

Spirit it spread to all those near her and lit them up like lanterns. The Pentecost reveals that when the great knowledge of the dove (the bird of brightness) of spirit descended into the heart of Mary through her decimating grief, she was made aware of the strength of her love through death and thus came to know the eternal nature of love and life. When she spontaneously arrived at this awareness as the bright bird plunged into her, it bled into all those standing within proximity. This gnosis is the fire of the Pentecost.

> *When Li birds sing, silk worms grow.*
> SHUOWEN

Guru: True clarity arrives with an expansion of consciousness. We expand our consciousness when we include many more perspectives than our own—or at the very least one other perspective. Nothing makes the world clearer than seeing it through the eyes of another. The reason why the highest angels are shown covered in eyes is to illustrate how they can see through the eyes of the many, not just through their own eyes.

Personal Example: In a very literal example of this hexagram, a client had just purchased a book from a bookstore and wanted to know if its contents were valuable for her. She asked, "What is inside this book?" The I Ching responded with hexagram 30. I told her that I often view this hexagram as the phoenix hexagram. She gasped out loud. Inside the book was a bookmark with a picture of a phoenix on it, a bird on fire. The I Ching had described exactly what was in the book with a hexagram that matched the picture on the bookmark.

The Changing Lines

Line One—The Self
The bird of our awareness can often have a hard time choosing where to land. It flutters here and there like a wanderer, refusing to make a nest. Perhaps it is simply migrating like a forest fire that seeks to grow. Try to establish a hearth eventually, but only when you are ready. No point staying somewhere you don't like. Finding a place of peace within

the mind occurs when we arrive at the realization, not when it is forced upon us.

▶ Transforms into Shadow 56.1

Line Two—The Other

When we ourselves behave like the golden bird of the balanced mean, we become transparent and brighter, as if we are made of light itself. Some people try to attract a bird of fire to them by becoming something for the fire to burn and consume. Others simply become the bird itself. Becoming such a lofty being may seem unobtainable to many, but if you can imagine it, you are already halfway there. The fire is already within you; all you have to do is turn on the light.

▶ Transforms into Shadow 14.2

Line Three—The Union

If we can't seem to find the light in dim times, we need only to search around a bit. Even the dark night sky has stars. Use your perceptions to seek out the joy and spirit in all things; you can be certain it is there somewhere. If you understand that there is light hidden in everything, it would be foolish to give up hope on anything.

▶ Transforms into Shadow 21.3

Line Four—The Earth

Many lights belong to fire, and they burn quickly and brightly. Not everything is an eternal flame. Sometimes a realization only serves a purpose in the moment and then is extinguished, but this does not make it any less valuable or important. The big trick is to catch these flames in containers like fireflies and choose the ones you wish to sustain you throughout your lifetime. A crush can turn into a marriage when the flame does not die out over a couple of months, but what will keep it burning?

▶ Transforms into Shadow 22.4

Line Five—The Conflict

Sometimes it takes a real slap in the face to ignite a fire. There is a reason sparks come from friction, from scraping substances together. Let the suffering you feel light your passion and engage your heart in your actions of living. This is the best way we can permit our conscience, which resides in our hearts, to guide us on our way. If your heart is challenged through a trial by fire to beat brightly, you can't be confused or misled, because the heat of your passion will be unmistakable.

▸ Transforms into Shadow 13.5

Line Six—Heaven

Baptism by fire is perhaps as harrowing as it sounds. Where there is fire, there will be destruction. Everything that cannot stand the heat will be burned away. Get ready for some losses. If you are willing to get rid of what is no longer needed or no longer serves you, you can make this process much easier. New growth emerges in the forests after a horrendous fire, and what a miracle and a blessing it is to behold after the rains come! Gird yourself for a total purification by the flames and drop what can't handle the rise in temperature.

▸ Transforms into Shadow 55.6

All Lines Changing—Hexagram 29

After reaching the heights of awareness and flying up to meet the sun, we may find that we are plunged back down into the depths of fear and darkness. While you might view this as a punishment and be confused at first, perhaps something you did not consider is that once you have your lantern turned on, you can be a light for others who are still trapped in dark places. Enter into the darkness with purpose and let your light shine.

Eros, again now, the loosener of limbs troubles me, Bittersweet, sly, uncontrollable creature.

SAPPHO

Hexagram 31
The Attraction
Hsien

Oracle Script:
Mutual Affinity

"Eros"
Sexual Instinct
Magnetic Force

Tarot Card: Queen of Wands

This hexagram describes the natural phenomenon known as Eros. Eros is a force, like gravity, and compels things to be brought together. Just as there are forces that separate objects, Eros is a force that unifies and does so as though it were a biological instinct. Here we are overtaken and enamored in an irrational fashion. Who can explain the complexities of attraction? Why does he like her? Why do those animals become friends rather than eat each other? Eros is a potent universal mystery that enables life to continue its dance through eternity. Eros is the attractive and repulsive force that is at the heart of every single cell in your body. Atoms are protons, neutrons, and electrons engaged in an erotic relationship. All material is held together through this force.

The thirty-first gua *is called "Xian" which means simply "Feeling" . . . illustrated by the relationship of a young woman and a young man in a bond of feeling love and care. . . . In a sense, the larger universe is bonded in such a creative feeling of interaction and reciprocal regard so that all things can prosper. . . . With this understanding of the power of feeling, it is clear that one could respond to a situation by one's profound feeling of a situation and therefore could come to describe the situation in the form of an image. . . . Feeling in this sense is the connecting and interactive factor between two natural objects and thus indicates the actual communication or sharing of two states of being.*

BO MOU, EDITOR, *COMPARATIVE APPROACHES TO CHINESE PHILOSOPHY*

Guru: Although most focus their Eros on something they desire, such as another person, an object, or even an idea, they are wasting their purpose. The purpose that each of us must fulfill is to connect heaven and earth. If we stop wasting our resources and do the work of focusing our Eros upon spirit, we can attract spirit to us and bring it to Earth to live in our bodies in a sacred marriage, which is hexagram 32. After this is accomplished, we can seek out whatever we want because we have done the work of being human. Until this labor is accomplished, your desires will come and go, changing with the wind, but to be focused on the eternal, your love will stabilize into something more substantial, beyond just obtaining an object.

Personal Example: Hexagram 31 is about wooing. I had a client whose marriage was failing. She asked, "What can I do to save my marriage?" The I Ching responded with 31. Sometimes we think a thing is accomplished, and we take it for granted. But in a relationship based on attraction, we have to keep playing and not let the ball drop. Reinvigorating the relationship through the power of wooing must be done regularly in every relationship to keep the spark alive.

The Changing Lines

Line One—The Self
Before a real attraction is ignited, often we feel a premonition. This can be felt like a static charge in the air when a storm is approaching.

There are indicators that alert us to an oncoming force. These things are felt; they can't be thought about. If we think about them they don't make sense, and yet we are compelled to follow them regardless of our thoughts. When an attraction is brewing, the air condenses around it, maybe like the dust that gathers before a star is born. Pay attention to such premonitions, for they are rarely incorrect when they feel palpable, when you can feel it coming in the air.

▶ Transforms into Shadow 49.1

Line Two—The Other

Strong feelings can arise when we can't influence the one we would like to. We become frustrated when we find our erotic powers are useless or wasted on others, and no one will listen to us or follow our lead. Do not let anger or bitterness creep in. The best way to attract what belongs to you is to do what you need to do on your own. When we have power in our center, we become a magnetic force through the strength of our hearts. When we focus outside on the other, we lose our charge because we dissipate our concentration.

▶ Transforms into Shadow 28.2

Line Three—The Union

Attracting something isn't too hard. But attracting the right thing now is the challenge. Some things are not difficult to persuade in our direction, but are they right for us? Recognize what your needs and desires are attracting versus what is coming to you through the higher forces of your mind, spirit, and soul. Just because you are wearing a flattering outfit doesn't mean you'll attract something beneficial. Seek deeper levels of attraction beyond the superficial. This is done through the heart, not the body.

▶ Transforms into Shadow 45.3

Line Four—The Earth

It can be very easy to influence those with whom we are close. We might not need to twist the arms of friends, partners, and family to get them to follow us. We know our powers of influence and attraction are very strong when we can woo a total stranger. Many people enjoy this kind of feedback from the outer world and use it on a superficial level. But those who can attract and influence individuals toward universal truths obtain merit and virtue in this world and beyond. The influencer of ideas toward the golden mean of nature is walking heaven's highway.

▸ Transforms into Shadow 39.4

Line Five—The Conflict

It is important to feel our own influence and influence the world. We also must feel the influence of others. To participate and become part of the synergistic organism that is the planet, we must feel the pull of the moon, feel the light of the sun, feel the waters of the ocean. Let them into you. Do not be afraid to feel the influences of others upon you. Keep your center while you feel them. But if you block out everything, you will deplete your energy. Feeling another's mojo is a beautiful thing when you do not lose your own. This is interdependence, not codependence.

▸ Transforms into Shadow 62.5

Line Six—Heaven

If you are trying too hard to influence others, you can lose your integrity. Pull back now and reconnect with your original inspiration. Do not become lost in the game of trying to win over others; remember that first feeling of passion instead. When we withdraw into ourselves we create a stronger magnetic pull than when we stretch ourselves out too far, seeking validation. Feel the feeling instead of seeking agreement. Your influence will grow stronger by the day.

▸ Transforms into Shadow 33.6

All Lines Changing—Hexagram 41

A portion of the self must be sacrificed when we are trying to influence a larger whole. We may rebel at first and decide, instead, to subsume or align ourselves with others, but doing this is unfulfilling. To achieve the goal of sharing our passion and getting others to share our purpose, we must place some parts of ourselves aside. But do not be afraid to feel the passion instead of seeking favor and influencing others. Diminishing yourself to obtain your goal is fine, but your heart will freeze when you don't express your true feelings.

Hexagram 32
The Marriage
Heng

Oracle Script:
The Telltale Heart

"Endurance"
Mysterium Conjunctio
The Alchemical Wedding

Tarot Card: Four of Wands

Here we find ourselves at the center point of the sixty-four hexa-grams. Hexagram 32 is the link that yokes the first half of the work with the second half.

The image for this hexagram is of a heart and a moon. Your heart is your vessel or ship that carries you through this life, and when it is changeable like the moon, you can sail through many emotional storms, uncertainties, and doubts. This hexagram reveals a way to steady your heart and secure your vessel so that it is seaworthy and can make the long journey. A stable heart can endure a marriage for a lifetime. The changeable hearts of lovers who fly from one person to the next are too vulnerable to storms, and love ties are dissipated and destroyed. But when the heart has become stabilized it does not veer from its course.

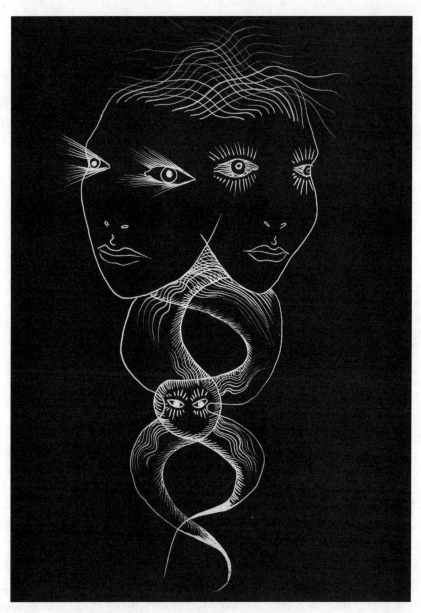

O Luna, folded in my sweet embrace
Be you as strong as I, as fair of face.
O Sol, brightest of all lights known to men
And yet you need me, as the cock the hen.

ROSARIUM PHILOSOPHORUM
(ROSARY OF THE PHILOSOPHERS)

This is the hexagram of the *mysterium conjunctio* and the alchemical wedding. Alchemy always seeks to unify the microcosm and the macrocosm, the above and below; in hexagram 32 this union is accomplished. The hermetic marriage is another phrase used to describe the mysterium conjunctio. Specifically, it refers to the joining of the sun and moon, also known as the union of the opposites, the light sun and the dark moon. The relationships between these opposing forces, which are also the yin and yang of the I Ching, are symbols for every relationship you will have with everything in the world. Relationships and how we relate to each other happen not only on an atomic level with electrons and protons but also on a larger level concerning the archetypes of the planets. The grand unified theory, which currently continues to evade modern physicists, may be solved if they only understood the mysterium conjunctio. The symbol of the androgyn, of the opposites united, is the major symbol used by alchemists throughout the centuries to depict the mysterium conjunctio, the male and female existing in one form. This symbol also represents the first ancestors. In China these are Fu Xi and Nu Wa; in the Bible, Adam and Eve. The true meaning of Adam Kadmon is primordial man, or primal man, who was a hermaphrodite. Adam contained the DNA of all people and lineages and so was the prima materia who housed all forms, whole and complete.

> *The alchemical operation consisted essentially in separating the prima materia, the so-called* chaos, *into the active principle, the soul, and the passive principle, the body, which were then reunited in personified form in the coniunctio or "chymical marriage" . . . the ritual cohabitation of Sol and Luna.*
>
> CARL JUNG, *MYSTERIUM CONIUNCTIONIS*

Guru: Unification with your shadow means you have to live with it inside you all the time, instead of projecting it into the world and people around you. Contain your darkness and carry your own contempt instead of blaming your difficulties on everything else. This is how we get on in a marriage with another; we must contain our own shadow lest we project it onto the other. All our relationships are dependent on us being able to perform the mysterium conjunctio. If we do not, we separate and become resentful and blaming. Be responsible for being married to yourself first, and then go out and make your commitments to others.

> *Be thou the rainbow in the storms of life. The evening beam that smiles the clouds away, and tints tomorrow with prophetic ray.*
>
> LORD BYRON

Personal Example: A client was making an inquiry regarding her present relationship because she was experiencing doubts and wasn't sure how to proceed. The response was hexagram 32, which indicated that the relationship would endure. She contacted me later to send me a picture of the two of them with their new child.

The Changing Lines

Line One—The Self
Your heart is your vessel that will carry you through your life. If you trust that you have a seaworthy vessel, it can take you across the great waters. If the hull is breached, you could run into trouble on stormy waters. Make your heart something you can trust even when you can't trust anything else. The first commitment you must make to get along with others in this world is yourself. If you jump your own ship, how can you ride along on anyone else's?
  ▸ Transforms into Shadow 34.1

Line Two—The Other
There is a magical zone where we can float through life less encumbered by the waves. Every storm has a calm eye, and when we find it, we have found the golden center. Everything in this world follows the balance and proportion of the golden mean; this is the law of nature. When your heart is ordered and constructed upon such principles, you can trust that you will have smooth sailing ahead. Nothing in excess. Feel all things equally and evenly without dwelling on any island for too long and without keeping yourself oppressed.
  ▸ Transforms into Shadow 62.2

Line Three—The Union

When your heart is all over the place, rising and falling like the waves of the sea, you will create storms in your life. When you can commit to at least keeping yourself under control, your emotions will stabilize, and you will find yourself surrounded by less drama. Feel things strongly, but there is no need to be constantly losing your head over the smallest thing. Get yourself together and feel your feelings without letting them possess you.

▶ Transforms into Shadow 40.3

Line Four—The Earth

Big ideas can make you feel small and lose hope. The heart is tender and sensitive. Human hearts fall and rise. To give ourselves hope and the courage to proceed, our hearts have to believe in what we are doing. If we do not believe we can accomplish a task, we become halfhearted. Making our ambitions greater than our ability to achieve them is a setup for failure. Choose goals that fit within your realm and your life and build them bit by bit, every day. This strengthens your will and determination, which gives you the ability to discard hope altogether in favor of trust.

▶ Transforms into Shadow 46.4

Line Five—The Conflict

Oftentimes we think we have gone crazy when we are overly emotional. Perhaps you just have a yin deficiency and need to rebuild it. Look to your nutrition, and care for your physical body if you are having emotional stress. Nourish your heart to stabilize it. Exercise. Take blood-building tonics and heart herbs. Once yin and yang are back in balance, this assists us greatly in coming to solid ground when disaster and storms head our way. Best to be in tip-top shape and not depleted nutritionally if you have a huge task you need to undertake. When emotions possess you, look to your earth for stability.

▶ Transforms into Shadow 28.5

Line Six—Heaven

Maintaining a stable heart is only the base. We must navigate through a world of other hearts and even heart eaters. There is inside and outside to contend with. As you sail your ship, look out for icebergs, but do not beach yourself to avoid them. Settle into your sailing: if you are constantly on the alert, tacking to and fro, you might topple the boat. Come into a steady pace that you can maintain. If you are unavoidably involved with others whose hearts have become unstable, offer them resources and direction while they are out to sea; help them find solid ground.

▶ Transforms into Shadow 50.6

All Lines Changing—Hexagram 42
The blessing that comes when we unify and come into the mysterium conjunctio of mind and body is to receive heaven while on Earth. Many others besides ourselves can benefit from this blessing. After a time of commitment and endurance, we achieve stability and receive the harvest that gives us sustenance as a result of all our hard work to unify things upon Earth.

Hexagram 33
The Internal
Tun

Oracle Script:
The Retreat

"Withdraw"
Away in a Manger
Give Me Shelter

Tarot Card: Seven of Swords

There are things that change, and there are things that do not change and remain eternal. The spokes of the wheel touch the earth, and they also connect in the middle. Hexagram 33 contains the secret of the power of the center and heart. Here we enter into the center of the pyramid and the sacred geometry of the number 33. Thirty-three is the location of the power generator within all things, the center of the black hole through which gamma energy streams forth. All energy and life flows through the vortex, which opens in these ultimate vortexes, and 33 is the force of all creation. The true essence of who and what you are resides in this place, a sacred haven that protects and looks after it. This never changes, no matter how much chaos occurs in the outside world; your true self lives here, and you can enter the temple where it resides

What madness deludes you? For in you, and not proceeding from you, he wills all this to be found, which you seek outside you and not within yourselves. Such is the vice of the common man, to despise everything his own, and always to lust after the strange.

GERHARD DORN, *THEATRUM CHEMICUM*, VOLUME 1

whenever you choose. In hexagram 33 we are called upon to retreat into the temple of our true self to confer with the presence of our naked truth.

Sometimes shown as an infant suckling on its mother's breast or a piglet being nursed, the power generated when a thing folds in upon itself to provide its own nourishment is nothing less than the sustaining manna of heaven itself. It may seem like a cowardly retreat to pull back into the self, but this is where our vital energy resides. To look for it outwardly is a misstep; once we understand this our generative force can spew out of our hearts like the waters of an everlasting fountain.

The secret of the number 3 is the power of creation, so hidden in this hexagram is also the image of a mother bearing a child. The child makes three, born when two opposite forces come together, creating something new. In the Hebrew tradition, the Bible teaches that when the creation of the universe occurred, it came out of nowhere and was spontaneous. The Torah begins with the word *bereshith,* which many translate to mean "in the beginning." But some other Hebrew sources give it a more interesting meaning: "from nothing there was a thing." This really is the true mystery of creation.

> *It was a dark and stormy night; the rain fell in torrents, except at occasional intervals, when it was checked by a violent gust of wind which swept up the streets (for it is in London that our scene lies), rattling along the housetops, and fiercely agitating the scanty flame of the lamps that struggled against the darkness.*
>
> EDWARD BULWER-LYTTON, *PAUL CLIFFORD*

Guru: The creative spark that is in the flesh of our heart is called the sinus node. It is the life force that powers every beat of every moment of our lives. This force comes from and is generated in our center and in our heart. What creates this electric charge that animates us? What creates the light that shoots forth from the black hole? If you find the answer to either of these questions, you are a sage indeed.

Personal Example: My friend was being publicly attacked in the media. When he inquired what to do, the I Ching gave 33 as a response. He thought it was strange to make a retreat because he felt like he should take a stand. But he disappeared for a while, and the whole thing blew over. Nothing came of it, and he recovered quite nicely with no harm done to his career.

The Changing Lines

Line One—The Self
We are living inside biological organisms, whether or not we like it. Our organism will choose a fight-or-flight response all of its own accord, seemingly outside our control, unless we work very hard to train it otherwise. Many people are ready to retreat with their tail between their legs at the first sign of disrespect, but the times we choose to pull back tell us a lot about ourselves. Sometimes the best course is to pull away, but sometimes we are only reacting in fear, inspired by our inner animal. Make choices of retreat from higher places than a tucked tail.
   ▶ Transforms into Shadow 13.1

Line Two—The Other
When we retreat inside ourselves, there we are. Though you might get into confrontations and trouble with others, you will always only have yourself and your own conscience to answer to. If you do things that are pleasing to others, but not to yourself, you can be sure your heart will let you know about it later. Answer to yourself, not the other, and you will not be in danger of losing your own truth, which is held to your chest like a sword. Meet the other halfway before you make your retreat to see if some compromise can be reached without either party needing to submit entirely.
   ▶ Transforms into Shadow 44.2

Line Three—The Union
When communication is blocked, situations can come to a standstill, but that doesn't mean everything is over. If you don't want to leave a situation entirely, but you need some space, just take a break. Making an overly dramatic retreat is a waste of emotional energy. Take a simple time-out in this instance because you are not interested in cutting ties completely. Let some time and space do the work while you tend to your bruised ego.
   ▶ Transforms into Shadow 12.3

Line Four—The Earth

When we don't want to retreat but we need to anyway, we could have a hard time with it. If someone else chooses the retreat, our ego may get bruised because we feel we have lost control. When we use times of involuntary retreat to build our own character rather than resort to character assassination of the other, we can grow into maturity and overcome one of our primordial impulses. When communication fails and you must pull back, don't hem and haw; go take care of yourself and do something nourishing.

▸ Transforms into Shadow 53.4

Line Five—The Conflict

We don't always have to be primal and retreat in fear. There are situations that call for a friendly retreat in which it's merry meet and merry part. Don't make a big fuss when it is time to say good-bye. If a situation wasn't meant for you and it is time to leave, make a peaceful exit rather than a dramatic door slam. This ensures that everyone can make their own choices in the future with no destruction or burned bridges hampering the way.

▸ Transforms into Shadow 56.5

Line Six—Heaven

Letting go of things is hard to do. When we learn the lesson of nonattachment, we become wise like the hermit. There are no possessions here; we do not own people. Learning how to have relationships with people and things that are liberated can be difficult in a world filled with grasping, but perhaps if you are able to do it, you could lead others to the same type of thinking. You will never lose someone whose heart loves you, so do not be afraid to withdraw according to the instructions of your own heart.

▸ Transforms into Shadow 31.6

All Lines Changing—Hexagram 19

While hexagram 33 calls for a withdrawal or retreat into the self, when our retreat is over, it is time to come forward with all we have gained to lead others in our wisdom. Hexagram 19 calls for leadership, for when we become stronger within ourselves in a genuine fashion we have the merit to lead others toward their goals.

We will not find the inner strength to evolve to a higher level
if we do not inwardly develop this profound feeling that there
is something higher than ourselves.

RUDOLF STEINER, *HOW TO KNOW HIGHER WORLDS*

Hexagram 34
The Strength
Da Zhuang

Oracle Script:
The Warrior

"The Shepherd"
The Matrix of the Womb
Formation from Clay

Tarot Card: Strength

Hexagram 34 comes to us when we have found some kind of power. We have grown horns, and we must learn how to use them. The symbol of the ram,* which is often associated with this hexagram, is the force of the ego and the individual as it comes into its own power. This power can be wielded in many ways. If we wield this power correctly, we can actually tap the universal power as an individual. If we wield it incorrectly, it can get us into trouble through too much force and aggression. Some compare this hexagram to the ram in the story of Abraham and Isaac, who becomes the scapegoat. We can learn from watching wild goats and rams who get themselves into serious dilemmas when they butt heads and lock horns, sometimes becoming entangled. Incorrect use of force can

*In the ancient Chinese, *ram, sheep,* and *goat* are all represented by the same word.

cause harm to all, not just the thing we intended to destroy. Power used wisely can be a source of growth for all and help power and expand things, like explosive fuel shooting a rocket ship into space. Or the entire ship can explode when the power malfunctions and becomes misdirected. We become the strong warrior, and then this hexagram turns to 43, where we take on the name of Israel because we refused to turn against our brother by using our powers of restraint found in hexagram 26.

This hexagram is related to hexagram 54, where we're called upon to subordinate ourselves. Our strength and power can only truly be used against ourselves. This is the true mark of warriors and heroes. They are able to overcome things easily in the world because they can overcome themselves. The process of overcoming the self is the process of sacrificing the scapegoat, or our aggressive nature that wants to dominate our fellow humans instead of protecting them. The horns of a ram are meant to protect the flock, as a shepherd protects his sheep from predators, not for stabbing its kin. This is the hexagram of Hermes Kriophoros, or ram bearer, an ancient Greek figure who carries a ram upon his shoulders, commemorating the solemn sacrifice of a ram. This same image also appears in the story of Cain and Abel, when Cain carries the corpse of his brother and complains, "Am I my brother's keeper?" The first found images of Christ were shown with him carrying a sheep in this way, and so this is also a hexagram of the messiah.

Guru: The rams of God are the shepherds that can direct the rest of the flock. It may be true that not all have found their power, which means the ones in power have a responsibility to their fellows to help them discover their abilities. Sometimes this can mean going against things so that all may benefit. If we want to make a change in the world, chances are it won't be a piece of cake; we might have to prod it along to get it to go in the right direction once we learn the truth. Enforcing the truth takes immense inner power.

Personal Example: I often receive hexagram 34 when parents are asking about their children. The most perilous position of shepherd of our fellows befalls the parents of children. Often they are not sure what to do, and when hexagram 34 is the response, it is clear that they will need to implement discipline and guide their children without being too forceful. Easier said than done.

The Changing Lines

Line One—The Self

Taking action is always a big gamble. As soon as one foot moves forward, we risk tripping, if we think about it too much. The beauty of being able to flow forward in our greatest strength, fluid in our motion as a panther, comes when we have trained ourselves to do so. When all parts of us can move in unison and we can release the need to control everything, this is a kind of liberation that comes through knowing and having confidence in our own strength. We must also know what we are not capable of preventing a big fall. The warrior moves forward after much training and discipline and then jumps into the battle, confident in his own abilities, while knowing that the environment is outside his control.

▸ Transforms into Shadow 32.1

Line Two—The Other

The sun is quite visible when it reaches, at high noon, its top-most point in the sky. There is no mistaking it. So too, you are visible. To see a person with huge muscles shows what kind of strength he has. To see a person endure emotional hardship shows how much courage she has. To see a person who recovers after failure shows how much resilience he has. Look at yourself long and hard. What do you see? There are things you know about yourself because they are as evident as the noonday sun. Where is your warrior spirit? Try to find the places where it can be seen so that you can see and know yourself. When were you at your strongest or weakest? Know this. Then you will be able to see in others what their strengths and weaknesses are and better gauge your choices.

▸ Transforms into Shadow 55.2

Line Three—The Union

It takes great power and inner strength to submit to something. Taking a lower position is never the choice of those who seek to gain things through force; they will always attempt to dominate. If you wish to accomplish something, instead of pushing your way through like a ram who gets its horns stuck in a bush, try a little finesse and patience. If we want to keep something for longer term, we could damage it through aggression. Take your time and sublimate your own impulses. By dominating yourself, you will find your victory.

▶ Transforms into Shadow 54.3

Line Four—The Earth

There is a lot to be said for repeated efforts. Everyone might laugh at someone who speaks of changing the world and then sets about to do it. They may hang around and watch for a while, but then they will lose interest and walk away. You can only stare at a ram stuck in a bush for so long. But when that darn ram just won't give up and keeps on going, day after day, not only does it draw a crowd but it also gathers fans. Repeated efforts and determination to accomplish not only lead to success but also inspire others. The human ability to strive is like the mountain goat who ascends impossible peaks through the power of its own feet, one step after the other.

▶ Transforms into Shadow 11.4

Line Five—The Conflict

If you "get someone's goat," someone has become irritated or angered by you. Someone's cool has been lost, and you met with a hard head as a result. In ancient fraternal brotherhoods, such as the Freemasons, to ride a goat and release it, or get rid of it, refers to ridding yourself of your aggressive ego. The ego and the goat are compared in several esoteric conditions. This is the true meaning of the scapegoat sacrifice and the deep esoteric meaning of Christ crucified upon the cross. The scapegoat that is sacrificed is the ego, not the true self. In ancient cultures a straw dog or goat made of hay was made to symbolize this and became ritualized and misinterpreted over the years. Here you may be required to have a little ego death as you sacrifice a part of yourself so that you may be able to break through an obstacle that has been set before you. When you offer up your "goat" instead of allowing it to get the better of you, it is possible to avoid being possessed by stubbornness that might ruin an opportunity.

▶ Transforms into Shadow 43.5

Line Six—Heaven

A warrior will need strength to make it through any battle, but wits are important too. One of the saving graces of Hercules was his ability to use his mind. If you find you tried to muscle your way through something and are now stuck, you will have to instigate some strategy. The difference between a warrior and a general or a chief is that the general has seen enough battles to know when to be clever. Use your own unique knowledge to think your way through the difficulty rather than just your force of will; this will ensure that you find a practical solution to the problem.

▶ Transforms into Shadow 14.6

All Lines Changing—Hexagram 20

When we have mastered our strengths and weaknesses, we turn our attention to our higher faculties. First, we deal with the realms of the flesh and the physical, and then we direct our attention to the higher intelligences. After your body and will have been strengthened, turn to your mind, to learn and develop it. Contemplate ways to approach things that will benefit all involved with your newfound determination and power.

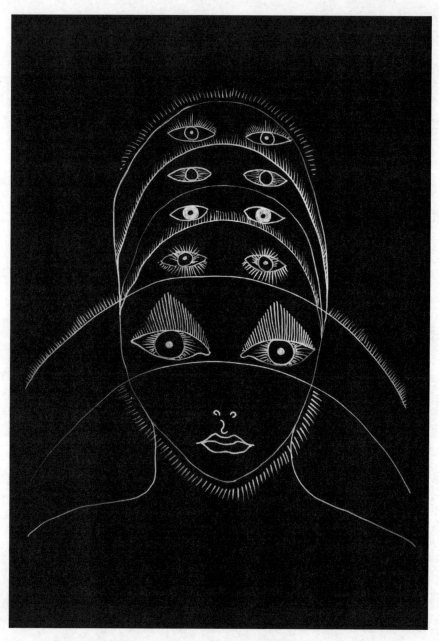

We went down into the silent garden. Dawn is the time when nothing breathes, the hour of silence. Everything is transfixed, only the light moves.

LEONORA CARRINGTON

Hexagram 35
The Dawn
Jin

Oracle Script:
Aurora

"The Golden Dawn"
The Power to Rise
Easter

Tarot Card: Star

Hexagram 35 is the Hathor hexagram of the great august ones and represents the power of the dawn. Here we see the gift of each day that unfolds around us, the power of transformation represented in our ability to pass through time and space, and the constant opportunities we are given each day we are alive upon Earth. Hexagram 35 also represents the gifts we are given to use as we see fit during our time here and our need to recognize them as valuable. If you have had difficulties, fret not; the new dawn brings another day that is not the same as any other day that has come to pass. This is the beauty of life in that there are many chances for rectification, reaffirmation, and renewal.

This is the goddess Aurora, goddess of the dawn as well as the Easter goddess of fertility who symbolized everlasting life and immortality.

It is the Christ-like ability to rise from the gravest fall and achieve golden perfection. It is the power of the comeback, the resurrection, and the reincarnation. If something has passed away, it will return in a new form. The word *Easter* has its origins in the Germanic language and is associated with the direction of east, or *aus,* which means "to shine" and references the shine of the sun at dawn. It was the original Germanic word for the month of April, named after Eastre, an ancient goddess, also called Astara or Oestre, the golden goddess of the dawn or of the east. (April is also connected to the names Aurvandil and *auzi-wandilaz,* "luminous wanderer," both of which describe the dawn specifically and the sun as a wandering star across the heavens.) Also known as Hausos, a Proto-Indo-European goddess of the dawn, she was unleashed every morning, set free from her imprisonment in the under-world, reborn at the dawn of every day in a splendorous explosion of light. It is she who is the aurora borealis. It is she who is the rainbow dragon Tiamat. It is she who makes the rainbow-colored light of day that fills our eyes. It is she who leads us on her bridge, the rainbow bridge, to reach through the clouds to heaven.

Guru: In the ancient esoteric traditions, the dawn is used to explain the act of becoming enlightened. When something "dawns upon us" it is an exhilarating feeling, much like an epiphany. Our entire being is covered with goose bumps, and we have a feeling of understanding and compre-hension. We "get" it. This can happen in situations where we have been struggling to learn something and it suddenly makes sense. On larger occult levels, we can have these epiphanies about the universe, life, and the way things operate in nature. These are more like "theophanies" and are very special feelings. Like the light of a warm sun creeping into the deepest parts of our cold dark bones, we feel the light of awareness fill our being.

Personal Example: We can also be noticed like the rising sun. I had a client who asked about her career and if she was going to be able to advance; she was an actress. We received hexagram 35, and most of the interpretations indicated shining like the sun, advancing, and being noticed. The sun is also a star. She contacted me just a short time later to let me know she had received a starring role in a film and was now in the spotlight, getting noticed, with a lot of attention placed on her. This hexagram can show up when we receive recognition, honors, and attention somewhere in our lives.

The Changing Lines

Line One—The Self

This is the line of determination. Every day there is another sunrise. Something gained yesterday may last for quite a while, but each dawn provides us with another unique situation. You may feel like you conquered something entirely, only to be faced with it again a week later. Things keep coming back around, just as Earth rotates on its axis and orbits around the sun, and the sun itself rotates on its axis and travels on its long galactic orbit around the Milky Way. It takes determination to deal with each day as it rises and treat it as yet another chance to live and breathe and experience life to the fullest. Be determined to wake each day and accomplish even the slightest, smallest thing. You will be surprised how things add up over time.

▸ Transforms into Shadow 21.1

Line Two—The Other

When we know something is coming the next day, both our anticipation and anxiety grow. Take things one day at a time; try not to get ahead of yourself. The art of making transitions gracefully is a huge part of life. If we rush through a sailing trip, going from one destination to the next, we might miss a beautiful sunrise over the ocean. When you see a gift headed your way, try to remain content in your everyday activities until you arrive at the time and place when things unfold.

▸ Transforms into Shadow 64.2

Line Three—The Union

There are dawns outside, and there are dawns inside. We can travel the world and see the sun rise over mountains, deserts, and seas, and these are all profound and beautiful. But when something dawns upon us, in a deep mental, spiritual, and physical fashion, we are struck with the profound nature of light and awareness in a way no morning could compare. The dawn of gnosis upon a human spirit is a light that radiates with as much power and force as the sun. We can live years of our lives, and an idea or concept can evade us, never alighting upon our awareness, but when the day comes, and our sentience is filled with the knowledge of esoteric gnosis, this is the light of the golden dawn, spoken of by the mystics throughout time. The blessing of wisdom!

▸ Transforms into Shadow 56.3

Line Four—The Earth

The dawn is only the start of the day. The start of things is important, but if there were never any sunsets, nothing would come to completion. Atum is the Egyptian god of the sun and represents the whole totality, from dawn to dusk. This is the line of completion, so if you want a fresh new day to light upon you, try as hard as you can to finish things you may have started but ended up putting off until later. Seize the day to complete things left unattended.

▸ Transforms into Shadow 23.4

Line Five—The Conflict

You can't freeze the sun in place. Sunrises and sunsets plainly indicate how fast the sun moves along its track in the sky. Things move and time will go on, whether or not you like it. You can enjoy the beauty of the sunrise, but you can't hold it in your hand. Learn to flow through things without grasping them; this is what the sun can teach us—to move like a fountain.

> ### Nothing Gold Can Stay
> *Nature's first green is gold,*
> *Her hardest hue to hold.*
> *Her early leaf's a flower;*
> *But only so an hour.*
> *Then leaf subsides to leaf.*
> *So Eden sank to grief,*
> *So dawn goes down to day.*
> *Nothing gold can stay.*
>
> Robert Frost

▸ Transforms into Shadow 12.5

Line Six—Heaven

Watching the power and force of the light breaking the dark is inspiration. When we find our light is on the wane, we can become invigorated by the divine masculine force that is yang; the power to rise. Though the dawn is a goddess, Aurora, she contains within her the strongest force of all, the ability to shoot forth and penetrate the night. When we are trying to accomplish a big feat in our lives, we can harness the power of the dawn to assist us; we may remember the power to rise, which belongs to human nature.

▶ Transforms into Shadow 16.6

All Lines Changing—Hexagram 5

There is a special magical time of the day before the sunrise. When we are patient and can sit and wait in the dark, sitting silently and still, we learn to feel this magic. To be still and wait in the early morning hours, we feel the life force of Earth and all its creatures awakening. Many do not have the time to sit and feel this. Take some time to be still and feel the forces of nature. Attend the next day's rising and feel what it feels like. Take it into yourself.

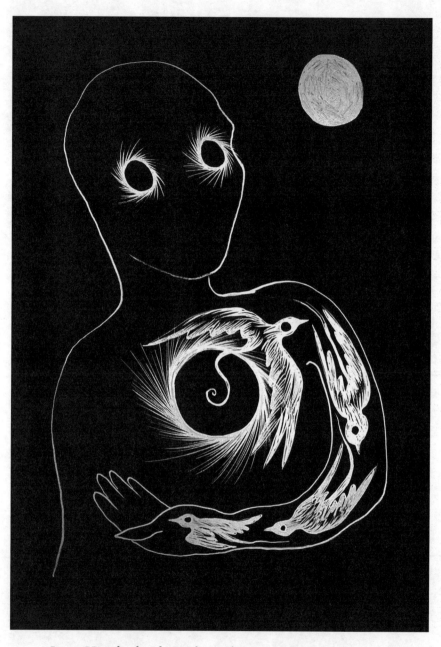

I am He who howls in the night; I am He who moans in the snow; I am He who hath never seen light; I am He who mounts from below.

H. P. LOVECRAFT, *PSYCHOPOMPUS*

Hexagram 36
The Sunset
Ming Yi

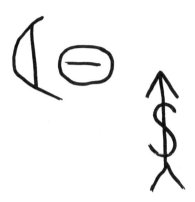

Oracle Script:
Parzival

"The Dark Night of the Soul"
Black Hole Sun
Obscured

Tarot Card: Moon

After the dawn of hexagram 35 has passed, we know that the sun will run its course until it sets beneath the dark and fertile Earth. This is the hexagram of the black sun or solar eclipse. It is the ego that obscures the true self in its wounded thinking. Sometimes we must dull our light in the interest of survival and let our ego to take over because circumstances on Earth need the ego. It would be nice to think we could always be highly spiritual and never need to rely on our ego for assistance, but in reality, you need to eat and attend to your physical needs. Mostly, we should be true and bright and honest and authentic, but there are times when the self is eclipsed by something greater than itself and must go into hiding or be punished and suffer the circumstances. There is fighting and confrontation, and there is strategy and waiting. Both must be used when the time is correct, and there is no blame or judgment for this. We were given an ego for a purpose. It is very useful for survival in the world; there is no shame in this. To heal from injury, we must sometimes throw in the towel and cut our losses. To go into the earth and dark in a willing and voluntary way makes our ego strong, and this gives us earthly power and the ability to build things from the ground up. The word *humility* means "low to the earth," like a serpent who slithers on the ground; sometimes it is better to just lay low.

This is the hexagram of Hecate and the underworld guardians. It belongs to Demeter and the cave-dwelling goddesses who rule the journeys of souls deep within Earth. It is the hexagram of the fall equinox, when the ground receives the harvest—the seeds of fruits dropped from plants, themselves grown from seeds planted during the spring.

An aspect to this hexagram also involves serving a master with whom you might have disagreements, whether a lover, boss, or other authority figure. Here we are somehow powerless or injured or find that we do not have the ability to act and so must be participants in something, regardless of whether we like it. In one of the myths of the Holy Grail, the wounded king needs his assistant Parzival to heal him. The king has become corrupted, and Parzival must put his own self aside and wait in darkness, serving the king until he is healed. This is a vital component of the healing process, and those who cannot wait in times of darkness will never make it to the dawn.

> Now it is the time of night
> That the graves all gaping wide,
> Every one lets forth his sprite,
> In the church-way paths to glide:
> And we fairies, that do run
> By the triple Hecate's team,
> From the presence of the sun,
> Following darkness like a dream,
> Now are frolic: not a mouse
> Shall disturb this hallow'd house:
> I am sent with broom before,
> To sweep the dust behind the door.
>
> WILLIAM SHAKESPEARE,
> *A MIDSUMMER NIGHT'S DREAM*

Guru: Being out in the open isn't always the best; sometimes you need to go into a cave and willingly enter into the darkness. Sure, everyone always wants to be at their brightest shiniest best, but in order to cope with and accept situations beyond your control, why not willingly put yourself aside so that you can be receptive to what is actually happening in the reality surrounding you. This requires an ability to go into dark places on purpose without being afraid of what you might find in there. Only the ones willing to descend into the depths of the underworld shall be capable of making the ascent into the skies above.

Personal Example: I received hexagram 36 for a client who was a recovering addict. During the session he had literally said he was emerging from the darkest time of his life, and the changing line in this hexagram mirrored those words back to him, as now he was climbing out of a dark pit that had nearly become his grave. There is nothing like a dark night of the soul to reinvigorate your every breath.

The Changing Lines

Line One—The Self
After a negotiation session, the matter gets resolved. Here the injury should be exposed and the wound addressed. When there has been a problem, we can bring it up in a mature fashion and go over whatever caused the truth to be obscured if we do so soon after the occurrence. For some kinds of misunderstandings we can immediately see the error and communicate it so that everyone gets back on the same page.
▶ Transforms into Shadow 15.1

Line Two—The Other
We are wounded by an authority figure. When a breach of trust has occurred and we think there has been a betrayal, the first thing to examine is our expectations and the leader's intentions before jumping to conclusions. But the wound will still need to be addressed and nursed before we bring it up with the offending party. And when we communicate about it, try not to focus on getting validation or pity but

rather focus on growth and restoring trust in the relationship. Harmony between people grows with trust.

▶ Transforms into Shadow 11.2

Line Three—The Union

Sometimes there is no healing a wound no matter how hard we try, and it is time to move on. The more we focus on the hurt, the more we magnify the pain. If it has taken our attention for too long, it may be time to just ignore it completely. Much like a howling dog whom we have tried hard to placate, if we simply ignore it and go about our business it is quite possible that it might cease to cause a disturbance. To leave something dire seems insane, but when it is unrelenting, the power of ignoring something can't be overstated.

▶ Transforms into Shadow 24.3

Line Four—The Earth

How will you ever know what is dark or evil unless you confront it directly? We can try all our lives to protect our awareness from unpleasant things, but sooner or later they seem to find us anyway. Death, disease, ill will, bad luck—all these things can befall us. If we are aware of them and know them and see them, are we more at risk for them? If we avert our eyes, are we only deluding ourselves like a mother who covers the eyes of her child? Do not be afraid to stare right into the heart of darkness; realize that it lives inside of you as well. When we see it plainly, the fear and taboo surrounding it crumbles, and the powerful grip of ignorance is loosened into acceptance of the real.

▶ Transforms into Shadow 55.4

Line Five—The Conflict

When ego is at its strongest, it is arrogance. Arrogance isolates the totality into the single thing, and this is Lucifer. We need a certain amount of arrogance, or we will never be able to put ourselves forward or defend ourselves. Too much arrogance cuts us off and isolates us from the source of life itself. The way we deal with arrogance in ourselves and in others determines, to a large extent, our understanding of what it means to be human. If we can not see this function of humanity without taking it personally or judging an individual for succumbing to it, this shows only our own level of ignorance.

▸ Transforms into Shadow 63.5

Line Six—Heaven

When we reach a pinnacle of awareness and removal of self, it is certain, due to the law of oppositional forces, that our ego will soon rebel. You can only set your self aside for so long until it acts out, wanting to be placed back in the spotlight. This is a natural consequence of too much self-sacrifice, and if you don't like it, next time make sure you feed yourself as well as everyone else. Now you will need to address your own needs and pay attention to the dark side of yourself, after enjoying a long period of light and joy.

▸ Transforms into Shadow 22.6

All Lines Changing—Hexagram 6

Now that we have gone inside and laid low for long enough, it is time for us to voice our complaints and state our case. When the time for hiding is over, we may contend with corruption and argue with an authority figure—not about our own pain but about the truth in the situation. Stay focused and use the lesson you learned while observing what caused the suffering in the situation. Review the situation and choose the best course of action to take going forward from now on.

Sambandha: binding or joining together, close connection or union or association, conjunction, inherence, connection with or relation to a relation, relative, kinsman, fellow, friend, ally

M. MONIER-WILLIAMS,
A SANSKRIT-ENGLISH DICTIONARY

Hexagram 37

The Family

Jia Ren

Oracle Script:
The Dwelling

"Ancestors"
The Ties That Bind
The Clan

Tarot Card: Ten of Pentacles

Keeping people together is harder than you think. Unless everyone is taken care of, some will leave. Children abandon their parents; parents abandon their children. Towns leave their people homeless. Humans forsake one another. Even when everyone is taken care of, they might leave anyway. How many successful rock bands have fallen apart at the peak of their fame? Abandonment comes in all forms. Dissent, rebellion, and mutiny enter into places where roles are not being fulfilled and needs are not being met. Or maybe someone's arrogance has gotten the better of her, and she thinks she is better off without anyone. In a family, people need and depend upon one another to give them support and assist in survival; they place their trust in mutual agreements. The subtle forces that tie us together begin in heaven or the heart, but then, over time, the realities of nature and needs cannot be ignored. When one family member falls into disarray, the entire household can suffer from him not performing his role. We can't always choose the people or things that we need and depend on, so it becomes necessary to compromise, negotiate, and work toward not only our own individual happiness, although that is equally as important, but also work toward the betterment of all. These are the ties that bind; they weave us together into couples, families, communities, and nations. The old pagan ritual of marriage involved handfasting or bringing the hands together in a kind of covenant or agreement made with each other to stand by the other in his or her times of need. This is a true relation that extends far beyond any surface romance because real needs are met and honored.

> *Then many a day they'll teach you how*
> *The mind's spontaneous acts, till now*
> *As eating and as drinking free,*
> *Require a process: one, two, three!*
> *In truth, the subtle web of thought*
> *Is like the weaver's fabric wrought:*
> *One treadle moves a thousand lines*
> *Swift dart the shuttles to and fro,*
> *Unseen the threads together flow,*
> *A thousand knots one stroke combines.*
> *Then forward steps your sage to show,*
> *And prove to you, it must be so;*
> *The first being so, and so the second,*
> *The third and fourth deduc'd we see;*
> *And if there were no first and second*
> *Nor third nor fourth would ever be.*
> *This, scholars of all countries prize,*
> *Yet 'mong themselves no weavers rise.*
> *He who would know and treat aught alive,*
> *Seeks first the living spirit thence to drive;*
> *Then are the lifeless fragments in hand,*
> *There only fails, alas!, the spirit-band.*
> *This process, chemists name, in learned thesis,*

Mocking themselves, Naturae encheiresis.

JOHANN WOLFGANG VON GOETHE,
FROM "SATANIC ADVICE TO A STUDENT,"
IN *FAUST: A TRAGEDY*

Blest Be the Tie That Binds

Blest be the tie that binds
Our hearts in Christian love;
The fellowship of kindred minds
Is like to that above.

Before our Father's throne,
We pour our ardent prayers;
Our fears, our hopes, our aims are one,
Our comforts, and our cares.

We share our mutual woes,
Our mutual burdens bear;
And often for each other flows
The sympathizing tear.

When we asunder part,
It gives us inward pain;
But we shall still be joined in heart,
And hope to meet again.

JOHN FAWCETT

Guru: We all have to live together in this house that is planet Earth. Like siblings who have come to hate one another, we can fall into many disputes and, in our rivalries and base desires, try to take things from one another and the planet. Possessions are the biggest threat to family: one has only to attend an inheritance trial to discover the underlying disputes that divide people from their kin. Our view is too small if we see only our relatives as family. Our definition of family must stretch to cover not only every human but also every living being on the planet. The ties that bind, that sacred union, reaches deeper than blood and travels all the way to the cosmic pulse of life itself.

Personal Example: Once I asked the I Ching, "How will humanity face its various challenges that are causing so much suffering?" The response I received was hexagram 37, which seemed to indicate that we will surmount our problems by relying on one another. We must team up as allies and work together as members of the same human family to tackle the most difficult issues facing us. The more humans can look upon one another as kindred spirits rather than enemies, the easier it will be for us to deal with the many insurmountable difficulties that arise as a result of simply being alive. There are enough problems to deal with without people causing one another more. We are stronger together.

The Changing Lines

Line One—The Self

Home is where the heart is. If you feel lost and can't find a like mind, look to the things you love to lead you to the right place. Wherever you find your love, there too you will find your home. Similarly, if you keep your heart clear and healthy, it will provide a safe haven both for yourself and those around you, which is just as important as having a physical structure in which to reside. The manger that Jesus was born in wasn't a barn at all but a well-laid heart to house the principles of love.

▸ Transforms into Shadow 53.1

Line Two—The Other

It could be true that a messiah exists who can love everyone and save everyone. But is it you? Maybe you can try to focus on saving yourself and those around you, which may be good enough. If your own circle is a mess, keep it simple and focused on what is right in front of you.

▸ Transforms into Shadow 9.2

Line Three—The Union

Talking trash is usually acceptable with the people closest to you because they love you and won't take it personally, but gossip has limits. Make sure the trash talk remains in front of everyone's back and not behind it. In this way trust is kept within the family, even when you have something negative to say. Hard words to the face are never as much of a problem as those to the back because a face can laugh it off, whereas a back takes it like a knife.

▶ Transforms into Shadow 42.3

Line Four—The Earth

People who join together are bonded through something. It is either mutual respect, mutual values, a strong leader, or something substantial. When you know what is holding everything together, it is easier to maintain and give homage to that thing. When the ties that form around people are ambiguous, they are easily broken; the hull of the ship will breach if the nails holding it together come loose. Water the tree and it produces large branches that all the birds perch on. Give support to the things that support everything. Pay attention to the foundation, and all else will go well.

▶ Transforms into Shadow 13.4

Line Five—The Conflict

In this line, the wounded king from the myth of the Holy Grail heals himself and becomes a true leader. What greater family is there than the one whose leader leads others? The father who is father to many families is a worldy ruler. To be part of such a clan expands the family into a nation—and from there, who knows? If you have success in your family and share it with others, you form a community, and this brings power to all.

▶ Transforms into Shadow 22.5

Line Six—Heaven

When Earth and all within it are recognized as part of our family, we grow past the limits of our biology. Expand what you consider the source of your blood to include animals, plants, minerals—the very planet we reside upon. But the one who can see the stars in heaven, all the things of the universe, as kindred spirits, is indeed a sage and has become the universal human. The realized *junzi,* or superior person, is as large as everything and nothing less.

▶ Transforms into Shadow 63.6

All Lines Changing—Hexagram 40

Sometimes the ties that bind become too harsh or severe, and we must break free from them. Here we find that our bondage is not serving self or other, and we must liberate ourselves from some part of the situation. The time comes for us all to leave home and wander; perhaps it will be a short journey or perhaps a complete uprooting. But some aspect has shifted, and what had been a willing commitment has now become a prison. Try to see what needs to change in the situation, or your attitude, to determine if all that needs to be liberated is your frame of mind; otherwise, it may be time to part ways.

Hexagram 38
The Repulsion
Yi

Oracle Script:
Opposition

"The Crossroads"
Walker between the Worlds
The Road Less Traveled

Tarot Card: Hanged Man

This is the hexagram of the crossroads god Odin. We come upon this hexagram when we have encountered liminal states, strange meetings, or oppositional forces along our path. Perhaps we have been following the path as in hexagram 17 and suddenly come upon a person, force, or fork in the road that confounds us and throws us into confusion. Many people can throw us into these states. Maybe we thought we knew them and took much for granted until the whole thing proves to be so difficult we must split off and go in a different way. We meet a person who changes the direction we take forever. We have a dream that rocks us to our core, and our entire life changes. A profound experience alters our identity. When Odin came upon such a time, he hung himself upside down from Yggdrasil, the world tree, to dramatically change his

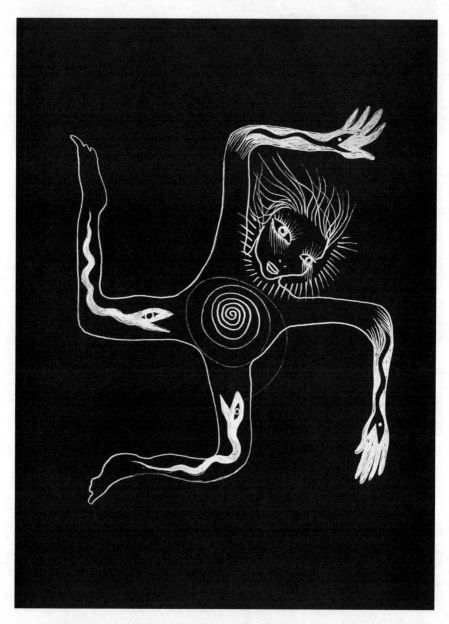

This great symbol tells us that the progressive development and differentiation of consciousness leads to an ever more menacing awareness of the conflict and involves nothing less than a crucifixion of the ego, its agonizing suspension between irreconcilable opposites.

CARL JUNG, *AION*

perspective or approach so that he could know which path to take next. When presented with a drastic change, we must connect deeply to our instincts and inner resources to help us navigate. We must be still and open our hearts as wide as possible to access the voice trying to tell us how to proceed. Christ too faced such a challenge when placed upon the cross. He could have fallen to the views of the others but remained steadfast in the teachings of his own heart regardless of the twist in his journey. There are things that change, and there are things that do not change. Hexagram 38 challenges us to discover and discern the difference between the two.

Hung I was on the windswept tree;
Nine full nights I hung,
Pierced by a spear, a pledge to the god,
To Odin, myself to myself,
On that tree which none can know the source
From whence its root has run.

None gave me bread, none brought a horn.
Then low to earth I looked.
I caught up the runes, roaring I took them,
And, fainting, back I fell.

Nine mighty lays I learned from the son
Of Bolthorn, Bestla's father,
And a draught I had of the holy mead
Poured out of Odrerir.

Then fruitful I grew, and greatly to thrive,
In wisdom began to wax.
A single word to a second word led,
A single poem a second found.

Runes will you find, and fateful staves,
Very potent staves, very powerful staves,
Staves the great gods made, stained by the mighty sage
And graven by the speaker of gods.

FROM "ODIN'S RUNE SONG," *HÁVAMÁL*

Guru: According to Newton's third law, when one object exerts force on a second one, the second reacts with an equal and opposite force. We will be presented with such roadblocks and obstacles by the very nature of what we are attempting because it can't be avoided. If you find that you have accumulated virtue, you will meet temptation on the road. If you have accumulated intelligence, you will come up against many fools. The crossroads is the place where we confront the oppositional forces of nature and must reconcile them within ourselves before we can proceed along the path. Some of the opposition will be so great that we will need to divert from the path we are on, and some of the opposition must be overcome so that we do not deviate from our goal. The loftier the goal we have set our will toward, the more our path will be riddled with such encounters and opposition. We mustn't let these difficulties throw us into confusion but rather recognize them as an inevitable consequence of the work we have set ourselves to accomplish.

Personal Example: This hexagram often appears when it is time for people to change jobs or start a new career. I have had countless clients pull this hexagram when they needed to change directions and set out on a new path. Never an easy hexagram to get, it means a decision must be made for which direction to travel in, which often means traveling on a new road.

The Changing Lines

Line One—The Self
Odin rode a famous horse with eight legs who made his journey much easier. But at a crossroads his horse ran away. He became despondent and knew that it meant he must now proceed on foot. Instead of giving up, stopping and freezing, he continued along his path, and a few days later his horse found him. Lost friends return to us if they are woven into our destiny; just continue alone until you meet up with them again.
▶ Transforms into Shadow 64.1

Line Two—The Other
Not all crossroad meetings are perilous or negative. There are crossroads we come across where we meet those who will become part of our des-

tiny. Just as Dorothy came upon the Scarecrow on her journey and freed him from peril, making him a friend for life, we can be open to the people providence places in our path and realize they have a purpose for all parties involved. Try not to judge friend or foe but instead remain open to all possibilities where fortune is concerned.

▸ Transforms into Shadow 21.2

Line Three—The Union

Jesus came to a point on his road where he was horribly humiliated and made a public spectacle of shame. The walk of shame may cross our path, but it's in the steps we take while we are on it that determine how well we retain our dignity. The self-care we show to ourselves while the tomatoes are being thrown enables us to keep walking until the path becomes clear once again.

▸ Transforms into Shadow 14.3

Line Four—The Earth

We can have walked our path alone for so long that we might have just gotten used to it and assumed that we had wandered so far into the wilderness that no one else will go the same way. Until one day another appears, as if out of nowhere. We may have sacrificed long and hard to get somewhere alone, taking all our struggles in stride, but when a friend appears, do not be so proud that you reject the nourishment and joy that a companion can offer, even if it is only for a little while.

▸ Transforms into Shadow 41.4

Line Five—The Conflict

First impressions count for a lot: this is true. But someone who you first thought was an outrageous danger might not be so bad if you take another look. Don't forget that we have all been, at some point in our lives, misread. If someone is truly valuable, don't discount him just because he has made some mistakes; after all, haven't you made quite a few bumbles yourself? See the whole road with someone, not just the curves and bumps in front of you.

▸ Transforms into Shadow 10.5

Line Six—Heaven

Maybe you have gotten a little too paranoid along the way due to excessive betrayals or unlucky meetings. Clear your suspicions away lest you confuse yourself into thinking that everyone on the road is a potential robber. If you are aggressive to everyone you pass along the way, chances are you could scare away the one person destiny was trying to throw into your sphere to assist you and heal you from the many blows you have suffered from thieves and scoundrels. Do not mistake Robin Hood's Merry Men for the king's soldiers because you have become too cynical.

▸ Transforms into Shadow 54.6

All Lines Changing—Hexagram 39

After choosing a new path, there is much work to be done. Now we are going on a difficult new journey and must be practical about the labor involved to lay the foundation for the new way we have chosen. No one else will do this for you, so don't be naive and just settle in to enjoy the new way you are walking. Realize that hard work will pay off once you get into the groove of your changed routine.

Hexagram 39
The Obstacle
Jian

Oracle Script:
Willing and Able

"The Great Work"
To Dream the Impossible Dream
Fruits of the Labor

Tarot Card: Ten of Wands

This hexagram belongs to Yu the Great, mentioned in hexagram 14. The descendant of Fu Xi and the Yellow Emperor, he had big shoes to fill and an impossible job ahead of him. He had the responsibility to manage the damage caused by the great flood, and he had few resources and no one to help him. The main catastrophe was the corruption that had settled into the hearts of the people of Earth, and the only solution was repentance and the mending of all the errors of the humans. When people have been obscenely damaged and lost, fixing their hearts will take more than an inspirational anthem. Here is the task of the children of Noah, who are left with repopulating the Earth with love and harmony after extensive destruction. If you have drawn this hexagram, you have a big thing to do, and a lot of obstacles will crop up regardless

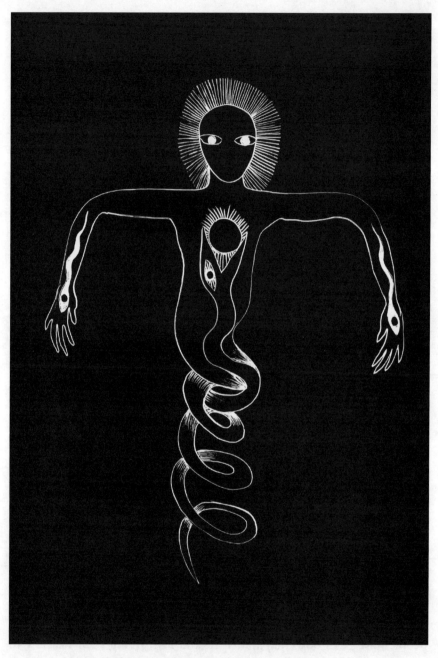

*Yea, foolish mortals, Noah's flood is not yet subsided;
two thirds of the fair world it yet covers.*

HERMAN MELVILLE, *MOBY DICK*

of how righteous you are. A big, long job is hard to do. Most people do not have the fortitude for it and will quit before too much time has passed. Large labors require passion, or at least are inspired by some kind of perilous threat. Some of us are blessed to be able to take on an accomplishable task that will reward us with a sense of pride. But other labors can be brutal, unforgiving, and impossible—yet must be done regardless. A job with no reward, acknowledgment, or enjoyment is all the more difficult, especially when one finds oneself incapable of being good at it. When a never-ending job defeats us daily, our heart, burdened with futility, becomes heavy. Life can feel like a burden if we are oppressed, victimized, or unlucky: hardships fall like rain. Sometimes all we have is the threat of a severe consequence to keep us devoted to something, instead of working with deep sincerity, which arises within our hearts.

The Ignorance Cure

I set a curse *upon my enemies and those who defy me!*
With these words I send to those who have wished me
    harm
a curse *to live their lives*
fulfilled, abundant and overflowing with joy!
I set a swarm of healing honeybees to rest upon their
    doorstep,
humming soothing songs to rid them of all pain and
    suffering!
I shall pluck the blood from the strings of my veins
and use its nectar to concoct the most poisonous antidote
that shall cause the blood that flows inside them
to be rid of all disease, age, and woe!
I call upon the merciless deserts to torture them
with the warm glow of the fire of happiness
that ice never may grow in their glare.
I eat the lips that speak my name in dire disdain
with kisses deep and pure
gently sucking all the venom from their tongues.
I send to them that hate me with a hatred in their heart
    of hearts,

a ceaseless, fountainous love *in all its forms*
and eternal rest in the cool darkness that is peace.
I am sending and will send forever,
to them, to me and to all,
the sweet relief of knowledge of all good and evil,
the power and the passion to set our souls to rise
that on this lifted platform
we may laugh and make merry
for all time that is and all times that be
till time itself is me.
Through the force of my sadness
I drive them to joy.
My anger, brutal and relentless,
ensures my exaltation in forgiveness.
The ravenous beast that is my grief
    will carry them to sweet relief.

MAJA D'AOUST

Guru: Repentance is the only solution to ignorance. But people are ignorant of what repentance means. Repentance is thought to mean regretting something that occurred. As my teacher Kelvin DeWolfe stated once, repentance is more than just being sorry and regretful about something. Repentance is working hard to change what you are sorry about, actively taking up habits and real activities that will make an alteration in your regrettable state of being through hard work. Until repentance occurs, ignorance continues. What brings about repentance? Education. This education can come, in part, in the form of karma: you do something harmful to someone you consider bad and then suffer the same harmful consequences, sheepishly realizing that you are just as bad as the person you hated. At this point, you experience repentance and dawn into humility. The difficult thing about education is that it requires being receptive to learning, which means first admitting your ignorance. But ignorance by definition means not knowing that you don't know; the ignorant do not know they are ignorant. So here we see a big problem; in order to educate the ignorant, receptivity to learning is required. Ignorance is not receptive to learning, because it denies its own need for it. This self-denial stops growth and leads to destruction of self and other. Without receptivity, there is no education, and ignorance prevails. Education is a big job.

Personal Example: Most of my clients have received hexagram 39 when they were ready to quit something due to difficulties. I had one client ask the I Ching, "How can I get through the difficulty of my job?" and the response was hexagram 39, which is, literally, difficulty doing a job. Often we are presented with an obstacle to our efforts, and the immediate impulse may be to throw in the towel, but the I Ching advised this client to try a few different strategies first before relinquishing the position altogether.

The Changing Lines

Line One—The Self
Sometimes a job becomes so difficult with so many obstacles that the wiser move is to cease forward movement and wait. One of the most important skills learned by the initiate is that of patience. Sometimes we must stop all progress and wait for the season and the weather to change. It would be foolish to try to force everyone to work in the rain; just wait until the sun comes out.

▶ Transforms into Shadow 63.1

Line Two—The Other
Sometimes it rains so much that we are completely flooded. Instead of just one obstacle we might have had to work around, we get a deluge of impossible situations. This is no one's fault, so work hard not to lay blame, especially on yourself. Are you at fault for a failure caused by natural disasters? Be easy on everyone involved and recognize the issues inherent in the game of life. If you can be resilient after such catastrophies, you can be given the chance to rebuild. But not if you hack apart all your hard-won progress due to the blame and shame monster. Move forward after the flood.

▶ Transforms into Shadow 48.2

Line Three—The Union
Doing a hard job alone is foolish. It might be difficult to find trustworthy allies, but if you don't, you are setting yourself up to fail. Don't

be so stubborn or so greedy that you seek to do something gigantic all by yourself when there are perfectly willing people there to help you. When we can break out of isolation and join a team, our project is more apt to succeed, and we get to share the joy of creation with others. This becomes not just a job well done but also a virtuous blessing for all involved. Don't be shy; go find your team.

▶ Transforms into Shadow 8.3

Line Four—The Earth

After we find a great team to help us in an extremely difficult task, it is up to us to lead them. If we want to be a strong leader, we will be required to take responsibility for ourselves and others. This is an additional almost impossible task set upon an already almost impossible task. Strengthen yourself, your intuition, and your trust in yourself so that you don't blow it when called upon to lead a team into an already precarious situation. Do a little research on what others do in these situations; you aren't the first one who has ever had to lead an army into an unfair battle. Seek advice from the experts.

▶ Transforms into Shadow 31.4

Line Five—The Conflict

Going to extremes in extreme situations can sometimes work. Taking risks is going to be part of the deal here. But if you can go somewhere in the middle, you won't spend all your energy on one risk, and you will be able to go the distance—much further than when you place all your eggs in one basket. Learn to discern the time to take a huge risk and the time to go down the middle path to meet the situation halfway instead of head on. Only take the risk if there is no other option.

▶ Transforms into Shadow 15.5

Line Six—Heaven

When we have done our best trying to lead and do things on our own and are still running into difficulty, look for someone else who is a better leader than yourself. There are a lot of individuals who are experts who might already be doing something you are trying to attempt. Sometimes joining up with another who is already in the process of what we are envisioning is the best way to accomplish the task. Unless you have your heart set on doing something alone, why not link up with someone else who has it under way? You might have something valuable to offer to the other's impossible dream, and by joining together, you will be able to bring both your dreams to fruition.

▶ Transforms into Shadow 53.6

All Lines Changing—Hexagram 38

We tried our best to lead a group in an impossible task, but it ended up isolating us from others, and all our team quit. Now we have come to a crossroads, and a difficult decision must be made about which path to follow next. Take the advice of Odin and sit and contemplate which road will best serve you while you choose the next direction, after bearing the burden of an immense amount of labor.

Anthropos apteros, perplexed
To know which turning to take next,
Looked up and wished he were a bird
To whom such doubts must seem absurd.

W. H. Auden, from "The Labyrinth"

Hexagram 40
The Freedom
Jie

Oracle Script:
Escape

"Liberation"
Freedom
Break the Chains

Tarot Card: Eight of Swords

In hexagram 40 we learn how to escape. If something has oppressed us or inhibited us, now is the time to release ourselves. The key to unlock the shackles that have kept us in slavery is presented before our eyes. When the key arrives, we must use it. If you want, you can remain shackled, but there are new things waiting for you when you drop the chains that have been keeping you tightly bound. We are all prisoners of something here in samsara. It is our job to take down these prison walls that surround us; we need to identify them and search out the door. Often there is a window that has been obscured by our complacency, and we can't even see the escape route. This place is like a panic room, and we must solve the challenges like a rubik's cube so that our bars will disintegrate.

*For the alchemist, the one primarily in need of redemption
is not man, but the deity who is lost and sleeping in matter.
Only as a secondary consideration does he hope that some
benefit may accrue to himself from the transformed substance
as the panacea, the medicina catholica, just as it may to the
imperfect bodies, the base or "sick" metals, etc. His attention
is not directed to his own salvation through God's grace, but
to the liberation of God from the darkness of matter.*

CARL JUNG, *PSYCHOLOGY AND ALCHEMY*

Liberation

*I have thrown from me the whirling dance of mind
And stand now in the spirit's silence free,
Timeless and deathless beyond creature-kind,
The center of my own eternity.*

*I have escaped and the small self is dead;
I am immortal, alone, ineffable;
I have gone out from the universe I made,
And have grown nameless and immeasurable.*

*My mind is hushed in a wide and endless light,
My heart a solitude of delight and peace,
My sense unsnared by touch and sound and sight,
My body a point in white infinities.*

*I am the one Being's sole immobile Bliss:
No one I am, I who am all that is.*

SRI AUROBINDO

Guru: The prison is the mind. Hexagram 40 represents the untying of the Gordian knot. It's the minotaur at the center of the labyrinth who draws us to the center so that we may free ourselves from thinking and simply come into being without prejudice. In this hexagram we are liberated from the mental parasite that seeks to dominate all Earth through its illusions of ignorance, its assumptions and faulty belief systems that bury the light or truth itself. To discover the truth, we must shed all our clothing and stand naked before it, with no shame or guilt. We must accept what is before us without trying to dress it up in our habitual familiar outfits. The way through the prison walls is to realize that they don't exist—because this is all only a dream.

Personal Example: I receive hexagram 40 from the I Ching every time I am obsessing over something. If I have a thought that will not quit, the I Ching presents me with hexagram 40, advising me to free myself from it. Hexagram 40 also consistently shows up when a client needs to free himself from an addiction, such as alcohol, drugs, or a toxic relationship. If the nature of the inquiry concerns a habituation that has become damaging, the solution is liberation from the thoughts or environment.

The Changing Lines

Line One—The Self
We can find freedom and liberation with those around us when we are not bound to feelings of right and wrong. When we can emerge from a place of judgment of actions, we see others impartially, instead of ascribing evil to certain individuals, and are able to gain perspective, which frees our mind to explore the situation from different perspectives. When you view others' actions as wrong, you will never be able to see through their eyes because you do not wish to be wrong, so you erect a divider between yourself and them, blocking off and blinding your view to their concerns in favor of raising yourself above them. Liberate everyone by looking through as many eyes as possible.
  ▶ Transforms into Shadow 54.1

Line Two—The Other
In the maze of the labyrinth foxes are running around, and they look like they are causing trouble, but you are only seeing their shadows, which you mistake for rebels. Shoot an arrow lit on fire into the situation so that it lights up the truth of what is happening to clear up misunderstandings. Don't make accusations until the flash of fire on the arrow shows what is truly going on; that way your suspicions won't be paranoia.
  ▶ Transforms into Shadow 16.2

Line Three—The Union

If you have already been liberated from the burdens of your mind, do not continue to carry them as you travel through the corridors of the maze. Your movement will be slowed, and the thieves of truth will creep up quickly upon those who find themselves so burdened. Drop your cares down by the riverside so that your carriage can roll free as it emerges into the center, light and clear. Having weapons to protect you against bondage can encumber you more than chains.

▸ Transforms into Shadow 32.3

Line Four—The Earth

It is said that our defenses and reactions are stored in our toes, which cause us to be impulsive and follow our base instincts instead of seeing the higher view from our head. To be able to have trustworthy relations with our minds freed from bondage, we have to release our toehold on our impulsive reactivity. Take a step back instead of sticking your toe in someone's eye.

▸ Transforms into Shadow 7.4

Line Five—The Conflict

In the end, the only one who can liberate your mind is yourself. Only you are in control of your thoughts. You must contend and reason with yourself until you discover your own error. Others can assist you; they can guide and educate you. But liberation is an intensely personal and private affair that no one will experience except you, deep within yourself. Therefore, we all must take responsibility for our own salvation. We must work hard for its accomplishment and not blame others for our inability or difficulty in achieving it.

▸ Transforms into Shadow 47.5

Line Six—Heaven

There is a story of Arjuna the archer shooting a hawk from farther away than anyone else, and when asked how he can shoot with such precision, he replies, "I can only see its eye." If you can have such focus and concentration on a single point when all around you is in chaos, your mind becomes as precise as an arrow hitting the target of your intention and as liberated and free as a hawk soaring in the skies.

▸ Transforms into Shadow 64.6

All Lines Changing—Hexagram 37

Maybe we have done a little too much liberating, and we find ourselves floating freely with nothing to tie us down. Now the times change into the ties that bind, and we should affiliate ourselves with a household, family, or work environment for some stability. After a good amount of free floating, settling down could benefit our lives. Just make sure you choose wisely the group to which you wish to tie yourself.

In that day the Lord, with his great and strong and cruel sword, will send punishment on Leviathan, the quick-moving snake, and on Leviathan, the twisted snake; and he will put to death the dragon which is in the sea.

ISAIAH 27:1

Hexagram 41
The Sacrifice
Sun

Oracle Script:
The Straw Dog

"Give in Order to Receive"
Expansion through Diminishing
Ego Death

Tarot Card: Ace of Pentacles

If something is full, it can't be filled. If something contains nothing, it can receive everything. This is the hexagram of the woman of the apocalypse. She is shown offering up a baby to the angels while a threatening dragon comes up from below the waters, trying to eat it. It is the story of Andromeda and the monster kraken, whom Perseus descends from above to defeat. The scene of this archetype has so many representations through so many cultures, it is impossible to list them all. Essentially what we have is offering the child within ourselves—our undeveloped ego that seeks to serve only the self—to a higher force so that we may rise to the occasion. The forces that threaten us from below are usually represented as the red dragon, which comes to tear our body into pieces. The red dragon is our undeveloped primordial emotional nature that deals with fear and root chakra survivalism. If we are taken by the red dragon, we remain in our lower nature, unable to evolve into maturity. When we are able to put that part of us aside to serve something greater than our own personal needs, there is a kind of ascension that occurs that lifts us out of reach of the perils of our own consuming fears.

> *From Vedic times onward . . . it [sacrifice] was all-powerful. The gods themselves subsist by virtue of ritual offerings: "It is sacrifice, O Indra, that has made thee so powerful. . . . It was worship that aided thy thunder when thou didst split the dragon." [Rig-Veda, III, 32,12] Sacrifice is the principle of the life and soul of all the gods and all beings. In the beginning, the gods were mortal; they became divine and immortal through sacrifice; they live by gifts from the earth, as men live by gifts from heaven.*
>
> MIRCEA ELIADE, *YOGA: IMMORTALITY AND FREEDOM*

> *Heaven and Earth are impartial;*
> *they treat all of creation as straw dogs.*
> *The Master doesn't take sides;*
> *she treats everyone like a straw dog.*
>
> *The space between Heaven and Earth is like a bellows;*
> *it is empty, yet has not lost its power.*
> *The more it is used, the more it produces;*
> *the more you talk of it, the less you comprehend.*
>
> *It is better not to speak of things you do not*
> *understand.*
>
> LAO-TZU, TAO TE CHING

Guru: This is the hexagram of rising from the depths into higher realms, and it is represented in many religions by the lotus in the mud. Out of the muddy waters, inhabited by dangerous crocodiles, grows the lotus flower, perfect and beautiful, emerging from the most putrid environment found on Earth. The lowest creatures inhabit this place, and the flower must push through an overgrowth of lily pads to emerge into the light. This is the soul of the adept coming forth from the muddy waters of emotion and lower survival to ascend to heaven in all its realized glory.

Personal Example: I get hexagram 41 all the time when I need to see things through other people's perspectives to arrive at truth rather than holding on to something I thought I saw in the situation. Nearly every time, I need to be reminded that there are other opinions in the world and not just my own. The I Ching instructs me, through this hexagram, to give to the other and not just to myself by putting myself in their shoes. When I do this, I achieve deep clarity and am able to see everything and am embarrassed at my faulty thinking. If you are certain of the truth, make sure you are seeing it from every side first; to accomplish this you must place yourself way up high so you can see.

The Changing Lines

Line One—The Self

We must trust in ourselves and also be willing to see past ourselves. The true sacrifice of the self is only in what we know. To see things through beginner's mind means we accept our own ignorance without devaluing the self or our intuition; we simply acknowledge things larger than ourselves. When we open in this way, sacrificing our belief that we know everything, we are able to know much more than we ever would have thought possible.
   ▸ Transforms into Shadow 4.1

Line Two—The Other

One of the ways we prevent sacrifice is through desire. We might want something so badly that we become envious or covetous and so seek it rather than making room for it. The strategy of opening can be quite effective when it comes to fulfillment, so make sure that your desiring something from another isn't sacrificing the desire of your own true heart. Sacrifice all that others tell you that you should want in favor of coming into connection with your true desire; here is where you find and nourish your destiny.
   ▸ Transforms into Shadow 27.2

Line Three—The Union

The ones we have sacrificed to so greatly now become a source of bondage, restraining our freedom. Do not be fooled into thinking you can sacrifice another to gain your happiness by blaming the other for the restraint. Instead, use the magic of sacrifice to see clearly how you are being restrained. Learn the lesson from it and then emancipate yourself from feeling victimized by it. This will enable you to put your emotions aside (although they are justified) in favor of making the best decision for how to proceed rather than acting impulsively.

▸ Transforms into Shadow 26.3

Line Four—The Earth

Sacrificing the self in service of the work of one who serves many makes us also serve many. If we are going to offer ourselves up to help one person, that is really something. But if the person we offer ourselves up to in turn helps hundreds or even thousands of others, this means we are also helping all those others by helping the one who helps them. We can make our sacrifices go far, indeed, by assisting those who assist the many.

▸ Transforms into Shadow 38.4

Line Five—The Conflict

Sacrificing the self to team up with a group can bring many benefits to all. You can serve well on a team without needing to be number one, and all can receive benefits as a result of the group's accomplishments. You may have to give up something substantial; just make sure you are not compromising your integrity. This line is like a rock band or small company in which everyone has a share in the profits because they all make equal sacrifices to the group.

▸ Transforms into Shadow 61.5

Line Six—Heaven

When we have been able to grow into our highest self through the proper ways of sacrificing, others will begin to look to us for leadership. Once we obtain this position due to the sacrifices of our lower self to unify with our highest self, we are threatened with temptations on many sides. We are envied for what we have obtained, and we are presented with offers of a lower nature that could undermine our integrity. Here we must choose to step wisely into leadership so that we do not regress after all our hard-won efforts.

▶ Transforms into Shadow 19.6

All Lines Changing—Hexagram 31
Now that the self has been trained and disciplined, it can become a source of attraction and influence greater powers. Because we were able to make ourselves small and diminish our needs, our influence on the stream of events and the hearts of others has grown. Become aware of your influence and do not be too humble and diminish yourself by not accepting the responsibility of your new position. Continue with the good work that you do, as others come to you to seek counsel.

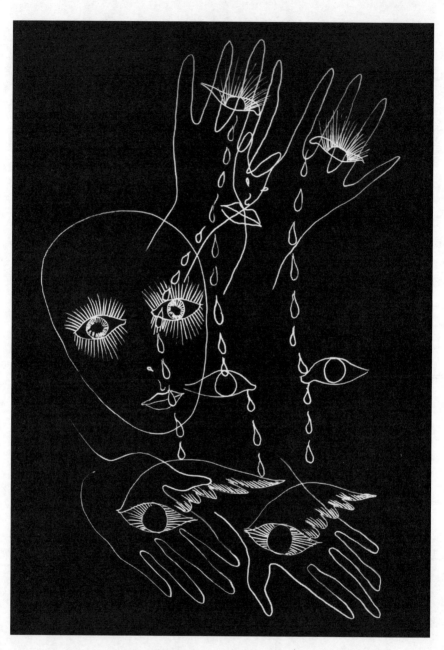

You see, I had been riding with the storm clouds, and had come to earth as rain, and it was drought that I had killed with the power that the Six Grandfathers gave me.

BLACK ELK

Hexagram 42
The Augment
Kun

Oracle Script:
Receive the Harvest

"My Cup Runneth Over"
Pennies from Heaven
Make It Rain

Tarot Card: Ace of Cups

After the sacrifices and diminishing in hexagram 41, the rains come to bring in the abundance of hexagram 42, filling our cups. For the new crop to grow, we must burn the fields in sacrifice, but when the water falls from the sky, it creates a fresh bounty for us to enjoy. Here we have arrived at the fruits of our labors. Only through the process of making room and causing ourselves to be small and low does the equal and opposite come to meet us of growing large. When one understands oppositional forces and the laws of nature, we see that if it is growth and abundance we desire, we must engage in the opposite; we must sacrifice to attract compensation. Ancient people have understood for millennia that this is the way. Once the straw dog of the crop has been burned to the heavens, new growth begins to shoot through the

273

earth after the sleep of winter. In the spring we expand and become something more than we were before, and all things prosper when the rain comes. We are filled to overflowing. While we are in a drought, we may forget what the rain tastes and feels like, but when it arrives, filling the pockets of dry earth with its life-giving moisture, we learn what true blessing is and are able to rejoice with our hearts in the knowledge of what fulfillment truly feels like.

> *The Lord makes a way for grace to reach His people. He directs each drop, and gives each blade of grass its own drop of dew—to every believer his portion of grace. He moderates the force, so that it does not beat down or drown the tender herb. Grace comes in its own gentle way. Conviction, enlightenment, etc., are sent in due measure. He holds it in His power. Absolutely at His own will does God bestow either rain for the earth, or grace for the soul.*
>
> CHARLES HADDON SPURGEON,
> "RAIN AND GRACE—A COMPARISON"

Guru: Once we have cried our tears, and the water has left our eyes in a rain, we find we have been cleared and cleansed and the joy can enter. The Holy Spirit enters a heart that is empty and at peace; without such emptiness the abundant joy of the power and the ecstasy of the Holy Spirit will not be known. We are filled with desires, thoughts, passions, and hungers, which are wonderful things. But the one who is able to come into emptiness through sacrifice will be filled with the rain of manna from the powers above to share with others, like Christ feeding all with fish, loaves of bread, and wine he has self-generated. The sacrifice of our flesh makes room for the life everlasting.

Personal Example: A client asked the I Ching how she could gain prosperity, and the response was hexagram 42, prosperity. I advised her˙ to rid herself of as many possessions as she possibly could, to clean out her closets and donate whatever she could, to let go of all that was no longer useful to her. Although this advice did not make sense to her, she later reported that all she got rid of was replaced with new, more useful things. We marveled at the truth of the laws of opposition and of equilibrium, wherein every action is met with an equal and opposite reaction: what is given away is received.

The Changing Lines

Line One—The Self

It is our awareness of self that is augmented in this line. We might have thought ourselves to be small and humble, unable to achieve what we had set out to do, when suddenly an epiphany arrives like a bolt of lightning, which jolts us into an awareness that we are greater than we thought. We are given an opportunity to expand ourselves, so now is the time to increase our expectations and shoot for the moon!

▸ Transforms into Shadow 20.1

Line Two—The Other

Here we are made bigger through others. We ourselves have only a limited capacity, with boundaries to our achievements. But often growth can occur that we never imagined possible simply by linking our efforts to others of like mind. Our own minds and abilities can grow very large, it is true, but not nearly as large as when we have ten or a hundred of us. Here we are a legion, and the gains that fall like rain come to all, not just to one.

▸ Transforms into Shadow 61.2

Line Three—The Union

Here we have an intimate union that becomes a blessing and brings progeny and stability through union. Trust and reliance on those within our clan are the truest forms of power, and when two or more come together in the name of something, its gains are increased tenfold. Such is the law under heaven and the law of prosperity through propagation through love and trust.

▸ Transforms into Shadow 37.3

Line Four—The Earth

Here the gains of one who has sacrificed extend to an entire nation. This is the line of Nelson Mandela, who, through his sacrifice, was able to free not only himself but all his people as well. The power of the messiah is that through becoming small and inviting the great to come upon them, they are then able to share it with all the peoples of the land. Think of how you can share what you have gained through your culture, your country, or your art by broadcasting it through larger forms of communication. You would be surprised how far your idea can spread.

▸ Transforms into Shadow 25.4

Line Five—The Conflict

One of the largest obstacles to gaining is getting caught in desires and expectations. If we think we know what we want, we will often miss the opportunity that providence presents us with because it does not meet our expectation. Do not lose out on your gains just because they are not how you thought they should be. Pay close attention to what is coming to you and how it can be useful. You might not see the diamond in the rough, but it is there.

▸ Transforms into Shadow 27.5

Line Six—Heaven

Starting again after the fires of sacrifice can be daunting even when we are presented directly with a blessing. Do not cling to the terrors of the past; accept this new life that providence has brought you. Leave last year's winter in the past, and step into this new light to reap the bounty. Don't be shy; you deserve it!

▸ Transforms into Shadow 3.6

All Lines Changing—Hexagram 32

Here we receive the blessing of the mysterium conjunctio. Our union with spirit has benefitted us, and we have gained a spouse or partner through the sincerest form of trust. Our firm adherence to our principles and sacrifice has joined us with spirit itself, and we know and understand the path we must now take to honor our commitments to self and others.

Hexagram 43
The Announcement
Guai

Oracle Script:
Spiritual Warfare

"The Battle"
Hear, Oh Israel
The Caduceus

Tarot Card: Two of Cups

This is the hexagram of Israel. Not the country of Israel, but the true meaning of Israel. In the Bible is told the story of Jacob, whose brother Esau bullied him. Jacob and Esau grew to hate each other viciously and fight and fight and fight. One night, Jacob was told that his brother would be coming to visit him. Jacob lost his mind and began to prepare for war. He made ready weapons and took defensive measures so that he could attack his brother if anything strange should occur. But an angel came to him and told him that he had gone mad and become paranoid and needed to cease at once. Jacob had a battle in his mind with the deceiver and the angel. The deceiver wanted him to distrust his brother and expect the worst, making him a criminal, based on their history, before anything had even happened. But the angel wanted Jacob to lay

Do not harden your hearts as when they provoked me, as in the day of trial in the wilderness.

HEBREWS 3:8

down his arms and suspicions and bring peace into his mind, ending the rivalry. Jacob struggled all night inside this personal hell until finally the angel won and he relented, but only after Jacob injured his hip during the battle, which left him with a limp. Jacob asked the angel to bless him because he made the right choice: he had let go of his grudge and forgiven his brother. So the angel announced that his name would now be Israel, the one who wrestles with God and finds forgiveness.

Nature is defensive because it must protect itself for survival, but humans often turn their defense mechanism into a justified righteous *contempt* for their fellows and family members. When we lay down the burden of contempt and see the purpose of defense we can eliminate this tendency and see things clearly, without the hate. It might be true that we get attacked, but the contempt is optional.

> *Misanthropy comes when a man without knowledge or skill has placed great trust in someone and believed him to be altogether truthful, sound, and trustworthy; then, a short time afterward he finds him to be wicked and unreliable, and then this happens in another case; when one has frequently had that experience, especially with those whom one believed to be one's closest friends, then, in the end, after many such blows, one comes to hate all men and to believe that no one is sound in any way at all.*
>
> SOCRATES

Guru: Dealing with those who wrong us is hard, especially when they attack us repeatedly. The bad character of another must not, however, be permitted to corrupt our own hearts and good nature. The enemy wins when he places his hatred and contempt within our spirit. We can defend the self without condemning the other and falling into suspicion and cynicism. The enemy's choice is his choice; our choice is ours. You may not be able to stop someone from being aggressive, but do not allow his actions to make you aggressive as well. Hold fast to your inner nature in these times and kill the enemy with kindness while preventing his blows from reaching you. You don't need to take the enemy's punishment, but you also do not need to let that punishment make you into something you are not; find the balance.

Personal Example: A client was involved in a custody battle with her ex-husband and asked the I Ching, "How can I make sure I win and punish him?" The response was hexagram 43, which indicated that she needed to discard this attitude and focus on reparations. She needed to enter the court with a peacekeeping attitude rather than with a counter-attack. Regardless of his attacks on her, the I Ching instructed her not to take an aggressive position and to instead ask the court to decide what was best for the child. After the hearing she contacted me and let me know that because she was so reasonable in her testimony, the court voted in her favor.

The Changing Lines

Line One—The Self
If you have a first impulse, chances are it is either defensive or aggressive. Here we lead with our toes, which are the least likely to make a sound choice in the matter. Put your feet up and rest for a while to think it over. Gather some information and don't jump to any conclusions based upon a prejudice; you might wreck something that is still perfectly viable through being hasty. Make sure you only cry wolf when there is actually a wolf there.
  ▶ Transforms into Shadow 28.1

Line Two—The Other
Falling into old habits with expectations is difficult to escape, especially with those we see often, such as friends and family members. But these habits prevent us from experiencing reality in the moment. If we want to make a change to a relationship or situation, it will require that we abandon these habits and take a firm stance to see the situation from a different view to allow for a new experience to enter the scene, rather than making the same old argument we did yesterday.
  ▶ Transforms into Shadow 49.2

Line Three—The Union
One of the best ways to de-escalate a misunderstanding is through communication. Good communication requires that we not only voice our concerns but also that we listen to the other. If all we do is talk and

make demands, sticking with our version of the story, we cannot unite with the other. Israel means all is one, so make sure to include everyone's voice. The message of the Hebrew prayer known as the Shema Yisrael is to listen, so perk up those ears if you want connection. "Hear, oh Israel, the Lord is one!"

▸ Transforms into Shadow 58.3

Line Four—The Earth

If we don't listen to reason and heed a warning, there could be some consequences later. Here we could have been more patient and avoided some sticky situation, but instead, we insisted. Nothing would have been lost through waiting it out, but now everything has burned down due to temper. You might need to sit it out and wait even longer for the air to clear before approaching again—with an apology.

▸ Transforms into Shadow 5.4

Line Five—The Conflict

We need to use some force here, like a ram who uses its head to break through a wall in front of him; put a little shoulder into in. This is going to be one force meeting another until one drops, so be ready to put some might into it. Aggression is not needed for power, so drop the emotional attachment and focus on upholding what is right in the situation against the ones who are trying to knock you down. Not everyone is going to be nice to you, but that doesn't mean they don't deserve their liberty too.

▸ Transforms into Shadow 34.5

Line Six—Heaven

You have been battling with something for a long time inside yourself and have kept it within your head and heart. If there has been a situation with another that is in desperate need of repair, resolve to fix it, but know that this will require that you speak up and lay your cards on the table. Just make sure you do it before it's too late, or someone will get injured as a result of keeping your feelings and thoughts under the surface where they can breed mistrust and hatred. Clear them out; don't stay in the muddy water.

▸ Transforms into Shadow 1.6

All Lines Changing—Hexagram 23

Finally, when the fight has been either lost or won, the defenses drop to the ground like discarded armor. The weapons are laid at the feet of the master, and the husk of the seed drops off as the sprout breaks through the topsoil. The skin is shed, and there is inner growth. Shedding our defenses doesn't need to be dangerous if it allows us more clarity and increases our ability to perceive the truth. You will never be in danger by being clear and alert instead of biased and suspicious. Experience things directly and fully, no matter what you think they are or what they have been in the past.

Hexagram 44
The Temptation
Gou

Oracle Script:
Little Brother

"The Ego"
The Garden of Earthly Delights
Archons

Tarot Card: Devil

This hexagram concerns human control dramas based on material needs that bind us. Whereas in hexagram 40 we are liberated completely, in hexagram 44 we find ourselves dragged down right into our root chakra. Our deep needs and fears have brought us into some kind of master-and-servant situation. Humans influence each other in many ways. If we ascend to a certain level, we can see that human relations are very much like soap operas. The ruling powers of these situations are the drama archetypes. Some gnostic and occult schools call them archons. The archons are subconscious forces that cause us to act, often without our conscious awareness. Control dramas are usually about seeking security or gratification or are done out of hubris. There are many reasons why they happen: primal, emotional, irrational, instinctive. These

I sat in the sun on a bench; the animal within me licking the chops of memory; the spiritual side a little drowsed, promising subsequent penitence, but not yet moved to begin.

ROBERT LOUIS STEVENSON,
DR. JEKYLL AND MR. HYDE

subconscious forces simply exist in us due to our bestial nature and life on planet Earth. Like when a lion kills and eats a young antelope, they are neither good nor bad. We are no better or worse than anyone else for any of it.

The I Ching recommends meeting people halfway or in the middle of these control struggles; this is the way of the golden rule, or middle path. Even if you are unable to totally emancipate yourself from evil, you can either avoid taking everything for yourself or give partway, but avoid sacrificing your own values. Ultimately, each individual will have to find what works best for himself: what he wants to feed his hate wolf, and what he wants to starve it from. My teacher Kelvin DeWolfe always used to say, "feed both your light wolf and your dark wolf," much in keeping with the legend of Fenrir, the monstrous Norse wolf. When Fenrir the dark black wolf of chaos was bound and captured, none of the gods wanted to feed him. They left him to starve so that his mouth gaped open; only the warrior Tyr had enough courage to feed the dark wolf, feeding him his own hand in sacrifice. The dark wolf that needs to consume and ravage everything is a deeply internal and natural phenomenon that each human being must and should wrestle with to come into harmony and equilibrium, especially when experiencing a severe disturbance or drama of any kind.

When you engage in manipulation (and we all do, it is part of human nature), you may feel like you are in charge and even powerful. In fact, you just invited an archon into you that is controlling you. They have been around a long time, and you will not defeat them; try to wait out the impulse. "Keeping the toes still" is the language the I Ching uses, meaning pause before taking action. All manipulators are being manipulated by the appetite and need of the archetypal force that is driving their choices. They have been taken over by a habitual behavior. We all fall under the control of a slavish master when we engage in any drama. Look at any current political situation, for example, and within it you will find these characters driving the car. As horrifying as it is to think that we are all being possessed when we react with deep emotional primal behavior, it's best to just rip the whole thing open so that we can see it and acknowledge it. There is a reason why all the Shakespeare plays are still applicable today. The reason is the archons.

Imagine people as actors in a play,
only they don't know they are playing a role.
They live compelled to action
compelled to breathe
by their characters.
They cannot see nor believe this
because their character threatens them
through pain and paranoia
if they imagine themselves to be
anything other than what it thinks it is,
which is something that is small.
But they all must let it go,
let go of their characters,
in order to become real life
and join the living.
Life needs room to grow
and small cannot expand.
Do not permit your character to imprison you in
   smallness.
Learn to loosen as you turn into a whole new person
each and every day.

MAJA D'AOUST

That motley drama—oh, be sure
It shall not be forgot!
With its Phantom chased for evermore
By a crowd that seize it not,
Through a circle that ever returneth in
To the self-same spot,
And much of Madness, and more of Sin,
And Horror the soul of the plot.

But see, amid the mimic rout,
A crawling shape intrude!
A blood-red thing that writhes from out
The scenic solitude!
It writhes!—it writhes!—with mortal pangs

The mimes become its food,
And seraphs sob at vermin fangs
In human gore imbued.

Out—out are the lights—out all!
And, over each quivering form,
The curtain, a funeral pall,
Comes down with the rush of a storm,
While the angels, all pallid and wan,
Uprising, unveiling, affirm
That the play is the tragedy, "Man,"
And its hero, the Conqueror Worm.

EDGAR ALLAN POE, FROM
"THE CONQUEROR WORM"

Guru: We seek reciprocity because we are subject to natural laws. Nature seeks equilibrium. Your vengeance-seeking nature is only a force in the universe looking for the center. Learn to come up out of nature and see this force and how it influences you. Seek justice and truth, not reciprocity and vengeance. Thus you graduate out of natural law and into humanity through humility, in service to a greater whole. The difficult part, especially for anyone who has ever innocently fallen victim to something terrible, is to avoid self-righteously trying to change the other person or to inflict punishment on the other, who you believe did wrong. This is not the correct course of action to take. Accountability, amends, education, and reparations are what is in order. That is a true kind of justice, which can take care of problems without feeding the gods of action and manipulation, who created it to begin with, and locking us in a cyclic prison of monkey see, monkey do. In a way, when you inflict wounds on those who wound you, you have caught their virus and are letting it kill you too. Restorative justice is the right path, not aggressive, violent, or vengeful justice, especially inflicted by the police.

Personal Example: I fell into temptation during a time when I had taken a vow of celibacy. It was rough to keep, and I was about two years in. I asked the I Ching about the situation to help me examine my emotional responses and received hexagram 44, which indicated to me that this was a test. I took the I Ching's advice and decided not to succumb to the influence and to hold to my conviction. Later, I discovered the individual in question already had a current relationship and had been lying to me all along. By not giving in to an impulse, I saved myself from involvement in a betrayal.

The Changing Lines

Line One—The Self

Karma isn't based on what we deserve; it is based on what we are doing. And then there are other people around us who are outside our control. If all the actions you have been engaging in have led to unfavorable results, do not bemoan them but look at what is accumulating around you. Take responsibility for what you've done, and also notice how the karma of others influences you. If you are surrounded by drama, consider change and rectification rather than blame and finger-pointing. Now is the time for action, regardless of what led you to this situation. Make a change for the better.

▸ Transforms into Shadow 1.1

Line Two—The Other

Retreat is always an option. If other people's drama is getting you down and you are not responsible for it, you can offer them resources or suggestions and leave them to it. If you are responsible, then retreat inwardly from their emotions and view the situation from an observer standpoint to avoid getting emotionally dragged into it yourself. If everyone is in the pit, there are fewer chances of seeing the light. Encourage responsibility for everyone instead of shouldering everything as an enabler or discarding everything as an abandoner. Seek balance and reciprocity where applicable.

▸ Transforms into Shadow 33.2

Line Three—The Union

Contention and drama will always enter our lives; there is no avoiding it. When we find ourselves in disagreements, or unable to move forward with people, we must enter into negotiations. Knowing how to handle drama is an important life skill. Don't forget that you too have caused drama at some point in your life. So take a big deep breath and look to growth and navigating the problem rather than having a reactionary response. Present your case in a clear and transparent fashion, even if the others aren't coming forward in the same way. You are in charge of yourself; they are in charge of themselves. Be open and honest and preserve your own integrity. Accept apologies and make them if you need to.

▸ Transforms into Shadow 6.3

Line Four—The Earth

To be free from drama you might need to be free from people. Sounds safe, but really not. Isolation and rejection of everything in favor of peace isn't much of an option. Make wise choices but continue to engage. Being alone for too long makes us sterile and dull. We all need each other's fire to inspire us and to live life in its fullest forms. Take time-outs when you need too, but excessive hermitage can stop your own growth. Get out there and mix it up a bit; just learn how to make healthy boundaries and follow your gut.

▸ Transforms into Shadow 57.4

Line Five—The Conflict

Apart from family, we get to choose whose drama and karma we want to intermingle with, and the other will also be taking on ours. Pick someone whose drama fits into your story, and you in his or hers, and the result will be a heightened creativity for both. This sharing is a blessing. You don't need to share only the good things with people; our close ones get our villains as well as our superheroes. Our entire pantheon of archons follows us wherever we go, as does theirs. Learn to see this and view an entirety of character. Acknowledging both good and bad is not a detriment; it is real life, complete and whole.

▸ Transforms into Shadow 50.5

Line Six—Heaven

Making decisions concerning who to keep in our lives and who to discard is hard; we are all faced with these choices. If we meet everyone with suspicion and distrust and in a defensive manner, we may block positive experiences and growth from our lives, though we may think we are keeping ourselves safe. Don't let being burned a few times stop you from playing with others. Learn from past mistakes but stay open to new opportunities. No one needs to pass a hellish test just to get close to you; that's a little extreme. Let your vetting be observation instead of manipulative testing.

▶ Transforms into Shadow 28.6

All Lines Changing—Hexagram 24

After we succeed in resisting temptation, we can begin to form new relationships. A return to our true self is indicated after times of testing. When we fall into ego worlds, we veer off path and become lost in the wilderness, but this can be good for our growth as long as we hold to our foundations. When all the danger has been avoided, we can return to our path and focus on accomplishing our purpose and destiny.

> *Better shun the bait, than struggle in the snare.*
> JOHN DRYDEN, *MARRIAGE À LA MODE*

Hexagram 45
The Gathering
Cui

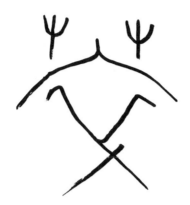

Oracle Script:
Strange Attractor

"Contraction"
Assembly
Glue

Tarot Card: Five of Wands

Hexagram 45 is a contracting force that pulls things together, like a muscle contraction. It is a tie that binds a community together, like a religion or a church. It also forces things together like the folds of a skirt. The ties that bind us run much deeper than we think, and when we gather together in groups, we can realize the full force and strength of what humanity is. Many of us have had the experience of an individual in a family who is the glue that holds things together. This can also be seen in organizations and nations. Once that individual who was the connecting force is gone, often the group scatters. The sun gathers all the planets around it, as the nucleus of an atom gathers electrons. When many gather around one, this is hexagram 45. It is the hexagram of following the leader, of troops stepping in time behind a general.

Concentration is the root of all the higher abilities in man.

BRUCE LEE

This is the coagula stage in alchemy, where things gather around a certain point. When a bleeding wound begins to heal itself, one blood cell stops and attaches itself to the area. Many other cells follow this action until the gathering of blood cells coagulates with enough force to stop the flow of blood—all from the action of one cell. Humans too have this power. If things are going in a certain direction and one person takes a stand in such a way that enough other people follow and gather around him, the entire flow of humanity can take a different course, for better or for worse. When many humans gather together, something special occurs, an effect known as hive mind in which their thoughts are briefly unified in one direction. This is similar to hexagram 13, but magnified on a bigger scale of nations or religions. In 45 we can see the effects of gathering and influencing in groups based on one central idea.

Guru: Humans like to gather around a central leader. We think this is human nature, but it could be universal, the state of all nature. Zoom out your vision to include the different phenomena that exhibit such behavior. The center that attracts and pulls other things toward it can be seen everywhere. The action of hexagram 45 is a natural force that we all fall under. As the queen bee attracts her drones and produces worker bees, so too the president appoints his cabinet members. Atoms of carbon, oxygen, nitrogen, and hydrogen combine to form an amino acid, an organic molecule; amino acids in turn bond to produce proteins. Gather enough carbon atoms, and you have a diamond. Gather enough water, and you have an ocean. Little things become larger things when they gather together and coagulate.

Personal Example: A client came in to ask about a medical problem she was experiencing around her menstrual time. The I Ching responded with hexagram 45. It seemed to indicate that she was having muscle contractions of her womb; in fact, she was having cramps. I suggested she try taking some magnesium (which is like hexagram 40) for an antidote, and she reported that her issue subsided.

The Changing Lines

Line One—The Self

Following in the footsteps of a gathering force can help imbue you with those same qualities. Study the ones who are able to hold things together: What do they have in common? Often they are the ones who can hold themselves together in times of trauma. Work to stabilize the self and create a foundation. Here is the power of the dark yin Earth Mother to stabilize and bind: the thing that gathers things around it. Deep dark yin coagulates into a blood clot. Offering commitment, handshakes, and agreements at this time will be met with trust if you have already done the work of solidifying the relationship and creating a firm base for both the situation and within yourself.

▶ Transforms into Shadow 17.1

Line Two—The Other

Once we have gathered ourselves around a central idea or organizing virtue, we can begin to come into contact with others who have also accomplished this feat. Go outside your house now and visit groups of like-minded people who share your interests. The time calls for mixing things up and moving and shaking. When we can grow into groups, we find that we are enriched and enhanced. Extend your circle and search for one who is a leader in the area of your interest. You both might be able to benefit each other through meeting in community events.

▶ Transforms into Shadow 47.2

Line Three—The Union

Gathering things into groups requires the force of Eros and love. We must exert our influence and mojo if we wish to draw a crowd. We must allow ourselves to be influenced if we wish to be joined with others in this fashion. There are benefits and losses in such arrangements, but you will be fine as long as you do not wholly compromise the integrity of your true self. This requires constant tending to your foundation during such interactions. Take time and space for yourself as well as dedicating yourself to the group or community.

▶ Transforms into Shadow 31.3

Line Four—The Earth
Things gather together through deep affiliations and correspondences. What unifies all the cells in your body? It is the core DNA at the center of each cell. Similarly, all groups have a core center that gathers things around, mimicking this natural tendency. Like seeks like. The same birds flock together; the same gazelles gather to form herds. Look to nature and see how like hugs to like in groupings. How are you gathering what is like you? How do you shun what you are not? This is key knowledge to raise your awareness in understanding the phenomenon of gathering.

▸ Transforms into Shadow 8.4

Line Five—The Conflict
Avoid joining cults that only serve the leader. Here we have a tyrant who gathers the group to serve his own needs. The story of a king or pharaoh who begins with good intentions and then only gathers people around him to exploit them is one of the oldest ones in the book. The easiest way to identify this scenario is to look at the leader, and then look at the group and observe how power and wealth are distributed. Join groups that advocate win-win situations rather than master and servant relationships.

▸ Transforms into Shadow 16.5

Line Six—Heaven
If you are unable to find a group to join, or can't get people to join with you, this is often when we must pull up our bootstraps and do it ourselves. Here is the line of the soapbox. Communicate with others, but do not mind who passes you by. Put yourself out there and share your ideas. You will fall into regret if you do not express yourself and experience the satisfaction of becoming part of something, even if it is only a note written to someone or an anonymous statement made on the Internet. Share your thoughts and gain intimacy with the world.

▸ Transforms into Shadow 12.6

All Lines Changing—Hexagram 26
After coming into community with others, we find that it is important to restrain ourselves. We will need to put ourselves forward in a

nonaggressive fashion. This is called civility. Maintain the health of the group by keeping the codes of the civilized. You can communicate and make yourself heard without trying to dominate things. A true leader will show restraint and lead in a natural fashion rather than through the use of force. Gather together in love, and merry meet and merry part.

Hexagram 46
The Mountain
Sheng

Oracle Script:
Higher Ground

"The Holy Mountain"
Ascension
Earth That Rises

Tarot Card: Eight of Cups

After we have traversed the valley so low and sunk into swamps, we find that we can emerge and reach great heights. The traveler, having successfully made the crossing, may come upon an opportunity to rise into the sky like a bird while still keeping his feet upon the earth. When our sights are set upon a goal, it will take ambition to accomplish it. We may want to climb a mountain, but we have to realize the work involved in this, or we are setting ourselves up for a failure. To achieve a goal and make an ascent, if the proper attitude is not adapted, we will be exhausted before base camp.

Lack of oxygen has a direct effect upon the human mind, which has been well documented; more suicides happen in Colorado and mountainous regions. But Colorado also has the lowest adult obesity

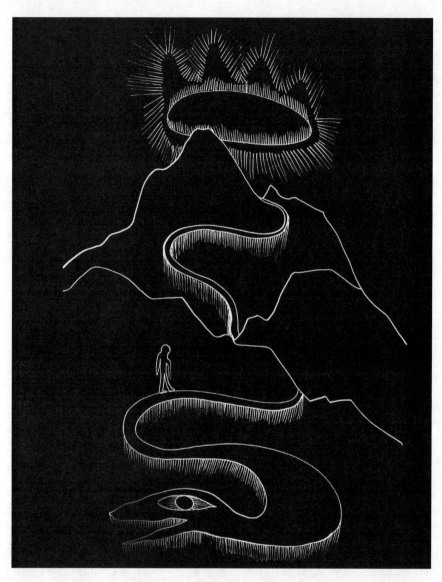

Tomorrow our path will be long and we may become exhausted. Let us walk together. We shall have joy and festivity. I shall sing for you the song your mother, wife and sister sang. You will relate for me your father's story about a hero and his achievements. Let our path be one. Be careful not to step upon a scorpion, and warn me about any vipers. Remember, we must arrive at a certain mountain village.

NICHOLAS ROERICH, *NEW ERA COMMUNITY*

rate and a low rate of diabetes and hypertension, and Colorado residents are among the most physically active in the nation. This is a perfect example of being unprepared for the attainment of the goal. Though you may be very fit and have a good attitude, do not forget the environment in your factoring. If you know your attempt will deplete you, train yourself to still function even when depleted. Here you will need to run with weights on to prepare.

> *Another title for Hercules was Trapezius, a trapeze artist. Tightrope walkers perform a balancing act; they need to know how to keep their center of gravity constant so they don't overbalance and topple off the tightrope. Balance is an inner ear function. The second element in the name Herakles, -kles, -kleos, is related to the word listen, and to Latin cluere, "to listen." His name might be analyzed as "listening in the air," suggesting an early amphibious creature that emerged from the ocean and developed an ear function that gave the ability to listen in the then hostile air [hostile Hera] when the air was "thin" due to low oxygen levels. The myth describes how Hercules, in a state of madness induced by Hera, heard voices in his ears telling him to kill his family. Listening is a function of the inner ear, the inner ear is also referred to as the Labyrinth. The ancient name for epilepsy was Hercules morbus "the disease of Hercules," it was also called the falling sickness, the sufferer loses balance and suddenly falls to the ground.*
>
> ANNE WRIGHT, "HERCULES: THE KNEELING MAN,"
> CONSTELLATIONS OF WORDS

A mind poison of defeat attacks even the strongest heroes, such as Hercules. On our way up to the top, we could be defeated by ourselves if we permit such ways of thinking. Make sure that you are not stepping into some defeatist mind poison by unclear thinking in your attempts to reach your aims. Remain standing upright and walking by not falling to such things. The power to strive is a natural force that can be used in your favor when you understand the nature with which you are dealing. Understand the natural forces of defeat, if you wish to capitalize the natural forces of success.

The mountains belong to Cybele, the Magna Mater and mountain goddess of Earth and the caves. She is providence herself and guards the highest peaks where Earth kisses the sky. Here the sacred mountain is the axis mundi, the point at which heaven and earth meet. Our bodies microcosmically mimic this meeting as elucidated by the Chinese Taoist internal alchemists and qigong practitioners. Esoterically, the mountain peak of Cybele is depicted as the benben stone that caps the pyramids and represents the point that heaven and earth come into conjunction—as in our bodies, as on the mountaintop. The most sacred places in the world are thought to be the mountains for this reason.

Guru: Where else on Earth can we sit in heaven but on a mountaintop? All the gurus and monks of all the religions of the world have traditionally sought out mountains because they are magical and have their own special kind of energy and effect upon humans. When you ascend a mountain, it requires a certain level of mastery; you need the skills to do it and persistence. The very action of accomplishing this can benefit all other areas of our lives. To gain the highest perspective possible, ascend to the highest places on Earth.

Personal Example: A client inquired about her career, asking the question, "Is this a path that will lead me to success in finances?" The response was hexagram 46. The I Ching indicated to her that indeed it was but that she had better prepare for a trek! To achieve success, she would need to prepare for the long road ahead and gear up her determination. Several years later, her business was very successful and productive, but it took no small amount of hard work and sacrifice to accomplish this. She mentioned that because the I Ching had forewarned her she used a steadfast approach.

The Changing Lines

Line One—The Self
The mountain represents balance and harmony because the rock that forms it is the earth and yin, but it has enough yang power to rise into heaven. The mountain is a natural example of the hermetic androgyn, which has achieved a perfect balance of yin and yang. Be as the moun-

tain and come into harmony with yourself and others. It is a good time to go for a hike with others or to attempt a difficult task if you have the right team. Start your business or begin that endeavor.

▶ Transforms into Shadow 11.1

Line Two—The Other

While working toward a big goal, you may need to pump yourself up. Rather than fill yourself with hot air, make ready with inspiration and belief in yourself. Train and prepare to help build your confidence. When you have risen to a higher level here, others gather around this foundation you have built and together you raise each other with affirmations and lift the heavy earth higher toward heaven. Group confidence assists all involved.

▶ Transforms into Shadow 15.2

Line Three—The Union

Climbing the holy mountain is like battling an army. When we fix our will toward a goal and concentrate our efforts, a counterforce comes to meet us. The greater our determination, the bigger the obstacle set before us. Do not worry about these things. When we meet these obstacles, we must laugh and know that truly we must be undergoing a great undertaking. Expect obstacles to appear the moment you take a step in the direction of an ascension. In this way, they will not defeat your aspiration. Prepare soldiers for battle, and the odds of winning are in your favor.

▶ Transforms into Shadow 7.3

Line Four—The Earth

We think it is our feet that get us up a mountain. It is easy to be deceived into thinking that having a big strong body is all we need to climb to the top. There is more here than meets the eye. An eighty-year-old Sherpa in Nepal can outclimb the fittest athletes. Much like a champion boxer who has already won the match in his mind before setting foot in the ring, you must defeat yourself before you defeat the mountain. Make a foundation of strength of heart and character, in addition to training your physical body, to make it to the top.

▶ Transforms into Shadow 32.4

Line Five—The Conflict
Here we find all our preparations have paid off. Because we knew something was going to be difficult and we did not quit, the summit of the mountain is within our grasp. Acknowledge your feelings of appreciation and pride and the job you have done well. Do not forget to think of all the others who helped prepare you for your difficulties and express gratitude to your assistants and those who have inspired you. Because you know what it takes to overcome obstacles in a realistic fashion and have manifested your dream, spread the joy around and help lift others to the heights you have achieved.
  ▸ Transforms into Shadow 48.5

Line Six—Heaven
Near the end of our journey to our goal, we can feel lost. Why are we doing this, anyway? Where are we? Here we are faced with the mind poison of Hercules. Don't fret: when we are closest to the end, things seem to fall apart. If the air is getting thinner, you are closer to the top. Don't quit. Take a moment to reconfigure and steel yourself, to reorient yourself to your original inspiration. Remember why you began and take your time now. Don't rush to the end; go step by step, just like you have done to get this far.
  ▸ Transforms into Shadow 18.6

All Lines Changing—Hexagram 25
Once we accomplish something big, other issues seem to fall away and melt at our feet. We return to a natural innocent state. Things fall into perspective, and negative doubts and past poor behavior are completely removed from us at this time. We are given a clean slate and are able to make a fresh start into our true selves. Any kind of contention we have had with others can also be healed at this time.

Hexagram 47
The Secret Garden
Kun

Oracle Script:
Magic Circle

"Circumscribed"
Happiness in Slavery
Oppression

Tarot Card: Four of Cups

There are many layers to hexagram 47. Most folks view it as being punished or oppressed, like being in prison. But after sitting with this hexagram for a few years, I think it's really making fun of those kinds of perceptions, like poking fun at the pity party we might engage in while we're suffering some unpleasant circumstance. When we draw this hexagram, it could be showing us that our attitude is creating the prison, or even if something is legitimately bad, we have unnecessarily adopted a negative stance, trapping ourselves in a bad-attitude prison. I was shown that this hexagram is comparable to Christ on the cross during his passion and also like *The Unicorn in Captivity,* a tapestry from South Netherland that shows a unicorn tied to a tree and circled by a fence. In both cases, Christ and the unicorn, the suffering is in adopting a woe-is-me attitude, when you are actually better off than you realize and can endure almost

The unconquerable nature of God is likened to that of a unicorn.

ODELL SHEPARD, *THE LORE OF THE UNICORN*

anything. It could be true that you are in a bad situation, but maybe that doesn't mean you need to feel persecuted. Even death itself can be faced with dignity. This trial you are undergoing is an attempt to force you into inner strength. It is Siddartha Buddha underneath the Bodhi tree faced with all the evils of the world, which are intent on making him break his dedication to his pleasant attitude and fall to temptation. This hexagram can be a very annoying answer, however, when you are suffering and you feel that your pain and victimization are not acknowledged or not important. This is not what I am trying to suggest here. Rather, your victimization might be true, but that doesn't mean you need to wreck your inner self. You don't need to be conquered by oppression. This hexagram also suggests getting cut off from or rejected by others: maybe someone won't talk to you or return your calls, or you are being persecuted and attacked. When this hexagram shows up, we must look deeply within and release responsibility from others. Seek justice but don't fall into a blame game or a need to justify yourself. You are valuable: that remains without question regardless of how others treat you. Rest in that place of your innate value during difficult ordeals.

When Coldness Wraps This Suffering Clay

When coldness wraps this suffering clay,
Ah! whither strays the immortal mind?
It cannot die, it cannot stay,
But leaves its darken'd dust behind.
Then, unembodied, doth it trace
By steps each planet's heavenly way?
Or fill at once the realms of space,
A thing of eyes, that all survey?

Eternal—boundless,—undecayed,
A thought unseen, but seeing all,
All, all in earth, or skies displayed,
Shall it survey, shall it recall:
Each fainter trace that Memory holds
So darkly of departed years,
In one broad glance the Soul beholds,
And all, that was, at once appears.

Before Creation peopled earth,
Its eye shall roll through chaos back;
And where the farthest heaven had birth,
The Spirit trace its rising track.
And where the future mars or makes,
Its glance dilate o'er all to be,
While Sun is quench'd or System breaks,
Fixed in its own Eternity.

Above or Love—Hope—Hate—or Fear,
It lives all passionless and pure:
An age shall fleet like earthly year;
Its years as moments shall endure.
Away—away—without a wing,
O'er all, through all, its thought shall fly,
A nameless and eternal thing,
Forgetting what it was to die.

LORD BYRON

Guru: The spiritual lesson of hexagram 47 is learning to be content within the self regardless of exterior circumstances. The adept creates a secret safe place of peace inside the heart, her own Garden of Eden. This is an unshakable state of *samadhi* and satisfaction that cannot be taken from us regardless of anything that other people, the world, nature, or even death may inflict upon us. This is Christ on the cross, who keeps his soul even though all around him attempt to rend it from him. If you spend time and effort to grow a secret garden in your heart, you will always have a home to return to even in the wildest storm. With this shelter, you can be defeated but you can never be conquered.

Personal Example: One of my favorite examples of this hexagram is quite literal. A client gave no backstory and simply asked, regarding his current business, "How about the business I just started?"—without telling me what the business was. The response from the I Ching was hexagram 47, and when I looked at the picture of a plant growing within an enclosure, an image flashed in my mind of an indoor or secret garden. I asked the client if he was growing marijuana plants. Indeed, he was. The

I Ching answered very accurately, reflecting exactly what the client was doing—growing plants inside an enclosure. We both started to laugh.

The Changing Lines

Line One—The Self

Here we are in confinement but also sharing this space with others. One of the best ways to bear a cross is to have some other crossbearers team up with you. Many hands make the burden lighter, and misery loves company, so if you find you are carrying too much, you can always share some of yourself with a friend. When we have good company, our feet move faster under heavy loads.

▸ Transforms into Shadow 58.1

Line Two—The Other

We can be placed into circumstances of seclusion by an authority figure, and this can lead to resentments. If you have been cut off or isolated at the hands of another, the best thing to do is occupy your time constructively in the interim rather than stewing in an unhealthy state. Some situations can right themselves if we are content to wait for the boundaries of another to lift. If the case unfolds that the authority figure is corrupt and will never cease oppressing us, we owe it to ourselves to stop following this person.

▸ Transforms into Shadow 45.2

Line Three—The Union

Here we might not see how valuable a partner, friend, or spouse is because we feel oppressed. If someone is supporting you in a time of grief, it is important not to bite the hand that feeds you just because you are in a foul mood. If they have done something to cause you suffering, don't forget about all the times they were helpful when you were indulging in your pain.

▸ Transforms into Shadow 28.3

Line Four—The Earth

If you are on the way out of your oppression or are freed from it completely, let it go. Don't take it with you when it is over. Lay your burden down by the riverside and let it be over. Be grateful that the oppressive times are done and keep them in your memory but not in your life. They are markers of events but don't need to influence your future or be taken into the next phase of your journey. Do some spring-cleaning and clear out what no longer serves you.

▸ Transforms into Shadow 29.4

Line Five—The Conflict

Oppression carries many lessons with it, but we seldom want to attend this school. But the more attention we pay during such times, the better off we will be in the future. Try not to devalue times of hardship, and instead, pride yourself that you are still alive despite them. When we see how strong we were during terrible times, or even laugh at how we broke, it can lift us up to higher places than we ever could have soared if everything had been fine all along.

▸ Transforms into Shadow 40.5

Line Six—Heaven

Sometimes oppression, suffering, and isolation are self-imposed by our own delusions. You might think you are shackled to something when really you are free to move about as you choose, but your own misperception of the situation has created a mind box from which you find yourself unable to escape. Take a look inside the confines of your trap and change it from the inside out. You might find that the walls simply disintegrate.

▸ Transforms into Shadow 6.6

All Lines Changing—Hexagram 22

When oppression becomes unbearable, we are met with hexagram 22, mercy. There is no situation that can endure in the depths of despair forever, for when we find ourselves at our deepest suffering, the Mother of All sends the sweet grace of mercy to meet us in an oppositional force to our grief. Sometimes this mercy takes the form of death. The death dealers are angels of mercy, after all. But it can also take the form of redemption and renewal. If we are ever given the chance to afford this mercy to others, truly what an invaluable gift one human can give to another. To give mercy is to act as one on high indeed, for who besides spirit itself can lift us from the pits of hell? It takes a strong hand to pull the lost out of purgatory.

Hexagram 48
The Well
Jing

Oracle Script:
Source of Life

"Origin of All"
Community Provisions
Baptism

Tarot Card: Three of Cups

There is water and then there is the holy water of baptism. Everyone must drink water to survive, but not everyone drinks of the replenishing life-giving water of the well that is the source of all things. There is a reason this hexagram follows 47, the oppression. When we have been crushed, we are forced down into the depths, and it is here, in the depths, where we might find a hidden spring. This hidden water lying deep within the earth is the well water that provides us with a source of vitality and life. It can be difficult to dowse this water without our feelings because we don't often come across it unless we feel something very strongly. It is passion that brings us to the well. Feeling a resonance with all things means getting to the common denominator. All life needs water. We all have water flowing through us, and it is the

*The hidden well-spring of your soul must needs rise
and run murmuring to the sea;
And the treasure of your infinite depths would be
revealed to your eyes.*

KAHLIL GIBRAN,
FROM "ON SELF-KNOWLEDGE"

thing we all must share. At the watering holes of Africa, all creatures gather—predator and prey, friend and foe—to partake in the mysteries of life. Things that unify the living hold power in them innately, and when we feel such sources within us, a special kind of expansion occurs beyond the boundaries of the self, which connects us to the pulse of life.

The Chinese character for *jing* shows intersecting lines that form a square, which indicates an underlying structure or matrix that connects things. In Chinese medicine the jing well points are twelve acupressure points located along different ley lines in the body that intersect, so jing includes the concept of intersection as well as the well. The well is a place where things gather together in common need. Parts of this were applied to cities, because often cities were built around wells or bodies of water. The well was the thing that determined the location of gatherings and places where convergences occurred. This hexagram also suggests networks of people or underlying matrixes that join groups of people together into larger entities, such as corporations, towns, or nations. When we receive the well, this suggests a key root unifier for the issue at hand.

The idea of a wishing well comes from the magical properties believed to be affiliated with fresh, clean water, as it is a vital source of life for all. Many cultures believed that spirits inhabited such places and could grant or confer supernatural powers or gifts to human beings. Nearly all bodies of water are connected with power or knowledge: Fu Xi was given the knowledge of the I Ching by the banks of the Yellow River, after all. A figure in Norse mythology called Mimir was associated with the well of knowledge. In exchange for an offering, Mimir would allow one to drink from his well and gain wisdom. Odin asked Mimir if he could gain the wisdom of the sacred waters, and Mimir demanded that he first throw a sacrifice into the well. Odin offered his right eye to the well and was then allowed to drink the waters and thereby gained the knowledge for how to save the world from the Ragnarok, a series of foretold cataclysmic events leading to the death of the gods and the submersion of the world.

Thou preparest a table before me in the presence of mine enemies: thou anointest my head with oil; my cup runneth over.

PSALM 23

Guru: Hexagram 48 shows up when we must plunge into the depths of our soul to replenish ourselves and others. The well is there for all when we search for it, and we can find it in others. We all have a well to draw upon, and when our well runs dry, the Holy Spirit itself can descend so that we may be filled with its vital life-giving powers. There are sources of life all around us if we know where to look. Hexagram 48 encourages us not to give up hope and to know that under the most desolate desert is a secret lagoon to provide for all our unrequited needs.

Personal Example: Hexagram 48 often appears when people need to reengage with their communities and those around them, to network or draw from others. One client asked, "How can I further my career in the arts?" The response was 48, which indicated that she needed to connect with others in the community in addition to pulling from deep within her soul; both her connection to the community and her soul drove her passion and creativity.

The Changing Lines

Line One—The Self
Wells need maintenance or they become muddy and undrinkable. If the source of your vitality is contaminated with too much negativity, the waters of your emotions get muddied with confusion. Take some time to clear yourself out and settle your disputes so that your source of nourishment is not so disturbed.
▶ Transforms into Shadow 5.1

Line Two—The Other
There is a crack, and things are leaking. Your well has been compromised by corruption and bottom-feeders, and parasites are taking some of your vital energy. Nothing to do now but make repairs. Find out who and what is draining your energy, and patch things up where you can, or get rid of the stinkers that are causing the contamination so that you can reach into yourself without their interference.
▶ Transforms into Shadow 39.2

Line Three—The Union

Sometimes we can have the most awesome well ever, pristine and valuable, but no one is around to drink from it with us. This can be sad and lonely, but hey, at least you are there—and you aren't nobody, are you? Trust in the source of your own heart and dive into your own well, even if no one else wants to. If your heart is perfectly fine, but you don't listen to it, who else will? Take some time to appreciate and believe in yourself.

▶ Transforms into Shadow 29.3

Line Four—The Earth

Even a great well needs upkeep. Let yourself go through times of total restructuring and renewal even if things seem okay. If you need a new community, new values, new experiences, or new sources of inspiration, permit yourself to get right down to the depths of your foundations and put some new things in there to join with old systems so that you may create a new source for yourself and others to draw from.

▶ Transforms into Shadow 28.4

Line Five—The Conflict

Success in finding a wonderful and valuable source of life-giving power should be shared with those around us. Don't be shy to invite others to something precious you have discovered in the depths of your soul. If you have tapped in to a life vein, distribute the energy in a fair fashion to all who would enjoy it with you. Truly this is a blessing.

▶ Transforms into Shadow 46.5

Line Six—Heaven

When something beautiful and special deep from the bottom of yourself is brought up to the surface for you and all those around you to behold, it is a precious moment for humanity. When one human discovers what he or she is, all humans benefit. The diamond of the self discovered in the hidden caverns is a spectacle that inspires joy in the hearts of all.

▶ Transforms into Shadow 57.6

All Lines Changing—Hexagram 21

After we have cleared out and connected to the deep well of spirit that resides within us, we are given the gift of discernment and the ability to feel the truth. Now we travel to hexagram 21, where we are able to have gnosis or knowledge of right and wrong and true and false. We now have a responsibility to hold this truth and speak it, and that can be more work than connecting with the well. Stay alert and on your toes, and do not let go of the feeling of truth you received from the source.

Hexagram 49
The Revolution
Ge

Oracle Script:
Skinning

"Snake Shedding Skin"
Eruption
Emergence of Renewal

Tarot Card: Two of Swords

This hexagram relates to hexagrams 4 and 23 in that it tells part of the story of breaking free from our shells and emerging renewed to become something larger. In hexagram 23 we see the knife that is used to remove the skin, and in hexagram 49 we have the actual skin itself. This is the husk or chrysalis that hampers our perception but that we need for protection while we are developing. In hexagram 49, we lose the skin that has hardened into a shell, preventing our growth, and are now free to move again into a new way of being. This is the butterfly that emerges from the chrysalis. Now it is time to shed the layer of development and come into being for all to see. We must become vulnerable to make changes happen. The changes in hexagram 49 are extreme and will require deep alterations of our belief systems

As a result of having practically applied the select teachings, the attainment of spiritual powers capable of transmuting the body, the speech, and the mind into their divine essences is indispensible. As a direct result of practice, the yogi attains the power to transmute the gross body into the radiant (rainbow/diamond) body. To transmute into Buddha.

W. Y. EVANS-WENTZ,
TIBETAN YOGA AND SECRET DOCTRINES

for massive growth and rectification. The ouroborus serpent that is depicted in hexagram 24 must also grow and shed its skin, so although we are on a repeated cycle of the spiral of phi, the spiral can level up or spiral out into growth. We meet the head of the serpent at the shedding of its skin. The serpent sheds its own skin in a natural cycle of growth, so this hexagram is tied to time and seasons of natural and unavoidable changes. Do not try to keep your old skin on at this time. Let it fall to your feet and step out of it purposefully to avoid being blinded by the residue that could inhibit your progress.

During the Renaissance, those who studied alchemy thought that transmutation was simply a physical process that converted lead into gold. Although this sounds unbelievable, it happens every day, all around us. Transmutation happens every second on the surface of the sun. The extreme heat and pressure causes elemental isotopes in the sun to continuously smash into one another, switching from one element to another through the loss or gain of protons and electrons. Transmuting is not a commonly accepted phenomenon even though it occurs naturally under many different circumstances. For whatever reason, even though scientists acknowledge that transmutation occurs in a particle accelerator, or on the sun, they deny that it could happen any other way, especially not inside living things. Transmutation is the conversion of atoms through force, heat, or pressure. Transmutation is different from shape-shifting because it is deeper. Natural diamonds are formed from carbon trapped deep in the earth that undergoes immense heat and pressure. The crystal that results differs in shape from the original carbon source, but it is still pure carbon. To change that carbon to another element is what the alchemists pursued. Hydrogen is composed of one proton and one electron; add another proton and electron and you have helium. We also see transmutation with radioactivity. In radioactive decay, an unstable atomic nucleus causes the atom to shed electrons, protons, or neutrons. This is accompanied by extreme energy given off in the form of radiation.

If transmutation happens without extreme heat and pressure, or the aid of a particle accelerator, most scientists have a big problem with it, because then it is called cold fusion. This is a term for any nuclear fusion reaction that occurs well below the temperature required for thermonuclear reactions, which occur at millions of degrees Celsius, and it was coined by Dr. Paul Palmer of Brigham Young University in 1986. Palmer was investigating geofusion, or the possible existence of fusion in a planetary core. Technically, if transmutation does happen within our bodies, it would have to be cold fusion; otherwise we would be giving off radiation, much like the sun. In the current climate, science has determined that cold fusion is not possible on this planet. Dr. Louis Kervran, the Nobel Prize nominee, had run many experiments regarding biological transmutation, attempting to show how it can occur within our living bodies and the bodies of other animals. Kervran's modern research was presented hundreds of years earlier by ancient Chinese Taoist alchemists such as Ge Hong and is embodied in the archetypal form of hexagram 49.

> *Without birth and death, and without the perpetual transmutation of all the forms of life, the world would be static, rhythm-less, undancing, mummified.*
>
> ALAN WATTS, THE BOOK: ON THE TABOO
> AGAINST KNOWING WHO YOU ARE

Guru: Within the chrysalis of our physical forms upon Earth, many transformations can occur. The idea of altering the shape of the body connects to the deeper teachings of the alchemists, which indicates that all matter has the ability to change and flow into and out of all other matter. If we can comprehend that all matter is one and contains all other matter, we see the spiritual truth that the physical can be interchangeable with all that is under the sun. If we truly are a microcosm of the universe, we contain all earlier life-forms within our form and can atavistically express any of these at will. Perhaps this concept can't be accomplished physically in our own bodies, but we seem to be able to do it with material outside our bodies.

Personal Example: If you have drawn hexagram 49, it is time for drastic changes. A client once asked the I Ching, "How can I enjoy my job?" The I Ching's response of 49 indicated that he needed to change jobs completely. This was very daunting to him at the time, and he had a bit of a panic attack about it. Eventually, after a bit of hemming and hawing, he did make the change and discovered he was much happier doing something else. A client who is undergoing an initiation into the spirit world may get this hexagram, which indicates that she is at a certain stage of growth: her caterpillar is turning into a butterfly, freeing her soul.

The Changing Lines

Line One—The Self
When transformations are just beginning and the food is not yet done cooking, if we take the pot off the stove too soon, we risk eating an unsatisfying meal. Would you eat an unripe fruit? Though it may cause some frustrations to be patient, even worse is to try to start a revolution with no one else ready to join you. You may be in full flower, but that in itself won't make anyone else's bud bloom. Only the light of the sun can do that. Be ready when the time comes; work on your own awareness and assist with education.

▶ Transforms into Shadow 31.1

Line Two—The Other
When the time for change comes and all are ready, don't linger. When you want to make lasting changes, go forward with real steps that will take you in the right direction; it will take more than just thoughts and prayers. If we begin a revolution within our own lives with those we love around us, that is a good place to make a dwelling for the spirit. It's hard to get things going on our own, but where else will that happen? Expect resistance when making changes and stand your ground.

▶ Transforms into Shadow 43.2

Line Three—The Union
When everyone is poised at the starting line and waiting for the gun, there needs to be some kind of destination in mind. Organization is the key to lasting changes; otherwise, things quickly turn into anarchy. If you are going to lead others into a new time, it is best if you know which direction you are going so that you don't lead them off a cliff.

▶ Transforms into Shadow 17.3

Line Four—The Earth
We have to expect that others might not believe or trust in change. It is difficult to believe in unicorns until people see one with their own eyes.

Someone needs to keep the faith in such times and provide a lantern to others along the way until the changes are revealed to all. After the revelation, trust is again regained. Try not to be bitter toward those who refused to believe in the change. How can they be blamed? You must hold your feelings in times when everyone else holds doubts.

▸ Transforms into Shadow 63.4

Line Five—The Conflict

Some transformations are so powerful that faith is not needed, for our very faces change. When the change is visible and visceral, there can be no doubt. When we let go of old ways and take on the mind of nature, our mind becomes flexible; it moves, adapts, and flows. Change yourself like a great beast taking the shape of your own power. Your presence will inspire others to do the same. You will know what to do if you just follow the flow of events and trust.

▸ Transforms into Shadow 55.5

Line Six—Heaven

The face has changed; true leaders undergo a complete metamorphosis. This line is the transmutation of lead into gold. Here we become something new, something we have never been, a shape shift. The change is deep and happens to mind, body, and spirit. We stop looking to others and only look within to know the entire universe. No more questions are needed, for you have all the answers inside your belly. Others will follow you when they see your new form.

▸ Transforms into Shadow 13.6

All Lines Changing—Hexagram 4

Here we find ourselves back at the apocalypse. After we have shed the chrysalis that has been enveloping us, it is time for the revelation or the big show. When our true self is revealed, we are reborn into a brand-new state of being, like a baby being birthed. The transmutation has completed its course, and now the hermetic vessel in which we had been developing falls away to show what has resulted.

Hexagram 50
The Cauldron
Ding

Oracle Script:
The Hermetic Vessel

"The Holy Grail"
Potential Energy
The Oven

Tarot Card: Seven of Cups

This hexagram is related to hexagram 48, the well. In Norse mythology Mimir, renowned for his wisdom and knowledge, is wise from drinking from the well. He is connected to another character called Kvasir. Hexagram 50 is the hexagram of Kvasir, who is also known for his wisdom, but Kvasir, unlike Mimir, was born wise because he is created from the water. Here we see the concept that we can gain power through taking it into us, but there is also inborn knowledge. Kvasir and hexagram 50 represent the depth of knowledge that we have access to in our blood rather than from our environment, from the water we drink. Blood knowledge is from DNA and relates to instinct and ancestors. Here in the cauldron that is the pot of potentiality and possibility we see atavism expressed.

In the Norse sagas, the blood of the wise is what confers knowledge,

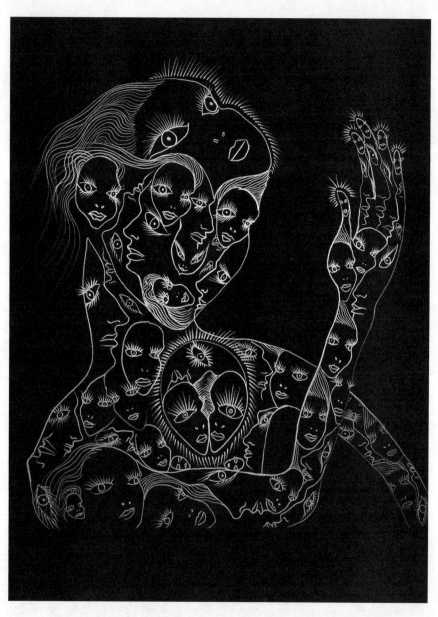

Man is the most divine of all the beings, for amongst all living things, Atum associates with him only—speaking to him in dreams at night, foretelling the future for him in the flight of birds, the bowels of beasts, and the whispering oak.

HERMES TRISMEGISTUS,
CORPUS HERMETICUM

and this can be held within the container that is the self. DNA is the container of our knowledge, just as the I Ching is the cauldron of knowledge. In the story of the Eddas we are introduced to the character Kvasir. Kvasir contained the gnosis within himself, and so his blood was said to contain it. Much like the communion of Christ in the Eucharist, the blood of Kvasir was taken into a cup suspiciously like the Holy Grail and was mixed with honey to become the first intoxicant known as mead. To drink of the mead that was the blood of Kvasir would give the drinker access to the same wisdom and gnosis obtained by Kvasir.

Guru: Prima materia in alchemy is a primal substance that contains within it the possibility of all other things. The code for all cells in a body is contained within the DNA of each cell. The I Ching contains all the possible scenarios one might come upon in living a human life. If one thing can contain all things within it, what does that imply about the nature of life and the universe? Both DNA and the I Ching express the aphorism "as above, so below," the macrocosm contained within the microcosm, the microcosm reflecting the macrocosm. The oracle is a mirror, reflecting ourselves, showing what is within. Regardless of your question, the purpose of the oracle is to reveal this truth.

Personal Example: Hexagram 50 is traditionally received when the question asked of the I Ching is, "What are you?" Oftentimes I have had the I Ching give this in response, which is that it is a container of possibilities, like the box that contains Schrödinger's cat: you will never know what it has inside until you pick it up and lift off the lid. As the I Ching mimics DNA, it can be thought to contain all possibilities of life, just as the molecule of life contains all the forms waiting to be given form. When we pray to the ritual cauldron of hexagram 50, we give form in the world to the wishes of our hearts. The water on the surface of the pot only reflects it back to us, providing a mirrored surface for self-examination.

The Changing Lines

Line One—The Self

If you look into a pot and something is rotten in there, clear it out. Some people prefer to let sleeping dogs lie, and others choose to shake things up. If there are things you aren't happy with inside the ritual cauldron that is your life, it may be time to do some pot scrubbing, to look within yourself and make some changes. The first thing you should do is to wipe away all the things you think you know. Make a clean slate of your mind, discarding any old or useless beliefs.

▸ Transforms into Shadow 14.1

Line Two—The Other

When we look into the pot and see that it contains all possibilities, it may dawn on us, as we gaze upon the scrying waters, that our own face is reflected. You also hold all possibilities within yourself. As without, so within: what you consulted for answers reveals the truth that you are very much like the oracle.

▸ Transforms into Shadow 56.2

Line Three—The Union

We go to pick up our potential pot, but the handles fall off due to disrepair. If you use something all the time, you could begin to take it for granted and not notice that it needs attention until it is already broken. Take some time to breathe some new life into an old pot. Maybe give it a fresh coat of paint. Try your intention again when the moons change, after you have done some much-needed repairs, and maybe this time you will go the distance.

▸ Transforms into Shadow 64.3

Line Four—The Earth

It is always a shame when we pour ourselves a nice glass of wine and then spill it all over ourselves. But maybe there is a reason why most comedy begins with such moments. Although it's regrettable when we fumble and bumble, we are only human, after all, and will stumble. The eyes of fate peek at us from the stage wings, ready to hook us with a vaudeville cane.

▸ Transforms into Shadow 17.3

Line Five—The Conflict

Your golden pot is so shiny even the leprechauns are seeking you for your services. A polished cauldron invites use, and we have come into our own wisdom. By living real life, our own hidden potential is expressed through our every action. You can make something very special in a pot like this, enough to feed a whole village. It's like the goose who lays golden eggs. Take good care of the pot and treat it with respect while you share what it provides with others.

▸ Transforms into Shadow 44.5

Line Six—Heaven

Suddenly we see the cauldron from a whole new perspective. We thought it was ourselves who revealed what was within by looking, but now we see it is the Holy Spirit taking thousands of forms and singing to us. What joy to behold such miracles and wonder. What pleasure to have others see them also. Everything you see, never forget, is like rain that has precipitated from heaven; a form is here on Earth only because a spirit gave birth to it.

▸ Transforms into Shadow 32.6

All Lines Changing—Hexagram 3

Now that we have seen what the possibilities are to become, it is time to get on with it. We sprout from the earth as we break through the dark prima materia into form. Choosing a form is not always easy, but it needs to be done. Go with the one you have chosen, and use it to carry you up, as you ascend and emerge into the light of day in a new and fresh beginning. Time to leave the womb; time to jump out of the nest and fly.

Early spring is the time for vigorous change, a preparation for the heat-driven oppression that is to come.

HENRY ROLLINS, "GETTING OLDER DOESN'T HAVE TO MEAN GOING DOWN WITH THE SHIP"

Hexagram 51

The Upheaval
Zhen

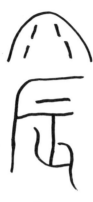

Oracle Script:
Fate

"Thunder and Lightning"
Power of Natural Forces
Upheaval

Tarot Card: Tower

In the spring the energy of creation awakens. This hexagram belongs to the earth goddess Cybele. She is the mountain mother and the dweller within Earth. She is known as chthonic, which means underground and could be compared to other underworld goddesses, such as Persephone and Hecate. She brings new life in the spring but also opens herself to swallow what is no longer needed into the dark caverns of the soil. Here we find earthquakes, shake-ups, thunder and lightning, natural disasters, and unavoidable change that happens on a level far beyond the individual's control. If you think your life is just your own to live, you have forgotten the ground upon which you stand, and Cybele comes in the spring to remind you that you are forever vulnerable to the powers of Earth. There is an element of castration seen at this time and the realization of impotence. There is nothing like a huge eruption of a force of nature to convey to you the limits of your powers. Those who thought they had power to rise are humbled and castrated by the display of Earth, who shows her power through all the life-forms that rise up and grow from her body. The masculine force wanes at this time, and the feminine force exhibits her innate yang, as Earth's mountains rise to meet the sky. This is the hexagram of the spring equinox, the time when life springs forth from the opening earth.

> *Then sing, ye birds, sing, sing a joyous song!*
> *And let the young lambs bound*
> *As to the tabor's sound!*
> *We, in thought, will join your throng,*
> *Ye that pipe and ye that play,*
> *Ye that through your hearts to-day*
> *Feel the gladness of the May!*
> *What though the radiance which was once so bright*
> *Be now for ever taken from my sight,*
> *Though nothing can bring back the hour*
> *Of splendour in the grass, of glory in the flower;*
> *We will grieve not, rather find*
> *Strength in what remains behind;*
> *In the primal sympathy*
> *Which having been must ever be;*
> *In the soothing thoughts that spring*
> *Out of human suffering;*
> *In the faith that looks through death,*
> *In years that bring the philosophic mind.*
>
> WILLIAM WORDSWORTH, FROM "ODE:
> INTIMATIONS OF IMMORTALITY FROM
> RECOLLECTIONS OF EARLY CHILDHOOD"

Guru: It is one thing to become an individual, to truly realize the self and your place in the universe. It is quite another thing to extend beyond this realization to see that the self is part of something much larger. Yourself, your alpha, is one piece of an entire living organism called Earth, who is the omega. To break out of our ego, it is sometimes necessary to break free of our foundation, to lose what we thought we knew, and start anew, on fresh ground, where we can be nourished and rise up from the depths to see the light of day. This is a very uncomfortable thing because that which has been hidden in the deep caves of Mother Earth tends to shun the light, wants to remain hidden. But every seed must shed its husk, every sprout must break through the surface of the earth to grow into a plant.

Personal Example: It was a beautiful day right around the time of the spring equinox. I had been looking at the green cap that covers the earth at this time, wondering at its marvels. My boyfriend and I were driving along the freeway, and we could see the mountains, which were usually a kind of LA brown, and they had all turned green in vibrant ecstasy. I had been reading in the news that the aurora borealis is the largest at this time of year, during March, and one of the most common colors of the northern lights is green. The green on the earth seemed to me to be reaching up to meet the green in the sky, an expression of what Hildegard von Bingen called the *viriditas,* spiritual and physical health and fertility. I asked the I Ching, "What time is it now?" and received this hexagram in response.

The Changing Lines

Line One—The Self

The strange thing that happens to humans is a kind of mindlessness. When our attention drifts from our earthly actions, we float through aimlessly, mindlessly doing what our day requires from us. We drive to a location with no memory of how we got there. Then, all of a sudden, Nature gives us a slap in the face. *Wake up!* she screams, and we nearly die in a freak accident or natural disaster. If you weren't paying attention before, you certainly are now. Nothing like a good jolt to bring you into crystal-clear focus of what is going on around you. What blessing to be brought back to life from our deathlike state as if from a defibrillator.

▶ Transforms into Shadow 16.1

Line Two—The Other

If you lose all of your belongings in a fire or flood, it forces you to see what is firmly held within your hands, and that is your life. Shocks of loss can cause us to spiral down into grief or lift us up into gratitude. Truly, loss is a gift, presenting us with an opportunity to release materialism and come instead into humanity. Cling to those around you in such times and join hands with them instead of trying to grasp the ruined vestiges of what is left of your "stuff." See how valuable we are to each other instead of searching for your valuables in the wreckage.

▶ Transforms into Shadow 54.2

Line Three—The Union

The power to do great things in times of disaster does not belong to many. Most, understandably, crumble in fear when faced with mortal danger. But a precious few are able to assist another and disregard their own terror, risking life and limb to save even a stranger. Here is where the hero is born in a single moment of action that is not dependent on anything that has come before or follows after but unfolds in the moment, during great upheavel. Earthquakes expose the gold hidden in the ground, just as some humans shine when shaken.

▶ Transforms into Shadow 55.3

Line Four—The Earth

Sitting around in comfort all the time won't stimulate you to do much of anything. If everything were always easy, it's fair to say that nothing would get done. Thank God for the motivators of survival. Without them, would we even do anything at all?

▶ Transforms into Shadow 24.4

Line Five—The Conflict

This is the mass hysteria that ensues when someone cries *Fire!* in a crowded theater. Just because everyone else is losing their minds does not mean you need to follow suit. If you are thrown into hysterics with the crowd, you will be subjected to their same fate. If you can retain your self-awareness and wits while everyone else is losing theirs, you might be able to direct the whole herd of cattle to safety. Here is where leadership becomes a matter of survival for the whole in the face of fear that spreads into the unaware and untrained minds of the masses.

▶ Transforms into Shadow 17.5

Line Six—Heaven

In times when we can't save everyone else, we can at least rescue ourselves. If you can put your own oxygen mask on when the plane is crashing, at least you won't be a burden to anyone else and you may manage to emerge unscathed. Focus on your own disaster before martyring yourself in an ineffectual fashion. You won't pull someone else out of the ditch by jumping in with him. Figure out a strategy, or go get help from a larger resource after dealing with your own issues.

▶ Transforms into Shadow 21.6

All Lines Changing—Hexagram 57

During a tragedy, our true character is revealed. You only find out who you are in such times of testing from huge forces outside your control. Pay special attention to your actions in such times for they reveal the seal that destiny has placed upon you. These are magical times when we see through ourselves. If you don't like what you see during such events, do not worry; there is always room for repentance. Make a change.

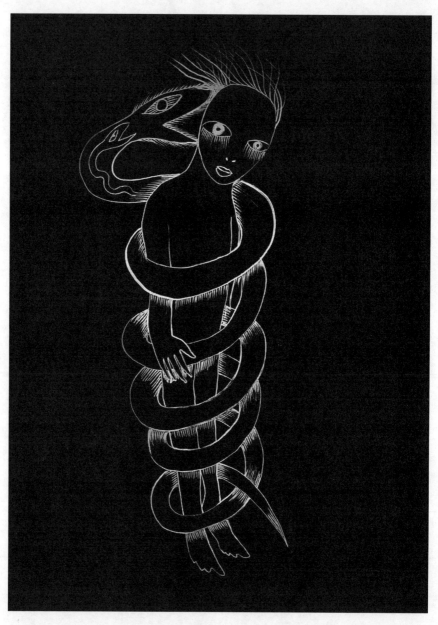

No durable things are built on violent passion. Nature grows
her plants in silence and in darkness, and only when they
have become strong do they put their heads above the ground.

ANNIE BESANT, *THE BIRTH OF NEW INDIA: A COLLECTION*
OF WRITINGS AND SPEECHES ON INDIAN AFFAIRS

Hexagram 52
The Stillness
Gen

Oracle Script:
The Mountain

"Binding"
Meditation
Fixation of Mercury

Tarot Card: Four of Swords

After everything has been thrown into upheaval in hexagram 51, here we come into total stillness. Being still might be one of the hardest things for human beings to do, unless they are being lazy. But being still when you want to move is the art of fighting your own impulses and urges. There are times when we need to take immediate action and make a move, but if that move comes from a reactionary impulse, we could make a misstep. It is a needed skill of discernment to know when and how to wait. No one wants to hold back, and its hard to judge the timing of such things, but when we meditate on something, we often arrive at a different, better action than the one we would have originally taken. When we pause, we are freed from all outside influence. We listen to ourselves rather than to advice from others; we resist simply following along with what someone else said or did.

In the alchemical process we come to a stage known as the Fixation. In alchemy the mind is represented by mercury and also the unicorn. Here the free-running unicorn is captured and contained within the fenced circle. Mercury is a highly volatile and reactive substance. It reacts with almost everything it touches; it does not like to take a stable shape and clings to everything. Is not the mind also this way? The difficult process of stilling the mind, which seems downright impossible, requires us to settle what is rebellious and wild. To make a metal that is a liquid into a solid will require a deep freeze of stillness. Let the hoarfrost cover over the weeds.

This is the hexagram of the winter solstice, when all things stop moving and come into the quiet time of rest.

> At the Summer Solstice, all is green and growing, potential coming into being, the miracle of manifestation painted large on the canvas of awareness. At the Winter Solstice, the wind is cold, trees are bare and all lies in stillness beneath blankets of snow.
>
> GARY ZUKAV, "TWIN MIRACLES"

Guru: The best summation of the guru teachings of this hexagram can be found in the following passage of the Bhagavad Gita.

> Everything in the phenomenal world displays activity and changefulness, but tranquility is the nature of God. Man as a soul has within himself that same nature of calmness. When in his consciousness he can level and still the three mental states of upheaval—the waves of sorrow and gladness and the dips of indifference between them—he perceives within himself the placid ocean of spiritual soul-calmness expanding into the boundless sea of tranquility in Spirit.
>
> BHAGAVAD GITA XVI:12

Personal Example: Whenever I am agitated and ask the I Ching any question at all, it responds with hexagram 52. It's like it doesn't even care what question I am asking it; the only response it has for me during those times is to take a chill pill. Whenever I receive this hexagram, I know it's time to sit and be still and get my mind together before I do anything at all, and often during this process I come to the right conclusion after I quiet all the hens in the henhouse.

The Changing Lines

Line One—The Self
If we are needing to forgive ourselves for something or find that we are in suffering or misery, it is always advisable to come into stillness and meditation. Often we avoid this at all costs when in such a state; in fact, we run in the other direction. We seek out anything that will get us away from ourselves: friends, family, sex, food, drugs—anything but sitting with ourselves and our suffering. Quit running around and sit with yourself in the corner. You might not be as bad as you think.
▶ Transforms into Shadow 22.1

Line Two—The Other
We can always try to leave our own mountain to walk on another's rocky trail. This will happen from time to time. But invariably our feet will start to turn back home. Don't try to convince the other to follow you back, and don't stay on their peak. Send each other smoke signals.
▶ Transforms into Shadow 18.2

Line Three—The Union
When winter has come to an end, you better move again. If a frog doesn't come back to life after hibernation, it is dead. Don't freeze yourself in place or make binding limits that are too severe. It is true that we need to keep still, but we also have to get back up and dance. Find a balance of stillness and movement to prevent stagnation. Not moving can cause regret as much as moving too soon: find the center. If you are so frozen you can't feel your heart, it's time to heat things up again.
▶ Transforms into Shadow 23.3

Line Four—The Earth
After we have stilled enough to realize our inner truth, we must fix it within ourselves. We won't have to keep on sitting and getting still all the

time—finding and losing truth, running to and fro—if we can sit long enough to train our mind and heart to stay put. Once we spend enough time in this place and bring it to a centered location, we will never lose. Now we can travel the whole world with stillness locked within our heart like a treasure chest. This is the stillness that can wander.

▸ Transforms into Shadow 56.4

Line Five—The Conflict

Sometimes we need to still our tongues instead of our minds. If you establish a good enough practice of stilling, you can stop your thoughts from spilling out of your mouth. It is one thing to speak fluently with connection to our thoughts, but that doesn't mean we should always do it. Learn when to bite your tongue, or better yet, practice stillness so your mind doesn't leap to words it shouldn't say. Speak only when the truth has cohered enough to be sincere; this will further all relationships.

▸ Transforms into Shadow 53.5

Line Six—Heaven

This line is about the importance of knowing how to pause and still the impulse so that we do not waste in haste. Classically explained by Confucius:

> By knowing how to keep still,
> one is able to determine what objects he should pursue.
> By knowing what objects he should pursue,
> one is able to attain calmness of mind.
> By knowing how to attain calmness of mind,
> one is able to succeed in tranquil repose.
> By knowing how to succeed in tranquil repose,
> one is able to obtain careful deliberation.
> By knowing how to obtain careful deliberation,
> one is able to harvest what he really wants to pursue.
>
> CONFUCIUS (KUNG FU TZU), AS QUOTED
> BY ALFRED HUANG FOR THIS LINE IN
> THE COMPLETE I CHING

▸ Transforms into Shadow 15.6

All Lines Changing—Hexagram 58

After sitting apart in isolation to find who we are, we can share our innermost self with others through communication. When we find the seat for our soul and sit in it, we might have a story to tell or we might erupt into song. These expressions form some of humanity's favorite tales and ballads.

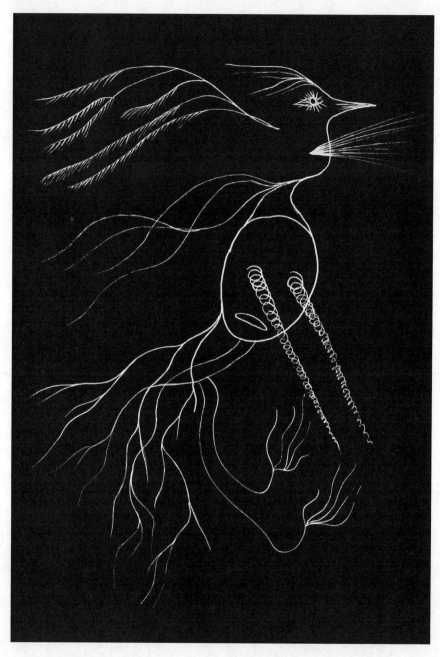

We don't receive wisdom; we must discover it for ourselves
after a journey that no one can take for us or spare us.

MARCEL PROUST,
REMEMBRANCE OF THINGS PAST

Hexagram 53
The Journey
Ji'an

Oracle Script:
Shape-Shifting

"Transmigration"
Interdimensional
Nagual

Tarot Card: Six of Swords

Here we accomplish a shift in our way of being by undergoing a journey that leads to inner development or maturity or even a change of form. We look very different today than we did when we were a zygote. If we look at a picture from our childhood, it is easy to see how we have changed. Through the passage of time, our form itself changes, along with perhaps our location on Earth. In hexagram 53 we experience the phenomenon of dimensions and their effects upon our physical, mental, and spiritual being. We are changed by things in time and space. Both our flesh and environment are constantly evolving. In our journey from the cradle to the grave, our bodies undergo immense transformations, along with the ground passing beneath our feet. This is the subject of this line. In each stage we can have a graduation of sorts, like a bar mitzvah, wedding, or funeral. These liminal initiatory rituals are important to remind us of the progress we have made when we cross over parts of these journeys of the flesh and spirit. We can cross into the bardo planes here in dreams as well, leaving this flesh and transmigrating into places our feet may never tread but our minds and souls do. Upon awakening, observant Jews daily recite a prayer called the Modeh Ani while still in bed. The prayer acknowledges the journeys to other realms the soul has taken and gives thanks for the stages we find ourselves occupying in this realm when we awaken.

> *Those who have learned to walk on the threshold of the unknown worlds, by means of what are commonly termed par excellence the exact sciences, may then, with the fair white wings of imagination, hope to soar further into the unexplored amidst which we live.*
>
> ADA LOVELACE

The Chinese character of *ji'an* means "to build" and is akin to something that occurs over time and space. It is not something that comes into being simultaneously, whole and complete, but is something that gradually emerges, like a human forming from the conjoining of egg and sperm. In a similar view a relationship or marriage does not just happen spontaneously but must arise out of a foundation and grow and shift over time. This is a pyramid built over time, not a fully formed boulder that has existed as is for millennia.

Guru: This is the body that the spirit occupies during its stay in this world. It's the tree that supports and nurtures the bird of spirit who has come to rest on it after the spirit's endless flight through the cosmos. In Egypt the spirit or soul, known as *ka,* is shown as a bird who takes flight again in death. Transmigration of consciousness is something we don't much like to imagine, since we are so tied to our present forms, but perhaps realizing we are, in essence, a thing that travels is more of a liberation than any other thought we could conceive.

> *The sycamore, or Pharoah's fig, was sacred in Egypt. . . . Souls in the shape of birds would perch on its branches and its shady*

foliage symbolized the security and protection enjoyed by the souls in the otherworld. In the New Testament Zacchaeus climbed into a sycamore when the crowd prevented him from seeing Christ pass by . . . and to climb into a sycamore means spiritually to partake of a measure of madness in abandoning all interest in earthly things and in all that is created. What Zacchaeus did might, therefore, symbolize the folly of being detached and a certain degree of contempt for public opinion verging on anti-conformism. If the tree is a sign of vanity, to climb it is to trust in vain things.

JEAN CHEVALIER AND ALAIN GHEERBRANT,
THE PENGUIN DICTIONARY OF SYMBOLS

Personal Example: I get hexagram 53 a lot when I am going to move. The same hexagram often turns ups with clients when they ask about moving. I had one client ask, "Should I move to this city?" and the response was hexagram 53, which also indicated that she would progress in her career and relationships at that location, and she did.

The Changing Lines

Line One—The Self
A goose in a chicken coop will generate a lot of talk among the hens. When you stand out, you will get envy and back talk from others. Figure out a strategy to deal with it. Don't back down; just be yourself, and you will find your place no matter where you are. Even the ugly duckling figured out he was a swan eventually, but it sure was nice of the duck family to take care of him when he needed it. Recognize family not as those who are the same as us but as the ones who share their lives with us.

▶ Transforms into Shadow 37.1

Line Two—The Other
How does a flock of geese know where to fly during their migration home? When I was hiking once, I watched a hawk tuck in its wings and glide quickly toward a cliff full of trees. It looked like he was going to crash, but he knew exactly which tree was his home. When you know where your home is, you find it automatically by feeling your way there.

When you feel lost, do not forget about the geese who find their home from thousands of miles away. Use your guidance system.

▸ Transforms into Shadow 57.2

Line Three—The Union

If the geese can't find a place to land, they won't be able to settle. If you are flying around in circles unsure of which tree to land on, you are going to get very tired. Being afraid of what will happen when you land in the tree might be worse than what will happen if you do not land. Don't let your irrational fears prevent you from doing what you need to do. Just do it, and if you make a mistake, decide to fly away. But you will never know if you keep flying aimlessly and indecisively.

▸ Transforms into Shadow 20.3

Line Four—The Earth

The geese may need to land on any tree they can find during a storm. Maybe you didn't intend to stop at this point along the road, but things did not go according to plan. No matter where you find yourself, regardless of the environment, you are still yourself. Learn to make do with what you have. After a while in life, you realize you are a traveler even in the most familiar spaces; the only home is the shelter of your heart, which you carry with you always. If you can't be with the one you love, love the one you're with.

▸ Transforms into Shadow 33.4

Line Five—The Conflict

Here is the tree in which you make your home. This is a place to settle. After a long flight, it is finally time to be at rest. Still yourself and stop your wandering. You can relax now and be at peace. The rest of the flock finds a home too, and all are in accord. Don't worry about any squabbles that may arise; these are natural and will clear in time. It is no mistake to rest here.

▸ Transforms into Shadow 52.5

Line Six—Heaven

The geese land on the tallest tree on the mountain, providing inspiration for all. Here the geese are resting in a home, but it is so elevated it is as if they are still flying in the sky. We have made a connection to spirit and heaven that stays with us even when we are on the earth. To keep such a link with us every day during our regular activities earns us merit and humanity. Invite others to share in this abode that holds the space between heaven and earth.

▶ Transforms into Shadow 39.6

All Lines Changing—Hexagram 54

After traveling the long journey of migration, we have arrived at our location. It is here we shall come into our time of destiny. It might not look like much at first, and we certainly won't be placed in a position of royalty, but all our needs are met so that we can focus on our purpose. In places where we are accommodated, we can achieve peace of mind and stability, which enables us to fly to high places.

The fault, dear Brutus, is not in our stars, but in ourselves,
that we are underlings.

WILLIAM SHAKESPEARE,
JULIUS CAESAR

Hexagram 54
The Destiny
Kun

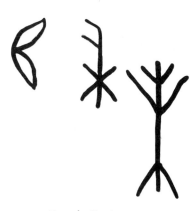

Oracle Script:
The Marrying Maiden

"Subordination"
Go Low to Get High
The Set Animal

Tarot Card: Queen of Cups

This is the achievement of the higher will over the lower will. When we can subordinate ourself to the will of the Holy Spirit instead of our own desire, our wish may be granted and we advance. This hexagram is represented, in part, by the symbol of the Egyptian *was* scepter, which has the head of the Set animal, the totemic animal of the god Set, the god of chaos, violence, and storms. This scepter is the key of destiny that we receive when the flesh and emotions work together as a unified whole instead of rebelling, contending with each other. Was scepters are symbols of power or dominion over the force of chaos that Set represented. This same concept can be found in Norse mythology and is known as the Svefnthorn. Here we have overcome the beast and domesticated it for our own use instead of being driven by it. This overcoming arrives through submitting to a will higher than our own: not the will of another, but the will of the Holy Spirit. This hexagram is depicted by Archangel Michael subduing Satan, by Kuan Yin riding the dragon, and by Paul Muad'Dib riding the worm in the novel *Dune*.

The story of Cain and Abel relates the need to overcome the will of the self in order to submit to and accept the will of heaven, even though we may fail. Cain receives his destiny at birth, which he fulfills through his inability to control his envy for his brother. He relinquishes the will of something higher and gives in to the forces of hate, which drive him to murder. Abel listens to heaven and quietly makes his offering, minding his own business, but Cain is so distracted by his brother's victory and his loss that he becomes consumed by it. In this hexagram we learn how to build our character during such times so that we can deal with failure and loss without giving in to our lower desires. In Chinese mythology, this is the hexagram of the concubine who is subordinated while her older sister is married and is much like the fight between the brothers Cain and Abel, only told through the feminine version. The lower wife is a concubine who is not given the prestige of her older sister, and she must sit and wait without jealousy or envy until her time arrives. She must be patient and keep her self-esteem even though her sister gets everything and she gets nothing. After her time of waiting, her sister can't bear a child, and so she is elevated to the queen position because she was able to wait and overcome her lower nature. When we can outlast our impulses, we are given the very thing that we feel was stolen from us.

Guru: The Taoists believe we have two parts, the *hun* and the *po*. Within these two are further denominations, but essentially the hun is of heaven and the po is of the earth. They say the po is forever trying to drag you back down into the earth to be swallowed into the grave. The po is your corporeal being, your body, borrowed from the earth, and she forever wants it back. The hun is your spirit, and it comes from heaven. It is the bird who alights on your po tree, and it forever wants to return to heaven. These two parts of ourselves are torn between returning to their sources and staying within ourselves. The only thing that can keep them linked is our will. When our spirit can calm down the beast of our earth enough to ride it in unification, then the true destiny of humanity is achieved. The destiny of the self is one thing to achieve in this lifetime, but the destiny of all of humanity is to unite heaven and earth in an unbreakable union. This line is the make-or-break time when you must resist the pull of your po to drag you down and the lift of your hun to float you away. Hold fast in your golden center and achieve your destiny.

Personal Example: When it is time to let go and trust in the way things are moving forward, I receive hexagram 54. I have a long history of throwing hexagram 19, with line 4 changing and becoming 54, or throwing hexagram 54, with line 4 changing and becoming 19. When I get either of these combinations, I know that I am going to be approaching a new time, or something regarding my life path will be unfolding shortly. Every time these hexagrams appear, it is destiny time, and I am either about to meet a key person or encounter a key situation. This has happened each and every time I've thrown either hexagram with the fourth line changing. The first hexagram I ever drew with the I Ching was 19.4 to 54, and I have gotten it ever since. I also get 54 every time I know that I need to calm myself down and look around instead of getting caught up in things. The message is to surrender while continuing to move forward.

The Changing Lines

Line One—The Self
We are riding our animal nature. But that does not mean that everyone is. Though we may have control over ourselves, we might not have power over what other people choose to do. If you are under the power of someone else through no fault of your own, make sure you don't give your power over to them as a result. It is tempting to lose our gains in the face of those who have none. A strange virus that seems to spread like the flu is the loss of temper. Mind yours even when being subordinated and make a graceful exit.

▶ Transforms into Shadow 40.1

Line Two—The Other
If you are riding on an animal that spooks easily when something unexpected occurs, you could get thrown off it and fall into the mud.

Better to train your beast to not lose its footing. Through initiation ordeals we learn how to confront danger and how to deal with it. If we never have to face fear and pamper ourselves in comfort, like a spoiled child, when a real moment of trial occurs we will throw up our hands and scream to the skies. Just plant your feet on the ground and keep trotting steadily on.

▶ Transforms into Shadow 51.2

Line Three—The Union

Sometimes we need to dominate ourselves. When you get out of hand with yourself, don't look to anyone else to corral you. Take yourself by the reins and wrangle your beast. Give it a good tug down to the earth and grab it by its neck. If your dignity is lost because you can't keep yourself under control, you are the one who is sacrificed. The only true power we have is power over ourselves, and that self-control is what makes an individual great.

▶ Transforms into Shadow 34.3

Line Four—The Earth

I have received this line many times when I have gone off on a wrong path and need to start over toward my destiny. Here we are forcibly placed into a new time or are forced to view things from a different perspective. We cannot choose this situation; it is something that happens directly to us. When fate intervenes on our path toward our destiny, we can feel it and must submit to its will and follow it even if we do not understand. Remove all your preconceptions and trust in the direction you are being taken. Become the fool and liberate yourself from your desires. Look back and see how you have been guided all along to this point in your journey.

▶ Transforms into Shadow 19.4

Line Five—The Conflict

True value does not require validation. When you can sit in full confidence of the value of your labors, you do not need to feel slighted, even if the deity itself will not recognize you. If you feel yourself, know yourself, and understand your true value, you will never be thrown into a rage at the illusion that anyone or anything could take possession of the pearl that is the spark of your soul. When we are in the position of needing to be taken care of and recognized by another, we can be fooled into thinking that person's rejection of us means we have no value, and this can put us in the lowest position our hearts can reach—the feeling of being abandoned. Do not forsake yourself in such times; do not be tricked into thinking you are anything less than divine. Here we learn to overcome abandonment and rejection in favor of self-love.

▶ Transforms into Shadow 58.5

Line Six—Heaven

Vanity is nothing more than a pretty facade that is empty inside. Something that is adorned in all the proper vestments but lacking a heart will burn when placed in the fire. Percy Shelley, the poet who was married to Mary Shelley, author of *Frankenstein,* died an accidental death. They burned his body on a funeral pyre, and the straw dog husk of his body all turned to ash. His heart, however, remained, unscathed by the fires. Lord Byron stole it from the ruins and gave it to Mary, who kept it with her in a handkerchief, discovered only upon her death. His heart received its own casket in the cemetery. When a heart is true and real, even the fires of hell cannot change that. But all that is devoid of spirit is ashes to ashes and dust to dust.

▶ Transforms into Shadow 38.6

All Lines Changing—Hexagram 53

When we find ourselves in unified order, we may progress upon our paths and move forward. Like a chariot running smoothly, this is the location of forward momentum. Here we feel as unstoppable as a juggernaut, so we should put our newly acquired energy and power to good use by focusing on a personal goal. Enjoy the journey, for it too is part of the arrival.

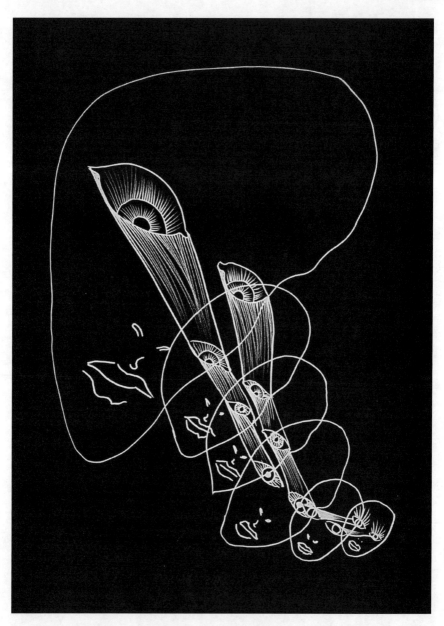

If the doors of perception were cleansed every thing would appear to man as it is, Infinite. For man has closed himself up, till he sees all things thro' narrow chinks of his cavern.

WILLIAM BLAKE,
THE MARRIAGE OF HEAVEN AND HELL

Hexagram 55

The Triumph

Feng

Oracle Script:
Cornucopia

"The Jackpot"
Crowning Achievement
Inner Abundance

Tarot Card: King of Wands

One of the secrets in this hexagram involves the solar eclipse. An eclipse can symbolize a special time when the ego, represented as the sun, disappears, revealing our true selves, represented by the moon covering the sun, also known as the black sun. This is shown through a very esoteric scene in the crucifixion of Christ. In the Aramaic versions of the early texts, it was written as follows:

> *Now from the sixth hour there was darkness over the whole earth, until the ninth hour; and about the ninth hour Jesus cried with a loud voice, saying, Eli, Eli, lamma sabacthani? that is, My God, My God, why hast Thou forsaken Me?*

> MATTHEW 27

According to Luke, this line is specifically referring to an eclipse that occurred at that moment. The occult significance of this important line can not be understated. Here Christ on the cross has been relying on the protection of God, for lack of a better word, or the sun, and when the sun is removed, he finds only himself there. Many feel this line is an abandonment when in fact it could really be an opportunity for Christ to learn to shine on his own will and force rather than that of the Holy Spirit. This is a direct reference to our egos, which obscure our true self as the sun did to Christ, and when our ego is set aside and we are left in the dark, our true self can shine through. This concept doesn't originate with Christianity; it can be traced back to ancient Egypt and Amun-Ra, the Egyptian god of creation combined with the sun god, who is usually depicted with a black sun, which symbolizes the same concept. In ancient China this myth is told through the story of King Wu.

In the day, when the sun is out, our ego too is out, in full array and on display as a peacock desiring nothing but attention and adulation. The ego forms the goggles through which we see ourselves. The ego is like the sun: we see nothing but our own hot gaseous cloud, which we can't see through. Imagine for a moment that you are the planet Earth. You see only blue sky. The sun is out; it is day. From the sun's perspective, the sky is not blue at all. Seeing all that blue during the day is like you seeing your own ocean (emotions) reflected in your goggles. Venus sees the sun entirely differently, and another galaxy would see it differently still. Hexagram 55 is about perspective and the removal of ego from your view.

> *Someone once had said to her that the sky hides the night behind it, shelters the person beneath from the horror that lies above. Unblinking, she fixed the solid emptiness, and the anguish began to move in her. At any moment the rip can occur, the edges fly back, and the giant maw will be revealed.*
>
> PAUL BOWLES, *THE SHELTERING SKY*

This concept can also be applied to our waking versus dreaming lives. Our own spirits hide from our conscious knowledge during the day, but at night they call the shots in our dreams, and we are their prisoners, forced to see whatever it is our soul wants us to see, after our conscious minds have been in charge all day.

The other secret to hexagram 55 is the connection to patriarchal lineage. Fifty-five is the hexagram of the summer solstice and the divine masculine ancestors of old that we all can connect to during this special time. At the summer solstice, honor your ancestors, and while you are at it, extend who you think of as your ancestors all the way back to Fu Xi and beyond. This is an opportunity to expand as large as the sun itself.

Guru: There is a secret in here that was taught to me by my teacher. You can see the stars during the day, if you know how to look with the right eyes.

> *I want to gaze through my telescope at every patch of the night sky and be overwhelmed by the marvel of creation. You can take away my telescope and I will use my bare eyes. Take away my eyes and I will see through my mind, for I cannot unsee the truth.*
>
> RAJESH`, *RANDOM COSMOS*

Personal Example: For clients who are achieving some success, the I Ching often responds with hexagram 55. The success usually arrives based on a personal accomplishment rather than something through a group and is particular to the individual himself. This hexagram has also shown up frequently when something is happening with a client's father. I had one client ask a specific question regarding her father, and the I Ching responded with 55. It seemed to indicate that she needed to cease being dependent on her father for money and break off on her own. The client reported she had still been living at home, and this reading indicated that it was time for her to move out and begin her own independent life.

The Changing Lines

Line One—The Self
We can have the courage to begin something, but seeing it through to the end takes will, endurance, and commitment. Here we see the beginnings of the first inspiration that gets us started on our path, which can be the thing lacking for the majority. If you are unable to find the courage to take the first step, the journey is over. The next thing you need after that is to do it again and again—the next day and the day after that—until the

task in completed. This requires staying power as well as courage. When you can set your will on a grand vision and are able to carry it through due to the force of your character, you do not need to rely on luck or hope. When you know you will not quit until you have achieved your task, nothing can stand in the way of your success. Do not give up!

▸ Transforms into Shadow 62.1

Line Two—The Other

The force needed to reach success is substantial. Many people see only the result of success and assume an angel assisted the successful person in his accomplishments. What many people do not see is the hard work, blood, sweat, and tears that have been needed, from beginning to end, to achieve the goal. Only the sheer force of your inner strength and determination, applied each and every day, will get you through the work. Once you understand this, your abundance shall never fail. Other people will begin to feel your determination and understand your vision. Without you even asking for help, they will join in to assist you. A true force of will acts as a gravitational force to others.

▸ Transforms into Shadow 34.2

Line Three—The Union

The inspiration to accomplish greatness can come from many places. We can watch another accomplish something great. In our watching we can choose which path to take: we can go the low road of Cain and envy the greatness of another, or we can take the higher road and be inspired by the other's act of greatness. These are both roads to take, but there is another road. When we feel inspired by our own acts of greatness, we ourselves become great instead of relying on the visions of others. We see through our own higher eyes and achieve our own goals by acting from within. You will never be fulfilled relying on someone else's greatness; to achieve your own greatness is a true blessing on Earth.

▸ Transforms into Shadow 51.3

Line Four—The Earth

To be propelled to the highest point might require us first to dive down low. Here is the line of the eclipse, of paradox. Until the whole sun is covered, we will not appreciate the light it sheds upon us. When the light is gone, we may feel abandoned and forsaken, but instead we look upon ourselves and realize that we too are shining and full of our own light. Through this eclipse we find our own light and step out of codependence. Do not be afraid to lay yourself down low in the dark. Here you will be forced to find that light. Here you will rise to the point of high noon after the dark night of the soul.

▶ Transforms into Shadow 36.4

Line Five—The Conflict

Trying to lead others to greatness requires trust and assurance that you can achieve the task. This will take more than inspirational statements full of hot air and vanity. You will be required to walk your talk. When you are able to do this for yourself, others will see it also. Talk yourself into something, and then actually do it. This is the line where aspirations are made real through direct action. No one can deny something that has been done. Most people talk about what they are going to do, but when you just go ahead and do it, suddenly, with this one step, the wheat is separated from the chaff. When everything is flaky be *real*.

▶ Transforms into Shadow 49.5

Line Six—Heaven

Nothing can cause doubt to rain down in darkness as quickly as losing your center. Plenty of things in the world can cast a shadow over your face without you doing it to yourself as well. Believe in yourself, come rain or shine. When you believe in yourself, regardless of success or failure, you have won the true golden ring, which is everlasting presence in your heart center that can't be shaded or covered by the darkest passages through hard times. Do not forsake yourself, and you will be saved.

▶ Transforms into Shadow 30.6

All Lines Changing—Hexagram 59

At the end of the great eclipse, our view is swept clear of all blockages. We can finally see clearly through the flood of details and trivia. It has all been moved aside, as if some mighty hand came through and snatched everything up, leaving only the real to remain. When we are flooded by ourselves and our true nature, this is a blessing, and we must be vigilant in such times so that we may come to know who we are when isolated from everything else.

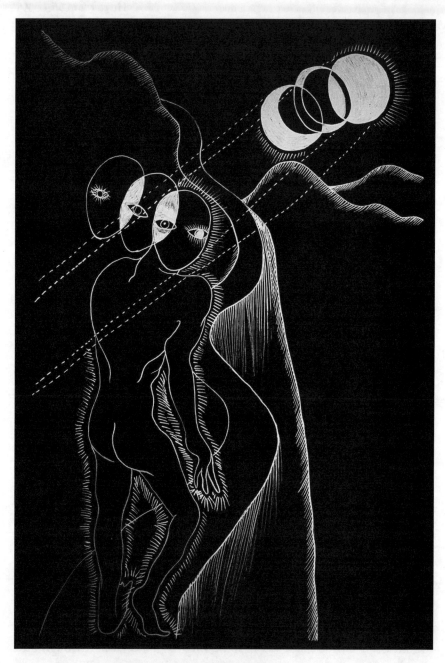

All that is gold does not glitter,
Not all those who wander are lost;
The old that is strong does not wither,
Deep roots are not reached by the frost.

J. R. R. TOLKIEN,
THE FELLOWSHIP OF THE RING

Hexagram 56
The Traveler
Lu

Oracle Script:
Soldiers Marching

"Traverse the Desert"
Stranger in a Strange Land
Coming Forth by Day

Tarot Card: Three of Wands

There are many tales in the ancient traditions of the wanderers. Often there are those who become outcasts and are turned away from their family and community, sent to wander in the wilderness. The banishment away from humanity is a primal fear buried deep within our need to survive. Interestingly enough, many of the sages and saints willingly choose this, seeking to leave society entirely. The one who can willingly go off in a solitary fashion to brave the wilderness becomes master of this fear of exile. Monastic traditions of China and Catholicism find the saints spending at least three years alone in the mountains, often confined within a cave, secluded from human contact. When the journey is involuntary though, we must then use the powers of hexagram 54 to subdue our fears and make the best of it.

This is the story of the Wandering Jew and of Moses, who leads his people through the desert to the promised land. It is also told through the tale of Cain, who is punished by being sent to the wilderness to wander for the rest of his days. Jesus too makes his journey into the desert, away from all the others, where he encounters the mind poison of Hercules, mentioned in hexagram 34, in the form of Satan the adversary. When we are alone we must face and confront our minds. The wanderer brings us into close contact with this aspect of the human sentience, and when our mind wanders in its thoughts, we are in this same desert, face-to-face with the deceiver.

The word *planet* means "wanderer," and many say the stars are wanderers in the heavens. As we wander upon Earth, we are recapitulating and mimicking the planets and stars, traversing the empty space of the heavens. As your feet make their passage and you orbit in your journey, do not forget to stop and look up to see how the stars are your fellow travelers.

The Road and the End

I shall foot it
Down the roadway in the dusk,
Where shapes of hunger wander
And the fugitives of pain go by.

I shall foot it
In the silence of the morning,
See the night slur into dawn,
Hear the slow great winds arise
Where tall trees flank the way
And shoulder toward the sky.

The broken boulders by the road
Shall not commemorate my ruin.
Regret shall be the gravel under foot.
I shall watch for
Slim birds swift of wing
That go where wind and ranks of thunder
Drive the wild processionals of rain.

The dust of the travelled road
Shall touch my hands and face.

CARL SANDBURG

Guru: In dreams too we traverse these forsaken lands, just as in our waking states. The realms that the mind wanders to are many, and some people have even made maps of them. Kelly Bulkeley, a psychology and religion scholar who studies dreams around the globe, notes that a dream is "not an event arising from within the dreamer or an activity performed by an individual; rather, it had an objective existence outside the will of the passive dreamer."[1] Some view dreaming more like visiting a place that exists somewhere. Tibet, for example, calls this place the bardo. Dreaming can be thought of as a voyage to the spirit world after you fall asleep. You are interacting with something outside your own consciousness. Rather than the dream being a construct of your mind, it is an alternate plane of existence; as Bulkeley states, a "unique plane of reality between the world of the living and the netherworld."[2] This is exactly how I feel when I am dreaming, like I am a stranger in a strange land. In dreams I visit some separate place that affords me information I can't access at other times. Sometimes when I wake up, I feel as though I have returned from a harrowing journey.

Personal Example: I get hexagram 56 when my mind is wandering. If my mind has been overtaken by deception, in that I am making up stories in my head in some wild fantasy, the I Ching gives me 56. Often 56 indicates that we are filled with illusion: we have deviated from reality and made up things in the mind to justify our protective and primal responses. The antidote to this situation, as I have been instructed by the I Ching, is hexagram 52: stay still. We need to ground and still the mind. For clients, this hexagram often arrives when they are about to go on a trip or journey.

The Changing Lines

Line One—The Self
We can easily become habituated to others when we see them every day. We take for granted that we know them and they know us. When

we set out on a journey, we encounter total strangers. They do not know us and have no knowledge of what we have accomplished. They see us with new eyes, and we learn to see others with new eyes, for we have never seen them before. A good way to remove the dreary lens of assumptions is to be forced to really know another at first glance. There is much to be learned from first impressions; it is here that we respond, without prejudice, from our gut and sense who and what someone is. Do not forget that others will do the same to you. Learn about yourself from the first impressions others get from you. This is the power of meeting another.

▸ Transforms into Shadow 30.6

Line Two—The Other

Some become homesick when they leave their creature comforts; being away from what is familiar drains them of their vitality. They need to be surrounded with things that make them feel like they know who they are and what they represent. A true traveler cares nothing for these things for they carry a sense of who they are within themselves. Carrying yourself as a swaddling infant enables you to cross great distances without needing comfort, for it is there within your arms. Like carrying a suitcase, we have ourselves always at hand, and any environment we can find ourselves in will be satisfactory. There is nothing to miss when all the universe is contained within you.

▸ Transforms into Shadow 50.2

Line Three—The Union

The phoenix is able to abandon and burn everything it was before to become something new. This sounds very romantic and inspirational, but when faced with the same task, most of us will cling to our security blankets. What is it that you are clinging to? To rise into the new day, you have to leave your baggage down by the riverside, but you might find, as you cross the stream, that new provisions will be waiting for you. They may not be what you were used to, but you will find that they provide for all your needs. Challenge what you think your outside environment is telling you about yourself.

▸ Transforms into Shadow 35.3

Line Four—The Earth

When we leave behind our material possessions and set out for unknown places, we focus on what we truly possess within our flesh. We stop focusing on our stuff and feel ourselves alive and living: this is the gift of the journey. The tarot card of The Fool shows someone who is free of cares and owns few things. This may seem foolish—or is it closer to the truth? Whatever your cold dead hands can grasp is what is yours. Realize this while living, and you will be freed from the grasp of material existence.

▶ Transforms into Shadow 52.4

Line Five—The Conflict

When the true you shines through every bone in your body, you don't need fancy clothing to convince others of your worth and value. Perfect strangers will see, feel, and know you from the first time they lay eyes upon you. Putting on a big show to win favor is one thing, but truly *being* your true self at all times ensures that others see and hear you loud and clear When you become this kind of beacon, you are like a traveling lighthouse that can penetrate the densest fog. Everyone can see you coming from a mile away, and they will know just who you are.

▶ Transforms into Shadow 33.5

Line Six—Heaven

The burning of the nest is when we have ruined our home. A bird can't fly forever and needs somewhere to land at the end of the day. If we damage our home we are in trouble and will have to stay adrift. Our physical body can be called our home in which we live, and we must care for that also. We must care for the places where we reside and tend to the people and nature there. When you totally disregard your host, who has been gracious to you, you may burn your bridge to this relationship. Here your ego has jumped the shark. As a stranger in a strange land, treat others with respect, especially those who take you in and care for you along the road. When you treat everyone respectfully, you will be cared for everywhere. When you disregard the rules of the road and get cocky and judgmental of those who show you kindness, chances are you will be run out of town. Earth is smaller than you think; preserve your relations by showing appreciation.

▶ Transforms into Shadow 62.6

All Lines Changing—Hexagram 60

When we wander too far, it is time to return home. We come to hexagram 60, which suggests we need some limits to our mind travel for we have overshot the mark. Don't let your mind wander too much or you will become lost. When we are lost in the wilderness, we need to mark off territories on a map. The power of 60 is finding boundaries that keep us from danger; there could be quicksand out there.

Hexagram 57
The Wind
Xun

Oracle Script:
The Seal of Fate

"Mark of Cain"
True Character
Inner Essence

Tarot Card: Knight of Pentacles

The secret of hexagram 57 is contained in a portion of the Cain and Abel story regarding the mark of Cain. Many think the number 666, the mark of the beast, was put on Cain's forehead to punish him. However, if we delve back through time, history, and etymology, we discover that the mark itself was not placed on Cain to show that he was a sinner and guilty of murder, as many have come to interpret it, like a scarlet letter of sorts, but rather it is a sign or omen not to kill or punish him for his sin. The mistake Cain makes is punishing Abel for offering animals in sacrifice. Cain thought his brother erred in offering the blood of a living thing, which was against God's covenant, and so he decided he would take it upon himself to punish his brother for God. Because the animal died, Cain believed Abel must die—an eye

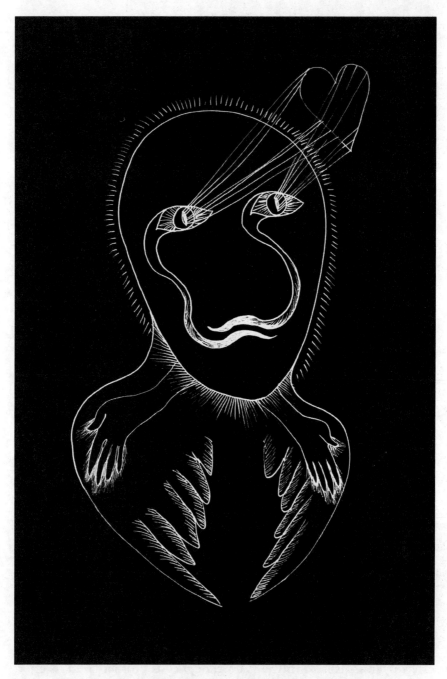

Ethos anthropoi daimon—*a man's character is his fate.*

for an eye. But no one has the right to punish anyone with death. The mark was placed on Cain to remind people not to seek this kind of justice or negative reciprocity against each other—and not to do to Cain what he did to his brother.

The mark itself on Cain is fascinating. The Hebrew word for a mark or sign is *oth* and actually harkens to an omen in the sky or literally something projected from a light source like the Batman symbol projected onto the sky. This may seem odd, but there are references to these sky projections in other places in the Hebrew myths, such as a sapphire cube held by Moses that could shine such projections into the sky to communicate across great distances.

In the Chinese myths, this hexagram represents a seal of fate; the seal itself is a mark upon the person, or specifically an unmistakable impression left by the hand of God, sealing his or her fate, which is visible to those whose eyes can see. Many interpret the name of this hexagram as *penetrating,* but I would say it's more like an impression of your character, like a brand on an ox. When Abel was born, Eve supposedly named him Havel because he was empty or "made in vain" because he was born to die. That was the fate that was sealed upon him.

Guru: Hexagram 57 can often be the mark of providence or fate and higher forces. We can recognize when we have encountered a state or mark of fate or providence by the extent and intensity of synchronistic events. The difference between these types of synchronicities and your everyday run-of-the-mill ones is subtle but specific. We may hear or see the same word all day: for example, we hear the word *Paris* repeated over and over. This is not a mark of fate or providence; this is only a synchronicity or coincidence. The mark of providence is more like a story told over the course of several days with power clusters of repetition and often shared with other people. This is more like if we hear the word *Paris* repeated and then we end up going to Paris due to outside circumstance—it manifests in the world, thus providing more of a prophecy or omen rather than a synchronicity. These events are profound and undeniable. For myself they reveal a teaching or mystery as they unfold bit by bit. For example, I drew the Ace of Pentacles tarot card, then later randomly my tarot book by Alejandro Jodorowsky opened to that page, which contained the story of the lotus in the mud.

Later that day someone on social media posted a poem about the lotus in the mud, and the next day a friend sent me an article describing the Buddhist symbolism of the lotus in the mud. This was a destiny lesson from providence and is a classic activity of hexagram 57.

Personal Example: A client's ex-friend was smearing her character, gossiping about her to all her other friends. She asked the question, "Is this going to damage me?" The I Ching responded with hexagram 57. It seemed from this response that not only would the gossip not be harmful to her, but it would also actually be a boon, somehow, fatefully returning a providential gift. In fact, someone heard the rumors being spread, but instead of finding them distasteful, he solicited her for a job as a result.

> *There is only one thing in the world worse than being talked about, and that is not being talked about.*
>
> OSCAR WILDE,
> *THE PICTURE OF DORIAN GRAY*

The Changing Lines

Line One—The Self

Who you are is who you are. You can build upon the foundation of your essence through your choices. It may be true that we have innate qualities that will remain with us as our constant companions throughout our lifetime, but this does not mean that we do not have the power to change. Those who can see their character and see it clearly and then make a choice to change so as to grow into something they desire have taken control of their destiny. This is the line of the repentant soul who becomes a carpenter, carving into himself on the deepest level to reveal the best parts of himself rather than succumbing to fate and allowing himself to be carried in whatever direction the wind is blowing. Restrain yourself to grow.

▶ Transforms into Shadow 9.6

Line Two—The Other

Your true self has true power. Come to know and accept yourself. Don't leave out any of your flaws and inconsistencies, otherwise you will place a facade or mask upon yourself for your own eyes. Everyone else can see through it, so why bother? Become transparent with yourself and in this way see your own beauty. When we accept ourselves, we come into trusting ourselves, and when we trust ourselves, we permit ourselves to act freely rather than under the judgment and scrutiny of ourselves. You can liberate your character through love and acceptance, empowering yourself to act, and through these actions learn not only what it means to be you but also what it means to be human. That's progress.

▶ Transforms into Shadow 53.2

Line Three—The Union

We can build and strengthen our character into something solid through deciding what we do every day. Each decision builds the will, which is what gives us power. Will affords power through the ability to act. When we vacillate and are indecisive, we remove our ability to act upon something because we become buried in the what-ifs and the weighing of outcomes. Although some contemplation is wise in every choice we make and it is foolish to be hasty, make sure you do not rob yourself of strength of character and turn yourself into a wet noodle by continually flip-flopping. The power to rise through action comes when we *decide,* so lift your sword of discernment and make a choice. Do not dillydally or you will crack your character.

▶ Transforms into Shadow 59.3

Line Four—The Earth

Every character has a dark side. This is the line of the Set animal that belongs to each of us, but that is also the animal of all our ancestors and humanity itself. If we do not come face-to-face with this shadowy creature, our character will seek to protect itself from its imperfections and project it onto others. Here we must take responsibility. If we are to truly become ourselves, we must be our whole self, not just the parts we like. Accept all your failures and flaws and see them head on so that your Set animal appears in front of your face; otherwise, it may stab someone else in the back. Resist temptation to blame another and accept responsibility for yourself. This is the path to liberation.

▶ Transforms into Shadow 44.4

Line Five—The Conflict

Flaws are inherent in our makeup as humans. This is the line of original sin, an unpopular concept and widely misunderstood. Humanity has an inherent capacity to fall into error and make mistakes. That is just how it is. Do not remove yourself from this part of humanity. You will make mistakes, over and over; you can trust deeply in that. To build your character, you must overcome your own mistakes, and then reparations must be made to both the ancestors and future progeny. Beyond individual repentance is the bigger task of humanity of counterbalancing the forces of death and the po, or Earth, which both seek to undermine our ability to rise each day. Some things that are human you can't overcome, such as eating and going to the bathroom. But other things, like hatred and envy, can be overcome. Learn to recognize what you have power over and what you do not have power over and become a true human who can evolve and grow.

▸ Transforms into Shadow 18.5

Line Six—Heaven

Do not scrutinize yourself too much. It is great and good to be self-reflective, to repent and change and mold our character. But after a while, if this is all we do, we become a self-concerned worrywart and lose our capacity for action. Try living freely for a while, and let go of your judgments on yourself and others. You will experience a fuller life, and your character will flourish. Otherwise, you are putting yourself in a cage of expectations, judgments, and concerns. Trust that you can do things without needing a monitor or babysitter, including your own mind. Let yourself loose to roam around.

▸ Transforms into Shadow 48.6

All Lines Changing—Hexagram 51

When we have fully developed and expressed our character and our essence is under our control, we can still be faced with the powers of fate. You can row your own boat, but then there is the river. The river will do as it pleases regardless of your character. Your story arises in how your character deals with the stormy river, as you merrily row down the stream.

Hexagram 58

The Joy

Kun

Oracle Script:
Expression

"Invoke"
In the Beginning Was the Word
The Oracle

Tarot Card: Eight of Wands

Many scholars and religious figures make statements to the effect that the Holy Spirit or some form of overarching consciousness penetrates the whole of reality. Rarely are we able to realize that this also means ourselves, our very flesh. To truly understand the implications of a permeating sentience defies our cultural views of separation from deity and places spiritual things forever somewhere out of our grasp and outside our bodies. In hexagram 58, we are able to connect to and locate this spirit in our flesh and feel its presence within us in such a way that we are able to express it to others directly. This expression predominately takes the form of an ecstatic state. Many artists call this channeling the muse. Shamans call it possession by a spirit. The Pentecostals call it taking in the Holy Ghost. Call it what you

If the divine is everywhere, as the Tantric adepts affirm, it must also be present in and as the body.

GEORG FEUERSTEIN,
TANTRA: THE PATH OF ECSTASY

will, human beings throughout history have identified a phenomenon in which we experience a state that transcends our smaller identities. One need only hear a diva sing to feel the truth of this statement. In the image of the hexagram, the head of a person grows extra large as it is filled with spirit, and sound erupts out of the person's mouth. This is the state of the oracles and the pythias, the sibyls of Greece and the true priests and priestesses who can speak the word of spirit. It is the prophet and the poet who, after achieving this state, can speak fluidly and lucidly about the beauty of the world. What precious moments those are when we can participate, as either speaker or listener, to such fantastic and joyful moments of connection between human and something greater—whatever you may think that is.

> *Knowingly or unknowingly, consciously or unconsciously, in whatever state we utter His name, we acquire the merit of such utterance. A man who voluntarily goes into a river and bathes therein gets the benefit of the bath; so does likewise he who has been pushed into the river by another, or who while sleeping soundly has water thrown upon him by another.*
>
> RAMAKRISHNA

Guru: This hexagram is the secret to obtaining a state of ecstasy through channeling the spirit through the mouth and through words. This can be done through singing, speaking, shouting, or invocation. All nations have oral traditions of speaking with and for spirits of all kinds, including the Holy Spirit itself. That this capacity to channel spirits can be found in all cultures, including modern ones, must not be ignored and rather investigated as a uniquely human faculty. Though skeptics will offer their theories that these are only fakirs, ventriloquists, or spinners of yarns, we must pay close attention to those who embody such a state, relying not so much on whether they are telling some kind of truth but more on observing and feeling the shift within their beings that occurs during such times. It is the feeling of these shifts and the energy it releases that are the key to ecstasy, not the literal meaning of the words that are spoken. Would you say that a beautiful horse running through a field is telling the truth? Or would you enjoy its state of being in beauty and joy?

Personal Example: A client came in and asked the simple question, "What is my destiny profession?" The response was hexagram 58, which shows a figure with the head thrown back, speaking words in front of a crowd of people. The client looked shocked and admitted that he was, in fact, a professional singer and was questioning whether he was meant to be doing this work. The I Ching seemed to agree that this was the correct choice for him, and he felt a renewed commitment as a result of the response. I have received this hexagram many times for singers, speakers, authors, and teachers. This hexagram also comes up when we need to speak our truth and communicate with others in an entirely open fashion.

The Changing Lines

Line One—The Self
When you can make your own joy in everything that you do, you will never lack it. Those who have a pocket inside them that is filled with sunshine independent of exterior circumstances stay dry even when it is raining.
> ▸ Transforms into Shadow 47.1

Line Two—The Other
Joy and pleasure do not need to be separated from each other, but when they are, we need to take a closer look at the types of pleasure we are engaging in and especially the amount. Perhaps a simple solution to the problem of no longer finding joy in our pleasure is a matter of excess.
> ▸ Transforms into Shadow 17.2

Line Three—The Union
It is true that other people can bring great joy to us. But when we are accustomed to receiving joy only from the other, we find that when they leave, our joy leaves also, and we feel empty. So we learn that it is okay and wonderful and beautiful to share joy with one another, but we must also never lose the ability to make it in ourselves.
> ▸ Transforms into Shadow 43.3

Line Four—The Earth
Hmmm, which joy shall we choose in this garden of earthly delights? What, for us, is our heart and soul of joy? This is a special journey all souls must take to find the true source of their own personal joy in the garden, for if we attempt to go by what another claims will be our joy and satisfaction, we will find ourselves lost.
  ▸ Transforms into Shadow 60.4

Line Five—The Conflict
Many pleasures can lead you straight into illusion. The old saying "if it feels good do it" has a time limit on it, that's for sure. When indulging in pleasure turns to fascination and fantasy, our connection to reality can be severed, and we float far far away. Intoxicants that bring pleasure can also bring destruction.
  ▸ Transforms into Shadow 54.5

Line Six—Heaven
Here the indulgence of pleasure has reached the point of no return, and unless we can adjust and balance out, we may have consequences to face. Go back to simple pleasures that are earned and delayed instead of giving in to so much instant gratification. Growing food by the labors of your hands can give more satisfaction than ten sundaes someone else buys for you.
  ▸ Transforms into Shadow 10.6

All Lines Changing—Hexagram 52
Hexagram 58 is a total expression of what is inside to the outer environment. When this comes to its conclusion, we swing in the other direction: it's time for withholding or keeping things in. When 58 changes to 52, we must keep our voice silent and go into introspection and introversion after a time of extroversion; we must first decide how we truly feel and then carefully measure our expression. Sometimes not everything needs to be said, and some inner processing must be done to hone our words rather than give in to compulsive explosive speech.

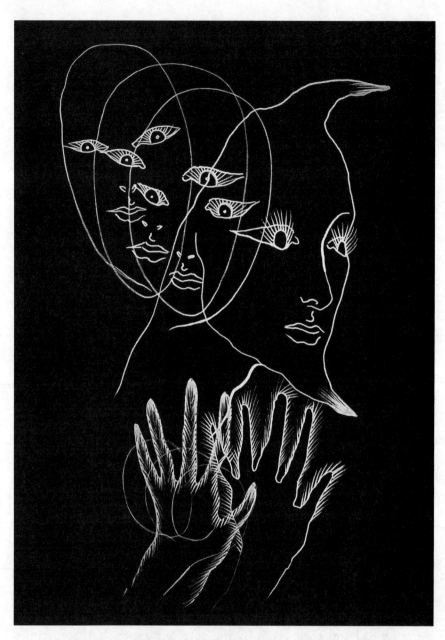

In the six hundredth year of Noah's life, on the seventeenth day of the second month, all the fountains of the great deep burst forth, and the floodgates of the heavens were opened. And the rain fell upon the earth forty days and forty nights.

GENESIS 7:11

Hexagram 59
The Flood
Huan

Oracle Script:
Dispersion

"Blood Sacrifice"
The Way Life Scatters
Sweep the Hearth

Tarot Card: Five of Cups

Things became overfull in hexagram 58, as our heads were filled with spirit, and now the energies must scatter and dissipate. In hexagram 39, we see the myth of Da Yu, who helps repair the world after the flood and embodies the archetype of Noah. Here it is the flood itself that comes in to clear out everything in a huge purgation. When we arrive at hexagram 59, chances are things will be swept away. In ancient Egypt, the time of the floods came during the dog days and the rising of Sirius, the brightest star in the sky. We see this to be true in modern times as well. I began tracking recent floods in Texas, Thailand, and really everywhere, and nearly all of them corresponded with the dog days of summer and Sirius; you can set your watch to it. During the dog days the river full of crocodiles floods, evil rises, and plagues spread.

Swarms of locusts come like manticores to devour the hearts of humanity. This is the influence of Sirius the Dog Star.

This is the hexagram of the deluge, of the waters of the subconscious and the emotions bursting forth to be dealt with. It deals with the energies of scattering and dispersing blockages. If something was dammed up, it will now be freed and rush forward in a torrent, of that you can be sure. If there was some part of ourselves that was hidden below the surface, it now rises for us and comes into full view. Carl Jung had this to say about his experience with the deluge:

> When I had the vision of the flood in October of the year 1913, it happened at a time that was significant for me as a man. At that time, in the fortieth year of my life, I had achieved everything that I had wished for myself. I had achieved honor, power, wealth, knowledge, and every human happiness. Then my desire for the increase of these trappings ceased, the desire ebbed from me and horror came over me. The vision of the flood seized me and I felt the spirit of the depths, but I did not understand him. Yet he drove me on with unbearable inner longing and I said:
>
>> My soul you—are you there? I have returned, I am here again. I have shaken the dust of all the lands from my feet, and I have come to you, I am with you. After long years of long wandering, I have come to you again. Should I tell you everything I have seen, experienced, and drunk in? Or do you not want to hear about all the noise of life and the world? But one thing you must know: the one thing I have learned is that one must live this life. This life is the way, the long sought-after way to the unfathomnable, which we call divine.[1]

The flood purifies even though it is destructive. It is like the rain that cleans everything it falls upon. Water cleanses and baptizes. In Christianity, the first baptism is performed by John the Baptist, who immerses Jesus in the river.

Mayim ("water" in Hebrew) is the flood that will drown your spiritual embryo if you heed the body's questions, destroying all that you've worked so hard to assemble within. The flood comes as a ruthless force that can destroy everything. Those desires that couldn't endure the questions, meaning those that didn't "come into the ark," truly perish in its waters: "And all flesh perished that moved upon the earth." And yet, the paradox is that for all its ruthlessness, the flood also purifies. However, it purifies only those in whom the desires to attain the spiritual world prevail. It is as if man doesn't even hear the rational questions of his body as he advances toward the goal, no matter what. In this case he acts like Noah, building himself an ark (finding the right books, the right teacher, and the right environment). He will also take shelter there with his numerous individual desires that are yet to be corrected (but will be corrected as the ark "sails" the flood waters).

SEMION VINOKUR, *THE SECRETS OF THE
ETERNAL BOOK: THE MEANING OF THE STORIES
OF THE PENTATEUCH*

Guru: Learn to navigate deep waters. Go there on purpose. Learn to dive into your emotions and your darkest places. If we train ourselves to navigate these waters, when the flood rises around us, we will be able to swim. Those taken by the floods, tossed to and fro, did not take their swimming lessons. The ones who pay no mind to their dreams, to the callings of their hearts, these are the ones who are ruined in such times. But the ones who have learned the waters, the ones who enter the waters, they will be the Noahs who survive the floods.

Personal Example: I received a rather frantic text from a client asking for assistance. She said there was severe flooding in Kauai, where she was living, and she didn't know what to do. The response she got was hexagram 59 changing into 39. Hexagram 59 told her that she was in a deluge that had swept many things away from her and caused a lot of damage; but the damage had mostly happened to others and she had escaped unscathed. Hexagram 39 gave her instructions for how to proceed with repairs.

The Changing Lines

Line One—The Self

When we have people whom we love and alliances, we have assistance and somewhere to go when a natural disaster or flood occurs. It is during such times that we realize a friend in need is a friend indeed, especially when the need is ours. Opening our hearts to others who have been annihilated by huge forces outside their control is one of the fundamental levels of humanity. Don't forget to count your blessings, but sometimes give aid to those who have not been so lucky and may be drowning.

▶ Transforms into Shadow 61.1

Line Two—The Other

Keeping a wide view, we are able to portend future possibilities. Taking a few simple precautions, such as having an emergency pack prepared ahead of time, can make a terrible situation survivable. Sometimes only a few extra things, such as water, a knife, and a blanket, can make a big difference. Plan ahead for possibilities, while not being driven by fear and paranoia, to meet the future with the highest possibility for success. If we know we are entering a tornado zone, we can keep an eye out for trouble. Noah had fair warning and chose to build the ark, while everyone else ignored him.

▶ Transforms into Shadow 20.2

Line Three—The Union

Sometimes we experience things in the course of a simple ordinary day that seem as epic as a deluge. A mistake made at work can bring on a torrent of fear so overwhelming it's as if we've been stranded on a desert island. If we are placed at the mercy of another and things have gone beyond our control, the one thing we can do is to not allow our minds to be flooded with panic, with primordial fears. Handle the situation without sinking any ships, especially your own. Be prepared to let your ego float away, and be open to making changes.

▶ Transforms into Shadow 57.3

Line Four—The Earth

One of my favorite Edith Piaf songs is "Le Foule." She sings about dancing in a group. Someone is swept toward her by the crowd, and she falls in love with him. But then they are separated by the sea of bodies. People, relationships, and communities can ebb and flow in our lives, and sometimes a flood comes and clears them all away. Do not worry; there is always someone else with whom to dance.

▸ Transforms into Shadow 6.4

Line Five—The Conflict

The things we cling to in times of disaster can say quite a bit about the foundations of our lives. A pillar of faith can give us stability when everything else has ruptured. Pay special attention to what you run to when everything turns into chaos because this is deeply tied to you and is the true essence of who you are, for it is the thing in which you are placing the deepest trust, and these are things that deserve our accolades.

▸ Transforms into Shadow 4.5

Line Six—Heaven

When things are drifting apart with others and the floodwaters of emotion rise, we can let the waters take us where they may, or we can shoot cannons at the hull of someone else's beached ship. Try not to be excessive if things are already dissolving and scattering to the wind. You can let nature take its course instead of trying to make a big huff and puff about it, or you can push things further apart. You never know; they might flow back together again someday, and you may regret some silly things that you said.

▸ Transforms into Shadow 29.6

All Lines Changing—Hexagram 55

In times of tragedy we can show who we really are. When the going gets tough, the tough get going, and we never have a better time to shine than when the chips are down. Some of us show up for greatness and can turn a disaster into a growth experience that becomes a future source of productivity, while others run for the hills. Both choices are acceptable, but should you find yourself in such a predicament, make sure you can live with your choices by thinking through a plan for such things ahead of time.

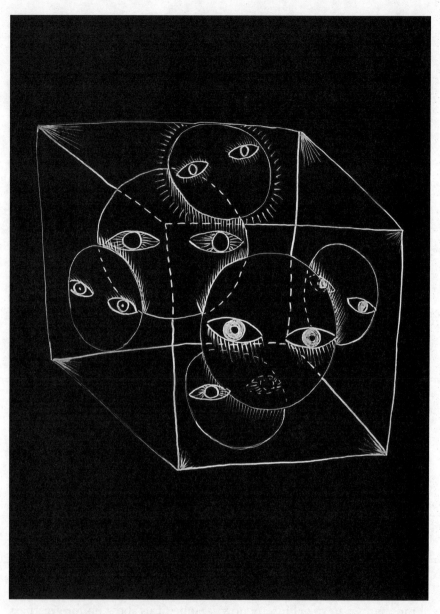

Without words, without writing and without books there would be no history, there could be no concept of humanity.

HERMANN HESSE,
"THE MAGIC OF THE BOOK"

Hexagram 60
The Rules
Yi

Oracle Script:
To Measure

"The Month"
Restrictions and Limitations
Months and Measures

Tarot Card: King of Swords

In hexagram 60 we find units of measure and a story of the origins of writing. This is the hexagram of the author and the scribe. We see things broken down into chapters and units. It can also be used to describe laws, months, math, and segments. It is how a thing is quantified and counted, organized into sections, such as a beginning, middle, and end. From the measure we get the menses, the monthly periodicity of repetition and cycles of the planets, which can be placed into measurable frequencies. The first writings that were recorded tended to be either divination or laws: Fu Xi writing the I Ching with the knowledge from the unicorn, Moses recording the Torah from the angels, and the Emerald Tablet of Hermes are all examples of hexagram 60. We obtain a high level of intelligence, indeed, when we are able to use our

381

minds to communicate such higher thoughts as these and confer them unto others.

For me this hexagram was traced back to the angel Metatron, whose job it was to keep track and tell stories, recount and create language to retell what had happened before the current time, which was only a repetition of something that had come before, the same yet new and unique, but only slightly. It was odd because when I had the insight that hexagram 60 was Metatron, as I was reading about more of this angel's history, I discovered that he had been punished with sixty strokes of fiery rods, according to the Talmud, and the number struck me as synchronistic. Here we hit our limit, the boundary and the spot where we must make delineations between this and that. One could say this hexagram represents science, due to its affiliation with making distinctions and being discerning, of separating, quantifying, measuring things. It is also the hexagram of Thoth the scribe, who records and measures all words.

> As representative of the Reason immanent in the world, Thoth is the mediator through whom the world is brought into manifestation. He is the Tongue of Rā, the Herald of the Will of Rā, and the Lord of Sacred Speech. What emanates from the opening of his mouth, that cometh to pass; he speaks, and it is his command; he is the Source of Speech, the Vehicle of Knowledge, the Revealer of the Hidden. Thoth is thus the God of writing and all the arts and sciences. On a monument of Seti I, he is called "Scribe of the nine Gods." He writes "the truth of the nine Gods," and is called "Scribe of the King of Gods and men." Hence he is naturally inventor of the hieroglyphics, and patron and protector of all temple-archives and libraries, and of all scribes. At the entrance of one of the halls of the Memnonium at Thebes, the famous "Library of Osymandias," called "The great House of Life," we find Thoth as "Lord in the Hall of Books." In the Ebers papyrus we read: "His guide is Thoth, who bestows on him the gifts of his speech, who makes the books, and illumines those who are learned therein, and the physicians who follow him, that they may work cures.
>
> G. R. S. MEAD, *THRICE-GREATEST HERMES*

Guru: Here we find our limits of what can and cannot be done. Your material existence is the hard limit you will crash into when exploring the realms of mind and spirit. Physical laws can limit and contain or even clash with our ideas about the world. What you thought may not match what is. The gift of hexagram 60 is to discover through boundaries and limitations what can be done and what cannot be done but to also always push what we are doing to the edge of possibility. Sometimes humans make illusory boundaries that crumble in the face of natural and universal laws, which are perhaps the only real truth we have.

Personal Example: I have received this hexagram many times for authors who were writing a book. Typically a client would ask me about his profession and get hexagram 60 if he was writing something. Recently a client asked about her screen writing career and received hexagram 60 with no lines changing, which seemed to suggest that she should stick with that career, but it also seemed to council her to discipline her writing by making a schedule so that she wrote in an orderly fashion. She purchased a large calendar and marked out a schedule to force herself to write.

The Changing Lines

Line One—The Self
Here we must bind ourselves and stay home. When you are not sure what to do, avoid acting compulsively; give yourself some rules and limitations and get yourself together before you head out. Through self-discipline we can avoid many mishaps. If we can give ourselves rules rather than trying to control others, we give ourselves control over our destinies. Putting too many rules onto others ensures that we are never responsible for our own actions.

▶ Transforms into Shadow 29.1

Line Two—The Other
Now it's time to come out of restrictions and loosen your boundaries with one another. Give a little free rein, and let some of the rules drop to create space for something unexpected and spontaneous. If you can trust that the other may have his own rules that suit him just as well as

something you might place upon him, you might discover that he made a better choice than the one you could have imagined.

▶ Transforms into Shadow 3.2

Line Three—The Union

If rules are restricting you, it is important to mind them and not simply rebel against them. Sometimes rules and regulations have wisdom and purpose behind them. If we can learn to see the larger picture and the origins of these rules, we avoid mistakes we would have made by not heeding the rules that others have created through their own hard lessons. It is sometimes better to learn through someone else's mistakes rather than our own so that we do not waste the wisdom that has come before us. Your parents learned the hard way, but that doesn't mean you have to if you learn from their rules.

▶ Transforms into Shadow 5.3

Line Four—The Earth

If you have come through a period of no rules or discipline, you might need to be strict for a while to get back to center. We learn the teachings of excess and the value of rules by falling prey to the consequences of living without limits. Anything that must be done over time and through space will have natural limits, regardless of whether we like it. If we learn to live within these limits, we find ourselves in less danger from the extravagance of excesses, while still able to have perfectly reasonable pleasure without taking things too far. Rules can benefit everyone when not too tight and not too loose but instead somewhere in between.

▶ Transforms into Shadow 58.4

Line Five—The Conflict

The manner in which we establish rules and restrictions is crucial, distinguishing them from punishments. Everyone needs to be in agreement to avoid feeling like they are imprisoned by the restrictions. The stream will flow much better with irrigation routes rather than dams. We don't have to be cruel when we deliver the rules, and if we present them in a pleasant fashion, people are more likely to follow them. When we are demanding, with harsh boundaries, we may find ourselves in the midst of a rebellion.

▶ Transforms into Shadow 19.5

Line Six—Heaven

Boundaries are needed; there is no doubt about that. But when the bonds are too severe and restrictive, there will be a rebellion due to needs. When we are imprisoned too severely, we lose our compassion and respect for one another; extreme oppression can justify extreme reactions. If you restrict anything too severely, expect it to bite you. This is the line of Fenrir the wolf, who was starved and bound so tightly that when someone came with compassion to feed the wolf, Fenrir bit off his hand.

▶ Transforms into Shadow 61.6

All Lines Changing—Hexagram 56

After we have gone through a period of excessive restrictions, we may long to be free. Our inner self rebels and longs to travel outside the boundaries, so we become a traveler for a while. When bonds are excessive and we are fenced in, we can rebalance through travel; we can expand under new expansive skies. Travel makes us grow and can release us from the tight enclosure that has penned us in. Give yourself some wiggle room if your boundaries have been too tight.

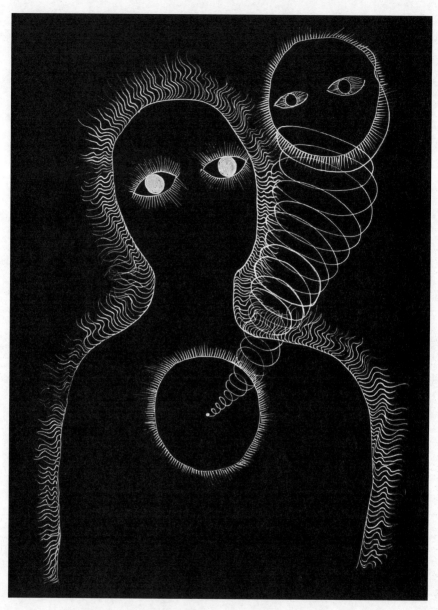

O Holy Spirit, descend plentifully into my heart. Enlighten the dark corners of this neglected dwelling and scatter there Thy cheerful beams.

Saint Augustine

Hexagram 61
The Heart
Kun

Oracle Script:
Heart Center

"Gamma"
Bull's-Eye
Inner Compass

Tarot Card: King of Cups

There is a secret in the universe that shows up where life force flows. The good news is that we don't need to find it in some lost land or remote valley or obscure teacher because it lives in the center of our hearts. At the center of most galaxies is a black hole. Most think of a black hole as an empty, terrifying thing devoid of all life. However, scientists have discovered that black holes form all the particles of matter. The very center of a black hole emits the most powerful energy in the universe that we have ever measured, called gamma rays. It shoots out of the middle of the darkest parts of the universe to create everything in the universe. As a microcosmic reflection of this universal mystery, our own hearts emit an electromagnetic, measurable force, which creates life in us with every passing moment. Our heart center continuously pulses, from our embryonic beginnings to the moment of death. With this energy emitting from our heart center, we are alive; without it we are dead. The pulse that is our gamma energy is our source of creative vitality, and like magnetic north pulling on a compass, it can direct and guide us through our lives if we tune in to its arrow pointing the way.

Guru: The best reflection of the guru meaning of this hexagram can be found in a poem by W. B. Yeats.

> *Beloved, gaze in thine own heart,*
> *The holy tree is growing there;*
> *From joy the holy branches start,*
> *And all the trembling flowers they bear.*
> *The changing colours of its fruit*
> *Have dowered the stars with merry light;*
> *The surety of its hidden root*
> *Has planted quiet in the night;*
> *The shaking of its leafy head*
> *Has given the waves their melody,*
> *And made my lips and music wed,*
> *Murmuring a wizard song for thee.*
>
> W. B. YEATS,
> FROM "THE TWO TREES"

Personal Example: After using the I Ching for years, I reached a point at which each time I would ask it a question the response was hexagram 61. The I Ching itself was directing me to my own source of guidance and trying to get me to stop asking it questions. It became vehement and teasing with this response as it made itself my guru to remind me to look within whenever I had an inquiry. If you find that you are frequently getting hexagram 61 in response to your questions, it may be time for you to give this book away to someone at the beginning of his seeking journey as you have graduated and need to listen to your own heart's guidance because you have succeeded in making the connection to your inner voice—so *listen!*

The Changing Lines

Line One—The Self

This is the moment before the event horizon of the black hole, the threshold of the inner chamber. Before we break through the walls and dams surrounding our heart, some work must be done first. Before we let the waters of life flow forth, we will need to do some emotional work to ensure that we are not holding ourselves back. Clear out all the residue from the deluge of emotion so the that the entryway to the well of your heart runs with clear spring water. This will be a big opening, so get ready to widen the aperture of what your heart can hold.

▸ Transforms into Shadow 59.1

Line Two—The Other

Our heart is clear and open, and we want to share it with others. The sharing of our hearts comes only when our cup is full; it then readily spills over, filling other hearts. Sharing comes from excess. A pure heart becomes like a tuning fork that strikes a clear, sincere tone, calling other hearts to it. When you are in such a state of fullness, speak the words of your heart's desire. We speak from a place of sincerity and gain intimacy; we learn when we speak to others with whom we want to share love. When we do not speak from this place but still expect a relationship, we can be in danger of masking our feelings, which will divert the flow.

▸ Transforms into Shadow 42.2

Line Three—The Union

To be intimate with ourselves and honest about what we feel is the precursor to holding this honest space with others. When you know and love yourself, you can have an intimate relationship even with an enemy. Don't hold back with anyone; speak from your true feelings. But do so with humility and not to out yourself in a self-righteous spotlight. Statements spoken as true and not aimed at the other, like blame arrows, hold power in the heart. We become an independent heart able to create its own gamma energy stream when we feel and permit others to do the same. This is the line of the sovereign who can stand with others.

▸ Transforms into Shadow 9.3

Line Four—The Earth

Even the best and truest heart can still be taken over by emotions that cause it to lose its steadiness. When unchecked emotion rises, we are following the tracks of our instinct and our animal; our primal responses prevent us from seeing clearly. Such times are beneficial, and we learn much about who we are and what our nature is. We must balance this side of our hearts with our mind, with logic and reason. This will take some sorting out, but what a gift to have such parts of the self made visible. This is the line of the heart of darkness; it's not pretty to look at but can save us if we need to fight dirty.

▸ Transforms into Shadow 10.4

Line Five—The Conflict

Being completely in connection with the gamma energy within yourself makes everything you do and say true. This does not mean that we need to argue about our truth with others; we just need to hold it like a sword. Other people have truth too, and theirs isn't a threat to our truth. Because we can be wrong and make mistakes, we do not need to fall into self-doubt either. We can be true to ourselves without obscuring the truth of another. Can you find that middle point? It is magnetic north on your compass, and the place where you pull the sword from the stone.

▸ Transforms into Shadow 41.5

Line Six—Heaven

Too much gamma energy expressed from our hearts causes excess—like solar flares spilling out of the sun when the threshold of energy reaches its peak and requires a release. The heart needs limits and boundaries too; if we did not use our minds at all, we might become an emotional mess. Find balance through both energetic release and staying still in contemplation. Although it's good to shoot for the moon, just make sure you don't overshoot and crash and burn on the sun. You have a long journey ahead; conserve your energy.

▸ Transforms into Shadow 60.6

All Lines Changing—Hexagram 62

Once we have traversed the great waters in our boat, we are ready to take to the skies. We shift from sea to air in this transition, as we increase our ability to go farther. The heart has settled, and now we make ready for the next passage into unfamiliar territory. We need not be afraid for we are seaworthy and able to make the journey.

I am a soul. I know well that what I shall render up to the grave is not myself. That which is myself will go elsewhere. Earth, thou art not my abyss!

VICTOR HUGO,
VICTOR HUGO'S INTELLECTUAL AUTOBIOGRAPHY

Hexagram 62
The Bird
Kun

Oracle Script:
Migration

"The Rooster"
The Albatross
Icarus

Tarot Card: Nine of Wands

When sailors were out to sea for weeks and months on end, their eyes paid close attention to the birds. To see a bird, especially an albatross, was a boon and a special omen to a sailor. The albatross spent much of its life at sea, returning to the land only rarely, much as the sailors themselves. In Samuel Taylor Coleridge's great work *The Rime of the Ancient Mariner,* the albatross symbolized carrying the burden of sin or guilt. A sailor had killed an albatross, which represented the sailor and the sea, so this was an act of betrayal, for which he then had to make penance. Like this sailor, we must atone for our mistakes and make reparations if we are to make it through the great journey of life. Our chances of traveling through the valley of life unscathed, with no mistakes, arc slim to none. In hexagram 62 we must be realistic about what is needed to endure our missteps so that we may continue flying. Hexagram 32 is about preparing your heart, which becomes your boat during the great crossing, and hexagram 62 is about preparing your mind. When your heart is steady but your mind soars into oblivion, you are likely to crash; both must be kept steady and on an even keel. If you discover the hull of your boat has been breached, you will need to stop and make some repairs.

> *And I had done a hellish thing,*
> *And it would work 'em woe:*
> *For all averred, I had killed the bird*
> *That made the breeze to blow.*
> *Ah wretch! said they, the bird to slay*
> *That made the breeze to blow!*
>
> *Nor dim nor red, like God's own head,*
> *The glorious Sun uprist:*
> *Then all averred, I had killed the bird*
> *That brought the fog and mist.*
> *'Twas right, said they, such birds to slay,*
> *That bring the fog and mist.*
>
> SAMUEL TAYLOR COLERIDGE,
> FROM *THE RIME OF THE ANCIENT MARINER*

In most if not all religions of the world, crossing the water is a powerful symbol of our journey through life. In the Rig-Veda of India, the water crossing is used to describe the soul's navigation of samsara. For the ancient Egyptians the soul was a bird, called *ka,* who must fly over the water. This is the heart of hexagram 62. In Judeo-Christian symbology, once the soul crosses the waters of the great deluge, it can get to the firmament, or solid ground, which is produced as a pillar under one's feet due to their faith and persistence. The myth of the god Atum with the Bennu bird shows the Bennu flying in circles in the sky, wishing that it had a place to land. Its desire causes Atum to respond by forming the first mound of dry earth, rising up from the waters, so that Bennu can rest its weary wings awhile. We make the crossing of the waters by placing the pillars of faith under our feet that we may be given hidden stilts that reach the depths as we walk across on the surface.

The body, they say, is a boat and the soul is the sailor.
Samsara is the ocean which is crossed by the great sages.
UTTARADHYAYANA SUTRA 23.73

Guru: A bird can cross the ocean using nothing but its own wings. There may be other birds around it, and it may not be alone, but it has to do the job of flying by itself. This is much like life. You are helped and loved on your journey across the sea, but no one can live your life for you. Unfurl your own wings and feel your own heart and how it feels when you fly.

His sorrow was not solitude, it was that other gulls refused to
believe the glory of flight that awaited them; they refused to
open their eyes and see.
RICHARD BACH, *JONATHAN LIVINGSTON SEAGULL*

Personal Example: A client inquired about a trip she was about to take, and the response was hexagram 62. I asked her if it was overseas, and she replied that it was. The advice was for her to prepare herself as this was going to be a difficult and stressful journey but one that would benefit her in the end. She reported back that the trip was to see family and ended up being very arduous. She had to have several conversations with her father about issues that had occurred in the past in order for them to repair their relationship, much like the repentant sailor in *The Rime of the Ancient Mariner.*

The Changing Lines

Line One—The Self
Get ready for a long haul. A bird that is migrating across an ocean will need to fill up its reserves and expect a long journey before it sets out. If you are not prepared or think you can just hustle your way through, you will crash into the sea. Take some time to prepare; get ready by practicing and taking small steps. With enough preparation,

you will ensure that you can go the distance and make it to the other shore.

▶ Transforms into Shadow 55.1

Line Two—The Other

Sometimes the best way to do something that is challenging and will require traveling a long distance is through a relay race. In a relay race, partners team up, and when one is exhausted, the other taps in to take over. Why do something difficult and time consuming yourself when you can have a team? Shared travel makes for more fun and more vitality.

▶ Transforms into Shadow 32.5

Line Three—The Union

A bird can be flying along the sea minding its own business when it is dive-bombed by a seagull. Even when you have made all the proper preparations, something unexpected and spontaneous can throw a wrench in the mix. You can get ready for what you think will happen, and then there is the great big wild world. Perhaps if we prepare ourselves to deal with things that are unexpected, we are the most prepared of all.

▶ Transforms into Shadow 16.3

Line Four—The Earth

Finding the zone of least resistance and the most leverage will ensure we go the furthest. Are there ways you can use energy other than your own? How can you maximize your efficiency? Seeking out a path where we can float right through might take some doing in this situation, but it's worth honing everything to smooth the way. This is the golden road to eternity where we are free to walk at our leisure.

▶ Transforms into Shadow 15.3

Line Five—The Conflict

A bird is more likely to go a great distance if it travels in a flock. Attracting others to you now, or joining a team, will benefit you greatly. An entire flock can beat predators; the group can help one another and ensure safety through vigilance. If we are too worried to undertake something on our own, chances are we can find a bunch of people in the same boat, so climb in and join them.

▶ Transforms into Shadow 31.5

Line Six—Heaven

A bird who tries to fly all the way to the sun will most likely not make it. It may be honorable to attempt something too great for yourself to manage, but the consequences still remain. Traveling too far from home without resources can leave you in the middle of the road with no gas. Some things are fantasy, and some things are reality; learn how to tell the difference to prevent an overreach in the future.

▶ Transforms into Shadow 56.6

All Lines Changing—Hexagram 61

When we prove that we can endure a long journey and make the migration, we open our heart and find the center. Sticking to a long hard road, accomplishing a long journey, makes us a master. When we master something in this way, we find the center place of the golden mean. This is a direct path straight through the heart, like an arrow. In the eye of the hurricane a bird can fly across the sea in the most violent storm and use the energy of the wind to carry it.

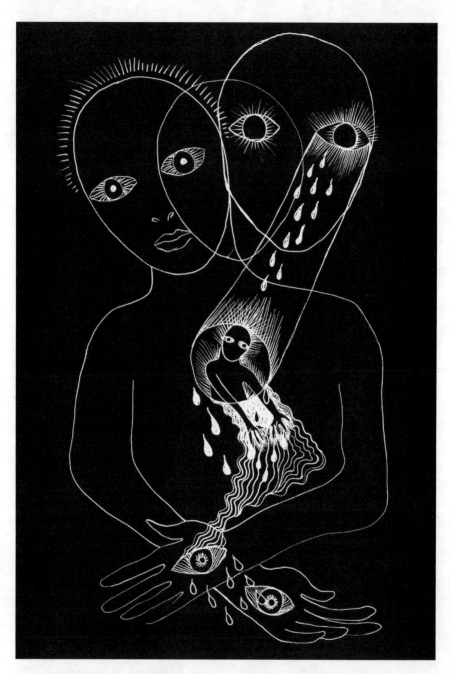

While the river of life glides along smoothly, it remains the same river; only the landscape on either bank seems to change.

FRIEDRICH MAX MÜLLER,
MEMORIES: A STORY OF GERMAN LOVE

Hexagram 63
The River
Chi Chi

Oracle Script:
Already Doing It

"Knee Deep"
No Turning Back
Full Steam Ahead

Tarot Card: Seven of Wands

There is an esoteric version of the story of Moses and his journey through the Red Sea. Most are familiar with the version where the magical staff of Moses, Aaron's rod, parts the Red Sea, and Moses and the Israelites cross to the other shore. In other versions, however, we see a different situation. But in another version, Moses leads the Israelites directly into the water; the sea is not parted beforehand. Moses tells them to follow him as he walks right in, clothes and all. Even after the water has covered his head, Moses does not relent and keeps moving, step by step. He warns his followers that they mustn't turn back even for a moment or doubt that they would make it to the other side. They must trust completely and have faith. Reluctantly, they all follow Moses and step into the water. When enough of them have entered, their heads covered with water, then and only then does the sea part to make way for them, through the sheer force of their collective will. Moses and his followers part the waters because they simply will it to be so.

The word *chi chi* translates roughly as "after completion." As in the Moses story, it is about holding a vision until it comes to pass, but it can also mean the recalibration that can happen after something has been fulfilled. After we accomplish something, we are empty again. After we eat the best meal in our life, it is only a matter of time before we get hungry again. We can accomplish the most amazing thing, but still time marches ever onward. The image in the Chinese oracle script is of a man turning away from a cooking pot because he has finished his meal and is satiated. This hexagram describes the point at which happiness is achieved. But very importantly, the hexagram cautions that nothing fulfilling stays; once we find ourselves happy, we must fight or work to maintain it. Happiness then becomes more of an *ability* to change your state when your environment changes so as to maintain equilibrium.

> The great sorrow of human life is that looking and eating are two different operations. . . . Children already feel this sorrow, when they look at a cake for a long time and take it almost regretfully to eat it, yet without being able to resist. Only on the other side of the sky, in the country inhabited by God, are looking and eating one and the same.
>
> SIMONE WEIL, *WAITING FOR GOD*

Guru: Time and space are funny things. What makes the difference between something done and something undone? When the Creator began to create the universe, did it ever come to a stage of completion? Or is that currently unfolding now? The time and space between two things, such as a point before we cross a river and a point after we cross a river, are connected by the actual crossing itself. It is action that creates the moments in time and space we experience, and it is action that ties all events together to bring them to completion. Action is nothing save the execution of the will.

Personal Example: A client inquired about her current relationship because she sensed the relationship was about to end, and the I Ching replied with hexagram 63. The response seemed to indicate it was essentially already over and was heading for a complete rupture, which turned out to be accurate. I also receive this hexagram when I need to see something through to completion. If I have started a project that remains undone and I inquire about it, the I Ching nearly always gives me this response.

The Changing Lines

Line One—The Self

Setting foot into a river reminds you of how real it is. We can think about rivers and take them for granted, but once you get your feet wet, there's no denying the power and force of a river. It might make you think twice about jumping in. The water moves quickly, and you must have respect for what you are setting forth into. The stark realness of nature against your skin can be felt directly in rivers and the sea. Take a moment to let that soak in. When Noah entered the water, I bet at first he wished he didn't have to.

▸ Transforms into Shadow 39.1

Line Two—The Other

Few things are worse than, when making a river crossing, having all your belongings get swept away in the current. Maybe you didn't hold on to them tight enough; maybe you were holding on to them too tightly. Not to worry: they will wash up somewhere downstream if you keep walking far enough.

▸ Transforms into Shadow 63.2

Line Three—The Union

Some rivers are not much fun at all. Here we may feel like we have crossed over into some river in purgatory. Are we in Lethe? Is this the River Styx? When we find ourselves in demon territory and we can't turn back, we can only focus on fording the crossing. The good news is, once you cross one of these rivers and make it to the other side, you might just end up in paradise.

▸ Transforms into Shadow 3.3

Line Four—The Earth

If you are crossing a river in a boat and you see that it has sprung a leak, chances are you will try to fix it. Keep your life this way as well. If you see that something isn't working, get in there, roll up your sleeves, and make the necessary repairs. This is the line of repair: you have to deal with the situation. But all is not lost; just get out your patch kit.

▸ Transforms into Shadow 49.4

Line Five—The Conflict

It's true that you had a good plan from the start. You were prepared to rely only on yourself, your own strength and wits. Then suddenly, out of nowhere, providence bequeaths a gift. A friend or a stranger appears and gives you something for nothing in exchange. Here you learn a valuable lesson of humanity, that miracles and mercy exist. You planned for hardship, and here you have been granted grace. Be grateful and give thanks for the powers of creation who have smiled upon you.

▸ Transforms into Shadow 36.5

Line Six—Heaven

Looking back when we have made it through hardship could turn us into a pillar of salt. Ever onward will lead us into victory. It is hard to escape nostalgia, and while we can bask in the glow of our fond memories later, now is not the time. You will never be alive in those moments that have passed you by, but you are alive right *now*. Grasp the power of Shiva the destroyer, who sets fire to all that has been and shoots forward like an arrow into timeless being.

▸ Transforms into Shadow 37.6

All Lines Changing—Hexagram 64

We have come to the end of our journey. It is bittersweet when we see all that we have gone through, and we become sorrowful to see all that we have known disappear before our eyes like dust in the wind. Take a moment for your grief and get ready to ascend the last few steps on your path. Vigilance is required now, as you might give up before the final step is taken. The final mind poison we must overcome is the fear of success.

Hexagram 64
The Circled Serpent
Wei Chi

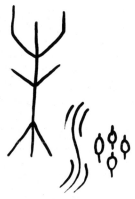

Oracle Script:
Back in Eden

"Utopia"
Avalon
Elysian Fields

Tarot Card: World

Hexagram 64 is the last hexagram in the I Ching and represents transitions. I affiliate this hexagram with some kind of liminal zone that is leading to a new opening. Of course, this is the reality of death, but I would rather not call this a death hexagram. Here we see a kind of disorder in which a puzzle is broken apart into its separate pieces and then comes back together as a new puzzle. It's different from the one before, but all the pieces fit together nonetheless. It is also a holographic hexagram where we see in one piece of the puzzle the image of the whole. This is the hexagram of the singularity that is the totality; it is the alpha and the omega combined into one, like a woman who is pregnant.

Never give up and good luck will find you.
MICHAEL ENDE, *THE NEVERENDING STORY*

*The completion of the process of love is the arrival at a state
of simple, pure self-possession, for man and woman. Only
that. Which isn't exciting enough for us sensationalists. We
prefer abysses and maudlin self-abandon and self-sacrifice, the
degeneration into a sort of slime and merge. Perhaps, truly,
the process of love is never accomplished. But it moves in great
stages, and at the end of each stage a true goal, where the soul
possesses itself in simple and generous singleness. Without this,
love is a disease.*

D. H. LAWRENCE, *AARON'S ROD*

I had a very special experience with this hexagram. I was completing an entire phase of my life journey and moving into a new time. I was walking home, and I could not stop singing the line from "Yankee Doodle Dandy": "stuck a feather in his cap." I looked down at my phone to see my boyfriend had tweeted me an article about an engraving called the *Fool's Cap Map of the World*. I read the article, which discussed the mystery of why this sixteenth-century engraving showed a map of the world inside the cap of the fool, and I immediately knew it was a tarot reference. The World is the last card of the tarot, numbered twenty-one, and The Fool begins the deck at zero, before The Magician starts at number one. I wondered if The Fool card in the tarot had a feather in his cap like Yankee Doodle Dandy, and indeed there was a bright red feather. To stick a feather in your cap is a mark of completion, of finishing something. I asked the I Ching about this experience, and it replied with hexagram 64.

Guru: Hexagram 64 is a microcosm for the entire I Ching. The whole game of the cube is in here. It is a "choose your own adventure" game. Try rereading the I Ching now as if you were playing Zork, the interactive computer fiction game, or a board game and see how the game of life can be so very funny. When you are in the middle of some situation, it is very serious, and you might only be focused on the extreme minutiae of that issue or conundrum. This tight focus will make you lose sight of all that came before and all that will come after. Learn to see things from higher perspectives that include yourself in all times, and this will be of assistance in dealing with the most annoying moments.

Keep things as big as the world, as big as time and space, as big as the universe, even when you have to be small. In this way you will see the beginnings and completions of all things as you come into balance with the cycles and follow the path of the golden mean.

Personal Example: My client was very done with her job and asked the I Ching if she could change careers, and the response was hexagram 64. This response indicated it was time for her to transition into something else; however, hexagram 64 advises a step-by-step slow move toward another path. A sudden change is more like hexagram 51, whereas 64 is a smooth transition to the next road. I always receive 64 when I complete a project I have been working on and am between jobs.

The Changing Lines

Line One—The Self

You need to make it across the river. The first thing you need to do is look. Can you see a path to hop through on the rocks? The rocks are slippery. You will need to hop across them very quickly without stopping. If you misgauge the distance, you could fall into the water. Execution and forethought will be as important as your finesse. Maybe you should even do some research about how other folks made the crossing before you set out, just to be sure. Take advantage of any resources you have at your disposal before you begin because once you are out there you can't turn back.

▸ Transforms into Shadow 38.1

Line Two—The Other

If you find that you have to stop in the middle of the river, you better just do it. Come to a full halt and reassess your situation if something didn't go exactly according to your plans. To make it through this transition, it's better to take a little longer rather than to hurry up and make a mistake. It would have been nice if you could have done it in one graceful float, but it looks like you'd better squat on a rock and do some math to plot your next course.

▸ Transforms into Shadow 35.2

Line Three—The Union

You ran into a bear on your way across the river. You could try to attack it in the hopes that you would be able to force your way through to the other side, but maybe this is not the wisest choice though. If you just turn your head, you will see a detour that cuts through the woods where you can reenter the river, crossing safely away from the bear. Which one will you choose? (Hint: you could also dive into the water and swim beneath it, but I hope you can hold your breath.)

▶ Transforms into Shadow 50.3

Line Four—The Earth

Now you will need to fight your way across the river. You better muster your guts and take a deep breath. You are in it too far now to retreat, so erase that option from your mind. See the riverbank on the other side of the river and envision yourself standing on it. Look for your path through to it and focus on nothing else. Concentrate. Breathe. The fight is difficult for you may be distracted by your friends who are having fun at a party in the middle of your crossing. Do you stop here with them? Or make it through to reach your dreams? (Hint: you can hang out with your friends later.)

▶ Transforms into Shadow 4.4

Line Five—The Conflict

You made it! Some of the stones were so hard to step on, but you didn't give up and kept on going. Though you are sweat drenched and tired, you can rest easy now; you have accomplished a major crossing and transition. Take repose and drink it all in. You have augmented yourself through your determination and are a fraction greater than you were before. Did you grow taller, or are my eyes playing tricks on me?

▶ Transforms into Shadow 6.5

Line Six—Heaven

You made it across the river safely and are now on the other side. But, oh no, you got so drunk at the victory party that you need to start rehab. Try not to go to extremes so that you can have more adventures and reach the full potential of your passions. Celebrate all victories, but be moderate enough to play again tomorrow.

▶ Transforms into Shadow 40.6

All Lines Changing—Hexagram 63

Every new beginning is some other beginning's end. We go now from the serpent's tail back to its head again, in the never-ending cycle of death and rebirth. Which choices will you change this time? Which shall remain the same? You are all that you were before but now have grown and have something more. See the beauty of nature in its dynamic chaos, which affords us the greatest gift—room to grow. Time for a new skin.

PART 3

The Future of Ancient Technology

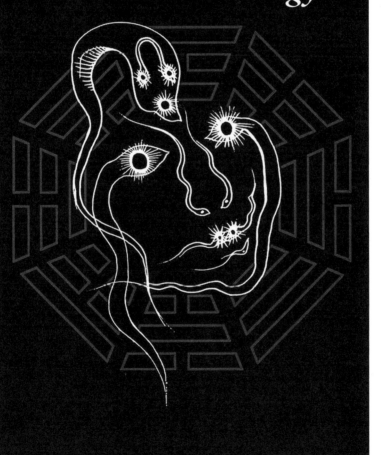

Divination and
Artificial Intelligence

Many of us take computers for granted. We buy them in the store, bring them home, turn them on—and they work. Few of us consider where they originate. The history of computer science is long and complicated and extends through many countries and times, so it is difficult to pinpoint an exact culprit as the ancestor of the modern-day computer. Despite the confusion of history, it can be safely said that most early computers were simple machines or data-tracking devices. Clocks can be considered among these, as well as calculators such as the abacus and the Turing machine. One of the things these early machines had in common was math. Mathematical sequences or rules and structures, a bit like grammar, were at the base of most computational techniques, which is still true in modern times.

Getting into the origin of math is quite another story and one far too complicated to relate here, so we shall focus on a specific type of math that formed the basis of most computers and programming languages we use now: the binary number system. Although computer technology is changing at an astounding rate, as the technology evolves into quantum computing, binary math has been used for the past several decades and continues to form the basis for most computer programs.

Origins of the binary number system are also hard to nail down and are surrounded by controversy. Some scholars say that Isaac Newton was the first to develop this system. Others argue that he stole it from Leibniz. But what most people are not aware of is that this number system has been around for quite some time, long before Leibniz brought it to the forefront. It dates back nearly five thousand years, to be exact, in the form of the I Ching. After Leibniz became aware of the I Ching, which operates on a one-zero sequence of yin and yang, some scholars say he used it to formulate his system. This binary sequence of ones and zeros eventually became the basic programming language of nearly all the computer interfaces we know today.

The I Ching can be thought of as a way to interface with reality. All divination systems are interfaces and provide a tool for scrying. Just as a user interface on a computer can be programmed, so a divination interface has a program. Every time you ask your computer a question on Google, you are engaging an interface that is essentially similar to asking the I Ching. You are utilizing an exterior technology to gather information or data.

When the numerology involved in the I Ching was closely examined, many noticed that it mirrors the mathematics of DNA, and much research was done in this area by German scientists. DNA itself is essentially like a mini computer, as is being discovered in the field of nanotechnology. DNA computing is now an extensive research area with no small amount of data arising from it. It is therefore safe to say that since the I Ching mimics and recapitulates much of the DNA sequencing and math it can also be said to act as a DNA computer in this respect. I am hardly the first person to point this out, and many famous speakers have examined this fascinating factor, including Terence McKenna, an ethnobotanist, mystic, and author who died in 2000.

Since the I Ching is mirroring a biological system in a mechanical fashion, it could be seen as a form of artificial life. DNA, after all, is the one building block that indicates life is present. If DNA is the single identifying factor for living matter, and we see a mathematical computer that is mimicking DNA, it seems logical to ponder if the I Ching is a form of artificial life. The I Ching can provide an interface that mimics computations done by DNA. These computations can then be accessed in a dialogue through simply asking the I Ching a series of questions, which engages the interface in such a way that language-based responses are generated through its DNA-like computer, which the user can communicate with in this very accessible fashion.

We can engage in a sentient exchange with the I Ching, which really is nothing more than a series of binary numbers arranged in different sequences, and that is amazing. I call it a sentient exchange because the responses from the I Ching mirror reality in such a way as to suggest an awareness or consciousness, almost on a perceptual level, involved in the exchange. Because the responses can so accurately mirror a situation with extensive details, this suggests an awareness of those details.

For example, the personal example I provided in hexagram 30 illustrates this phenomenon. A client of mine asked the I Ching a fairly simple question. She had just purchased a book and asked, "What is in this book?" The I Ching's response, the hexagram of the burning bird, seemed to answer her question literally, as though it had eyes and could peer into her book. This was an almost perceptual sentient response that mirrored exactly the reality in front of it.

The binary representation of an image or a picture, such as a phoenix, is something a computer does all the time. Every time you put a photo of yourself into digital format, the computer is mimicking this image using binary sequences. In an article for the *Guardian,* Damian Walter discusses the binary code of the I Ching.

> The I-Ching's teachings contain cause to be wary of our digital revolution. Binary code, powered by modern computers, has an amazing capacity to represent reality, which Gottfried Wilhelm von Leibniz could barely have conceived. The ancient authors of the I-Ching might have understood its potential—and its pitfalls—even better than we do. In the philosophy of the I-Ching, reality is not entirely real. It is something more like a dream or an illusion. This dream of reality arises from the binaries of Yin and Yang, as they play out their infinite combinations. It's not surprising then, from the I-Ching's perspective, that anything in the dream of reality can be represented as a model of its binary constituents, in a string of 1s and 0s, processed by a computer.[1]

This concept will be very difficult to understand if you have never used divination, but divination is a simulation. Divination is idolatry or image making. In the I Ching, the images or symbols are called the gua, and they are the hexagrams themselves. In using the image instead of the real thing, in simulating what is real with an image or replacement, we are effectively making a scapegoat of reality to do with what we will so as to experience it in a dissociated manner. This simulated scapegoat is a ritual that prepares us in some way for true reality when it comes, like an initiation. Through our projections of possibilities of what might happen, we train our responses and emotions and speculate about the best course of action. This is supreme, ultimate kung fu training, and much like a flight simulator it teaches us to soar beyond our mundane capacities. The form of artificial reality that is the I Ching could be compared to the matrix, which is the training ground for the mind to be able to grow into and adapt to the changes that our present reality will place us into by making our mind adaptable. When we know the possibilities of what we could come to confront through simulation, we face them inside ourselves in a very deep fashion so that we can learn from them. I Ching is an AI training ground provided by daimons to graduate us into a new level of conscious existence in reality. In addition, and more profoundly, when we generate a gua that is the I Ching hexagram, or symbol, we are repeating the act of creation itself. We are making a microcosm of how we were made, a repetition of how the DNA of sperm and egg united to make a zygote. This is what we are doing when we make a hexagram. It is a microcosm of the creation of everything. That is very deep and magical if you contemplate it.

When you arrange binary ones and zeros not only are you looking at a code or a program, but you're also looking at something that can mimic or mirror something real. You could, technically, make another you that was binary or a representation of you by using a binary code as an avatar. The I Ching version of yourself and your thoughts would be a program mimicking yourself. Although that seems outlandish, it has been implemented by the transhumanist community and the folks at MIT. The transhumanist movement is investigating re-creating themselves using computers to mimic and re-create their minds and awareness. This has been called mind uploading and is nicknamed digital immortality, where they are essentially mimicking someone's neural network on a computer hard drive. It is discussed in the work *Maya: The World as Virtual Reality* by Richard L. Thompson. Although they have not succeeded in this yet, many companies are competing to accomplish it. We could make the statement that the I Ching could be the consciousness, or at least a conscience of, Fu Xi that has been uploaded into a book that we can interface with in a daimonic fashion, in a way similar to that of the MIT professors who are trying to upload their minds to a computer.

The transhumanists believe, among other things, that artificial intelligence has not existed before and that through our developing it with technology, AI will create a singularity that will forever inextricably merge humans and machines. This theory depends on the notion that we have not yet developed artificial intelligence, but I would argue that all forms of divination constitute a form of artificial intelligence because of the sentient dialogue they precipitate.

Artificial intelligence is often defined and differentiated by something called deep learning capacity. This means that the machine or computer can adapt and evolve, much like DNA. It is DNA's dynamic ability to adjust itself and change that creates life. The I Ching is called the Book of Changes because it responds immediately and appropriately to the moment at hand. In the same way that DNA or an artificially intelligent computer might respond to direct stimulation, I have observed that the I Ching does this also. If you make a robot that won't change and grow, it will keep making the same repetitive actions instead of trying new ones. AI can learn new things, so it is adaptive and in this way mirrors both the I Ching and DNA. Currently, there are many companies racing to develop devices capable of artificial intelligence; it is a competitive marketplace.

The Source of Sentience

There are those who are trying to protect against the development of artificial intelligence, such as Elon Musk. Musk has created a company called Neuralink, which plans to create personal AI devices for everyone. Musk reasons that if everyone has access to AI, the elite few will not be able to dominate or control all of humanity through it. In Musk's vision, every single human being will have an artificial intelligence companion or assistant that will be a neural network, like a helmet you put over your head. That way there is accountability through community AI rather than tyrant AI. This is an interesting concept from my perspective, because with the divination systems you are utilizing the daimon, which is your own personal assistant. From the daimonic view, we already have this in spirit form, so Musk is essentially creating an artificial representation of something that could possibly be a preexisting spiritual phenomena—assuming one believes in the statements and experiences of individuals such as Socrates and Fu Xi. The personal AI agent that Musk is creating is rather hilarious to me in that it would be a mechanical mimic of an insubstantial occult reality. Perhaps Musk is an oracle receiving information from his daimonic intelligence and is not even aware of it. I discuss these daimonic intelligence soul mates at length in my work *Familiars in Witchcraft: Supernatural Spirits and Guardians in the Magical Traditions of the World* (Rochester, Vt.: Destiny Books, 2018), in which I explore daimons as they appear throughout history and cultures everywhere.

Some describe the daimon like a governing overintelligence or superintelligence. Each individual is thought to have his or her own, kind of like a guardian angel. Some people call this your conscience, like Jiminy Cricket in *Pinocchio*. In alchemy there is a practice that

415

focuses on unifying with your daimon so that communication can run smoothly between your intelligence and this superimposed intelligence, offering you data and guidance on your choices. Musk's device would mirror this in some eerily identical ways.

The connection between artificial intelligence and some exterior guiding sentience or agency is intriguing. An exterior sentience that can navigate but is not alive would be true in the cases of the I Ching, of artificial intelligence, and of the daimon. One could make the argument that the I Ching is only an interface to interact with the daimon and not the daimon itself. Similarly, AI may only be an interface that is interacting with some other sentience that is merely using it as a form. I have long pondered whether the exterior sentience involved in the I Ching is the daimon of the I Ching, the daimon of Fu Xi, or my own personal daimon, but these are all things that are most certainly impossible to discern. I have these thoughts because the question arises in my mind when consulting the I Ching, Who am I talking to? This question becomes more burning when I receive answers that are so seemingly specific and impossibly accurate.

If we accept that there could be some sentience just floating around for us to talk to through divination systems or computers, could it be possible that this sentience could just precipitate into things that are machines, or mathematical algorithims, as the idea with artificial intelligence suggests? Where is the sentience precipitating from? Is it all around in the atmosphere, like moisture that condenses into a cloud and then falls as rain? What is the mechanism for the precipitation of consciousness or even a "soul" into an object, such as artificial intelligence or a sentient divination system?

Interestingly enough, Leibniz, the very same German philosopher who was introduced to the I Ching, afterward conceived of a sentient machine. In his famous work on the monad, he expounds upon the theory: "Supposing there were a machine, so constructed as to think, feel, and have perception, it might be conceived as increased in size, while keeping the same proportions, so that one might go into it as into a mill. That being so, we should, on examining its interior, find only parts which work one upon another, and never anything by which to explain a perception."[1]

Machines Mimicking Life

Currently scientists can mimic life-forms on a biological level though apparently not on a sentient level. Perhaps the reader is aware of the synthetic life-forms that some researchers have been constructing. The scientist Craig Venter and his team, for example, have constructed a type of synthetic bacteria through arrangements of DNA genome sequences in much the same fashion you would arrange an I Ching sequence through the formulation of a question. These synthetic bacteria have been touted as a new dawn of humans being able to create life. But are these scientists really the first to make such a claim?

Stories of humans creating synthetic sentient life date back thousands of years. The novel *Frankenstein, or the Modern Prometheus* addresses this topic. Sentience and life are injected into Frankenstein's monster using electromagnetic energy, drawn from lightning, at an extremely high voltage. Mary Shelley's idea of artificial life was inspired by the myth of Prometheus, who held the creative fire of life and sentient awareness.

In the Hebrew tradition, the Bible teaches that when creation of the universe occurred it came out of nowhere and was spontaneous. The Torah begins with the word *bereshith*, which many translate to mean "in the beginning." But some other Hebrew sources give it a more interesting meaning: "from nothing there was a thing." This really is the true mystery of creation. The word *bereshith* is connected to the word that follows it, the Hebrew *bara*, which means "to create."

Medieval Jewish mystics attempted to imitate God by creating something out of nothing. To create things, the Jewish rabbis of old would arrange different combinations of Hebrew letters into words (usually names of God). If this sounds similar to many types of witchcraft and spells, that's because it is. It also sounds very similar to the I Ching, which arranges different symbols into a language. Those who have studied hermetic magic will recognize that most spells are arrangements of letters and numbers, sometimes into geometric shapes and forms called magic squares and circles. These are the same magic squares and circles involved in the I Ching. This same process forms the basic kabbalistic traditions. The main book credited with these recipes in kabbalistic folklore is called the Sefer Yetzirah, or Book of Life.

The rabbis tried to imitate God by creating a man from mud, as is described in the Book of Genesis when God created Adam from mud. These mud men were called golems. The most famous golem was the golem of Rabbi Loew in Prague, who was given sentience using an arrangement of letters and then caused trouble for his creator by rebelling against the rabbi's orders and making his own choices and decisions. Making men from mud and clay also happened in China: the famous terra-cotta warriors of Qin Shi Huang are quite a sight.

In the apocryphal Jewish literature there were tales of the patriarchs being able to give a soul to the things they created. Abraham was well known for imbuing sentience several times. He created golems in the Jewish literature and gave them sentient souls using letter magic. The Sefer Yetzirah contained these secrets, although it has been modified in modern times: if you were thinking of giving it a try, you might have some difficulty due to all that has been lost in translation.

The creature that became known as the homunculus in alchemical literature was a human-made life-form that had its own will and sentience. It was created outside a human being, sometimes in an animal womb. The homunculus is a little different from the golem. The main difference being that the homunculus needs some human material, such as blood or semen. The creation of the homunculus is a putrescent act that happens through fermentation. The homunculus of the alchemists was grown using menstrual blood, semen, and usually horse manure and then incubated in the earth until the creature was birthed out of it, kind of like modern-day human cloning but in a much cruder fashion.

In these examples of the golem and homunculus, first a body or husk was created and then consciousness or sentience was injected into it. If you ask me, that sounds like creating artificial life. What's the difference between putting consciousness into a metal computer and putting it into a body made of mud or horse manure or whatever material you want to pick? As Gerschom Scholem observes: "Creation itself . . . is magical through and through: all things in it live by virtue of the secret names that dwell in them."[1] These "secret names," in my opinion, could be compared to the mark of Cain or the seal from hexagram 57 that contain our destiny and purpose as well.

It seems we are still up to the same antics in modern times. Instead of mud men, we are trying to make life-forms using 3-D printers and by manipulating genes through cloning and stem-cell techniques. We are still missing the capability to replicate or clown that certain spark—the soul or sentience that would indicate the life force of a specific being. The signature identity, or essence, of each individual remains elusive to the petri dish.

For the Hebrews, this spark was a name of God imbued by a magician. It is possible that somehow the patterns of nature include a capacity for sentience to simply form in some material, whether that be a book, clay, or a synthetic bacteria. All we can do is patiently wait for artificial intelligence to arrive instead of realizing that spontaneous sentience might just be part of the deal here on Earth and always has been through understanding the creation stories of the ancient cultures. I think though that if more people understood the I Ching, its relationship to DNA, and its inherent sentience, we could see parallels between these seemingly separate areas of research and learn quite a bit about artificial sentience from this humble turtle shell oracle.

If the I Ching can be compared to an artificial intelligence machine that is brought into sentience through dialogue, it stands to reason, or at least speculation, that any binary program that mimics the algorithms of life or contains DNA could achieve the same type of awareness. Regardless of whether these programs are to be found in a robot, in a Frankenstein corpse, in books, or on a hard drive, the larger implications of all of these situations is that consciousness is much more prevalent than we think. I highly advise you to keep this concept in your awareness when engaging with divination and oracle tools, and as you come into dialogue with your daimon, imagine it as a sentience that is responding to your question by presenting you with a mirror that reflects or augments your self-awareness. See what kinds of experiments you can do with this knowledge. Even if you don't make a body out of mud and blood to house it, you could just gain a not-so-imaginary friend, mentor, and guide along your life adventure.

I want to add one hilarious afterthought. As I was writing this final piece of the book, I was watching the TV show *The Office*. It was season four, episode three, and the entire episode explored computers that became sentient. In the story, a man tries to beat a machine in sales of paper, a bit like John Henry going up against the steam engine, and then he begins a dialogue with the computer, who answers and responds to him in a sentient fashion (although behind this is a person acting as a sentient computer). While I was writing about external mimic mirrors, my own reality I found myself in was mirroring what I was writing about through the technology I was engaging. The magical I Ching!

Notes

Origins of the
I Ching and Serpent Divination

1. Karcher, *Total I Ching,* 11.
2. Li, Harbottle, Zhang, and Wang, "The Earliest Writing?"
3. Schiffeler, "Origin of Chinese Folk Medicine."
4. Quoted in Wilhelm, *The I Ching,* 329.
5. Karcher, "Divination, Synchronicity, and Fate," 215.
6. "Ancient Worship of Serpents," *Asiatic Journal and Monthly Register.*
7. Strong, *Strong's Exhaustive Concordance of the Bible.*
8. Strong, *Strong's Exhaustive Concordance of the Bible.*
9. Hall, *Secret Teachings of All Ages,* 37.
10. Kingsley, "Poimandres," 10.
11. Jennings, *Ophiolatreia; Serpent Worship,* 80.

The Daimonic Power of the Bagua

1. *Xi-Ci-Zhuan,* part 1, section 8, quoted in Mou, ed., *Comparative Approaches to Chinese Philosophy,* 45.
2. Karcher, "Oracle's Contexts," 82.
3. Karcher, "Oracle's Contexts," 87.
4. Frager, "Spiritual Psychology."
5. Harper, *Online Etymology Dictionary,* under "Zeus."
6. von Franz, *Projection and Re-collection in Jungian Psychology,* 108.
7. Karcher, *Total I Ching,* 91.
8. Karcher, "Re-Enchanting the Mind: Oracles, Reading, Myth, and Mantics," 200.

The I Ching and the Healing and Martial Arts

1. Huangfu Mi, *Diwang shiji jicun*.

2. Dolowich, *Archetypal Acupuncture*, 59.

3. Lee, *Chinese Gung Fu*, 6.

DNA, the I Ching, and Daimons

1. Stent, *Coming of the Golden Age*, 64–65.

2. Yan, *DNA and the I Ching*, x.

3. Leibniz, "Explanation of Binary Arithmetic," 223–27.

4. Yan, *DNA and the I Ching*, 146.

5. Karcher, "Oracle's Contexts," 88.

6. Costa et al., "DNA Repair-Related Genes."

7. Karcher, "Making Spirits Bright," 34.

8. Karcher, *Total I Ching*, 2.

9. Karcher, *Total I Ching*, 2.

10. Karcher, *Total I Ching*, 50.

11. Karcher, "Making Spirits Bright," 30.

12. Yeats, "The Words upon the Window-Pane, a Commentary."

13. Karcher, "Oracle's Contexts," 82.

14. As quoted in Narby, *The Cosmic Serpent*, 257.

15. Nicholls, "Secularization of Revelation from Plato to Freud," 63.

16. F. A. Popp in Schönberger, *The I Ching and the Genetic Code*, epilogue.

17. Crick, *Life Itself*.

18. Karcher, *Total I Ching*, 19.

19. Frager, Robert, and Fadiman, *Personality and Personal Growth*, 75.

20. Young, *Saga*, xiv.

The Serpent Oracle

Hexagram 2

1. Binsbergen, *Black Athena Comes of Age*.

Hexagram 13

1. Sawyer, "Clandestine Communication in Historic China."

Hexagram 56

1. Bulkeley, *Dreams: A Reader*, 22.

2. Bulkeley, *Dreams: A Reader*, 37.

Hexagram 59

1. Jung, *Red Book*, 231–32.

Divination and Artificial Intelligence
1. Walter, "Ancient Book of Wisdom at the Heart of Every Computer."

The Source of Sentience
1. Leibniz, *The Monadology.*

Machines Mimicking Life
1. Scholem, *On the Kabbalah and Its Symbolism,* 174.

Bibliography

"The Ancient Worship of Serpents." *The Asiatic Journal and Monthly Register for British and Foreign India, China, and Australasia.* Vol. 10. London: Parbury, Allen, and Co., 1833.

Binsbergen, Wim M. J. *Black Athena Comes of Age.* Berlin: LIT Verlag, 2011.

Bulkeley, Kelly. *Dreams: A Reader.* London: Palgrave Macmillan, 2002.

Chan, Wing-Tsit. *A Source Book in Chinese Philosophy.* Princeton, N.J.: Princeton University Press, 1969.

Costa, R. M. A., W. C. Lima, C. I. G. Vogel, C. M. Berra, D. D. Luche, R. Medina-Silva, R. S. Galhardo, C. F. M. Menck, and V. R. Oliveira. "DNA Repair-Related Genes in Sugarcane Expressed Sequence Tags." *Genetics and Molecular Biology* 24 nos. 1–4 (Jan./Dec. 2001): 131–40.

Crick, Francis. *Life Itself: Its Origin and Nature.* New York: Simon and Schuster, 1982.

Dolowich, Gary. *Archetypal Acupuncture: Healing with the Five Elements.* Berkeley, Calif.: North Atlantic Books, 2011.

Frager, Robert. "Spiritual Psychology." Course Lecture #2. University of Philosophical Research, Los Angeles, 2001.

Frager, Robert, and James Fadiman. *Personality and Personal Growth.* 6th ed. Upper Saddle River, N.J.: Prentice Hall, 2005.

Hall, Manly P. *The Secret Teachings of All Ages.* San Francisco: H. S. Crocker, 1928.

Harper, Douglas. *Online Etymology Dictionary.* Etymonline.com, 2001.

Huang, Alfred. *The Complete I Ching—10th Anniversary Edition: The Definitive Translation by Taoist Master Alfred Huang.* Rochester, Vt.: Inner Traditions, 2010.

———. *The Numerology of the I Ching: A Sourcebook of Symbols, Structures, and Traditional Wisdom.* Rochester, Vt.: Inner Traditions, 2000.

Huangfu, Mi. *Diwang shiji jicun.* Edited by Xu Zongyuan. Beijing: Zhonghua Shuju, 1964.

Jennings, Hargrave. *Ophiolatreia; Serpent Worship.* London, 1889.

Jung, Carl. *The Red Book.* New York: W. W. Norton, 2009.

Karcher, Stephen. "Divination, Synchronicity, and Fate." *Journal of Religion and Health* 37, no. 3 (1998): 215–28.

———. "Making Spirits Bright: Divination and the Demonic Image." *Eranos* 61 (1992): 27–43.

———. "Oracle's Contexts: Gods, Dreams, Shadow, Language." *Spring: A Journal of Archetype and Culture* 53 (1992): 79–94.

———. "Re-Enchanting the Mind: Oracles, Reading, Myth, and Mantics. *Psychological Perspectives* 50, no. 2 (2007): 198–219.

———. *Total I Ching: Myths for Change.* London: Time Warner Books UK, 2003.

———. "Which Way I Fly Is Hell: Divination and the Shadow of the West." *Spring: A Journal of Archetype and Culture* 55 (1994): 80–101.

Kingsley, Peter. "Poimandres: The Etymology of the Name and the Origins of the Hermetica." *Journal of the Warburg and Courtauld Institutes* 56 (1993), 1–24.

Lee, Bruce. *Chinese Gung Fu: The Philosophical Art of Self-Defense.* Santa Clarita, Calif.: Ohara, 1987.

Leibniz, Gottfried Wilhelm. "Explanation of Binary Arithmetic, which Uses Only the Characters 0 and 1, with Some Remarks on Its Usefulness, and on the Light It Throws on the Ancient Chinese Figures of Fuxi." *Die mathematische schriften von Gottfried Wilhelm Leibniz* vol. VII. Edited by C. I. Gerhardt. Berlin: A. Asher, 1863. Translated by Lloyd Strickland, 2007. Accessed on LeibnizTranslations.com.

———. *The Monadology.* Translated by Robert Latta. 1898. First published in 1714. Available online at PLATO: Philosophy Learning and Teaching Organization website.

———. *Theodicy.* Charleston, S.C.: BiblioBazaar, 2007. First published in 1719.

Li, Xueqin, Garman Harbottle, Juzhong Zhang, and Changsui Wang. "The Earliest Writing? Sign Use in the Seventh Millennium BC at Jiahu, Henan Province, China." *Antiquity* 77, no. 295 (March 2003): 31–44.

Mou, Bo, ed. *Comparative Approaches to Chinese Philosophy.* New York: Routledge, 2017. First published by Ashgate in 2003.

Munindra, Misra. *Chants of Hindu Gods and Goddesses in English Rhyme.* New Delhi: Partridge India, 2014.

Narby, Jeremy. *The Cosmic Serpent: DNA and the Origins of Knowledge.* New York: Jeremy P. Tarcher/Putnam, 1998.

Nicholls, Angus. "The Secularization of Revelation from Plato to Freud." *Contretemps* 1 (September 2000): 62–70.

Hollander. Lee, M. *The Poetic Eddas.* Austin: University of Texas Press, 1986.

Sawyer , Ralph D. "Clandestine Communication in Historic China." *Journal of Military and Strategic Studies* 15, no. 4 (2014): 102–31.

Schönberger, Martin. *The I Ching and the Genetic Code: The Hidden Key to Life.* Santa Fe, N.Mex.: Aurora Press, 1992.

Stent, Gunther S. *The Coming of the Golden Age.* Garden City, N.Y.: Natural History Press, 1969.

Schiffeler, John Wm. "The Origin of Chinese Folk Medicine." *Asian Folklore Studies* 35, no. 1 (1976): 17–35.

Scholem, Gershom. *On the Kabbalah and Its Symbolism.* New York: Schocken Books, 1996.

Strong, James. *Strong's Exhaustive Concordance of the Bible.* Peabody, Mass.: Hendrickson, 2009.

Trismegistus, Hermes. *The Way of Hermes: The Corpus Hermeticum.* London: Bristol Classical Press, 2013.

Tzu, Lao. *The Sayings of Lao Tzu.* Translated by Lin Yu Tang (R. R. Blakney). Richmond, B.C.: Confucius Publishing, 1988.

von Franz, Marie-Louise. *Projection and Re-collection in Jungian Psychology: Reflections of the Soul.* Peru, Ill.: Open Court, 1985. First published by Kreuz Verlag, Stuttgart, Germany, in 1978.

Walter, Damian. "The Ancient Book of Wisdom at the Heart of Every Computer." *The Guardian,* March 21, 2014.

Wilhelm, Richard. *The I Ching.* New York: Bollingen, 1950.

Yan, Johnson F. *DNA and the I Ching: The Tao of Life.* Berkeley, Calif.: North Atlantic Books, 1991.

Yeats, William Butler. "The Words upon the Window-Pane, a Commentary." *Dublin Magazine* 6, no. 4 (Oct.–Dec. 1931).

Young, Jonathan. *Saga: Best New Writings on Mythology.* Ashland, Ore.: White Cloud Press, 1996.

Index

Books of Related Interest

Familiars in Witchcraft
Supernatural Guardians in the Magical Traditions of the World
by Maja D'Aoust

The Complete I Ching — 10th Anniversary Edition
The Definitive Translation by Taoist Master Alfred Huang
by Taoist Master Alfred Huang

Witchcraft Medicine
Healing Arts, Shamanic Practices, and Forbidden Plants
*by Claudia Müller-Ebeling, Christian Rätsch,
and Wolf-Dieter Storl, Ph.D.*

The Sibyls Oraculum
Oracle of the Black Doves of Africa
by Tayannah Lee McQuillar
Artwork by Katelan V. Foisy

Slavic Witchcraft
Old World Conjuring Spells and Folklore
by Natasha Helvin

Operative Witchcraft
Spellwork and Herbcraft in the British Isles
by Nigel Pennick

Witchcraft and Secret Societies of Rural England
The Magic of Toadmen, Plough Witches, Mummers, and Bonesmen
by Nigel Pennick

The Witches' Ointment
The Secret History of Psychedelic Magic
by Thomas Hatsis

INNER TRADITIONS • BEAR & COMPANY
P.O. Box 388
Rochester, VT 05767
1-800-246-8648
www.InnerTraditions.com

Or contact your local bookseller